OCTAVIO PAZ

A study of his poetics

OCTAVIO PAZ
A study of his poetics

JASON WILSON

LECTURER IN LATIN AMERICAN LITERATURE
KING'S COLLEGE AND INSTITUTE OF LATIN AMERICAN STUDIES, LONDON

CAMBRIDGE UNIVERSITY PRESS
CAMBRIDGE
LONDON · NEW YORK · MELBOURNE

Published by the Syndics of the Cambridge University Press
The Pitt Building, Trumpington Street, Cambridge CB2 1RP
Bentley House, 200 Euston Road, London NW1 2DB
32 East 57th Street, New York, NY 10022, USA
296 Beaconsfield Parade, Middle Park, Melbourne 3206, Australia

© Cambridge University Press 1979

First published 1979

Printed litho in Great Britain
by W & J Mackay Ltd, Chatham

Library of Congress Cataloguing in Publication Data
Wilson, Jason, 1944–
Octavio Paz, a study of his poetics.
Bibliography: p.
Includes index.
1. Paz, Octavio, 1914– –Criticism and interpretation. I. Title
PQ7297. P285Z98   868   78–18108
ISBN 0 521 22306 7 hard covers
ISBN 0 521 29509 2 paperback

Contents

para Andrea

Preface

Parts of this study have appeared in different form in *The Bulletin of Hispanic Studies* (1971), *Symposium* (1975) and J. Ortega (ed.), *Convergencias y divergencias* (1973). The reader should be warned that the translations are all my own and are merely literal aids to a reading of the originals and in no way pretend to literary self-sufficiency. My thanks are due to the Fondo de Cultura Económica for permission to quote from *Libertad bajo palabra,* and to Editorial Joaquín Mortiz for permission to quote from *Salamandra* and *Ladera este.* Finally, many people, not least Sr Octavio Paz himself, have generously contributed to the elaboration of this study; I will not write a list as the debts are too complex and numerous, except mentioning the late Professor R. O. Jones who in a subtle and intelligent way started me off in the pleasure of criticism and Michael Black who skilfully tidied up my manuscript.

E. J. W.

Abbreviations

A	*El arco y la lira*
C	*Cuadrivio*
CA	*Corriente alterna*
CD	*Conjunciones y disyunciones*
CLS	*Claude Lévi-Strauss o el nuevo festín de Esopo*
LBP 60	*Libertad bajo palabra*, 1960 edition
L	*Libertad bajo palabra*, 1968 edition
LE	*Ladera este*
LS	*El laberinto de la soledad*, 1964 edition
Pe	*Las peras del olmo*
PEM	*Poesía en movimiento*
Pu	*Puertas al campo*
S	*Salamandra*
SG	*El signo y el garabato*
Singe	*Le Singe grammairien*
SR	*Los signos en rotación*

Introduction

1. The biographic prop

Octavio Paz was born in March 1914, in Mixcoac, Mexico City. He was the son of an eminent lawyer who had defended Emiliano Zapata, the peasant revolutionary leader. Paz first published poems in reviews such as *Barandal* (1931–2) and *Cuadernos del valle de México* (1933–4). His first book, *Luna silvestre* (1933; Rustic Moon), was printed in an edition of sixty-five copies, and consisted of seven poems invoking 'poetry' with subdued echoes of Juan Ramón Jiménez; it has not been re-issued. In 1937 Paz went to Spain for the Writers' Congress (1938), meeting many of the twentieth century's most exciting poets. He contributed to Republican magazines (such as *Hoja de España*), edited anthologies (e.g. *Voces de España*) and published a book of poems (*Bajo tu clara sombra*, Valencia 1937; Under your Clear Shadow). From these decisive experiences in Spain onward, this study traces Paz's relationships with the surrealists, from friendship to metaphysics. The first book of poems that concerns us is the first edition of *Libertad bajo palabra* (1949; Liberty on Oath; or under Word), a selection of his poems. This was expanded to include his work in the 1950s, again as *Libertad bajo palabra* (1960); a 1968 edition excised some forty poems. Then followed *Salamandra* (1962; Salamander) and *Ladera este* (1969; Eastern Slope). Paz has also written criticism: from uncollected articles in the 1930s and 1940s to *El laberinto de la soledad* (1950, enlarged 1959; Labyrinth of Solitude), *El arco y la lira* (1956; The Bow and the Lyre), *Las peras del olmo* (1957; Pears from the Elm), *Cuadrivio* (1965; Quadrivium), *Los signos en rotación* (1965; Signs in Rotation), *Puertas al campo* (1966; Doors to the Field), *Corriente alterna* (1967; Alternating Current), *Conjunciones y disyunciones* (1969; Conjunctions and Disjunctions), *Le Singe grammairien* (1972; The Grammatical Monkey), *El signo y el garabato* (1973; The Sign and the Scrawl) and *Children of the Mire* (1974). He has edited anthologies (*Poesía en movimiento*, 1966; Poetry in Movement), collected his translations (*Versiones y diversiones*, 1974; Versions and Diversions), collaborated with other poets (*Renga*, 1971) and edited prestigious magazines like *Taller* (1938–41; Workshop), *El hijo pródigo* (1943–6; Prodigal Son), the magnificent *Plural* (1971–6) and *Vuelta* (1976– ; Return). He continually revises, excises and adds to his writings. He has written lucidly and excitingly on Michaux, William Carlos Williams, Cernuda, Darío, Pessoa, López Velarde, Duchamp, Tamayo, Breton, Lévi-Strauss, Fourier, Sade, Bashō – the list gets out of hand. He writes prolifically, his books pile up, his work expands with translations, new editions, interviews and innumerable studies on him. In the bibliography some of these are noted.

I have chosen 1968 as a symbolic date. After 1945 Paz represented his country as a diplomat; from 1962 he was Ambassador in India, then, following the atrocious massacre of Mexican students just before the Mexican Olympic Games (see Paz's *Posdata* (1970; Postscript)) he resigned in protest, returned home and participated polemically in Mexican life. If I have underplayed the biographic approach, more can be found in Claire Céa's *Octavio Paz* and I. Ivask's collection of studies on Paz.

In order to avoid attempting a general survey, for Sr Octavio Paz is still very much alive, I have focussed on a moment in his poetic life – surrealism – and seen this as a centre, symbolic of an *actitud vital* (vital attitude), and stretched it over the rest like a net. To attempt anything else would be absurd.

2. The critic

It is a commonplace to talk about the 'crisis' in literary criticism, and the critic can no longer feign innocence. He has to explain himself, defend his views, reveal his position. This critic's relation to Octavio Paz's *obra* (work) has developed in a schizoid way, divided between 'private' enthusiasm (he first read Paz in English in *Evergreen Review*) and academic concern, in that Paz's *obra* was the centre of an eight-year exploration of Paz's vision, surrealism, the nature and function of poetry and so on, pursued through the repressive and deforming convention of the doctoral thesis. That he occasionally writes about himself in the third person singular or in the self-effacing first person plural underlines the consequent distance (alienation?) of this writer from the texts. This loss of 'heat' and this numbing of enthusiasm contradict the essential, ecstatic vision of the poetry, and casts a 'cold' eye.

However, Paz is not a poet locked in the intensities of poetic language; as a concerned critic he is obliged, with a minimum of sacrifice, to water down his heady vision. He can expound in prose, in an amenable, immediately consumable language that is rooted in common sense, not ecstasy. In his case, as a critical poet and poet–critic, the need to *descend* from metaphoric heights, from hermetic song, and to relate his critical perceptions in prose to a shared body of thought, is symptomatic of the *absence* of those sensed, invisible meanings that weave poetry into the fabric which is called culture.

Further, the critic is not only an intermediary or more thorough 'reader', but creates a sense of tradition by relating works together, as Paz himself claims (*CA* 41). The critic discovers those texts and readings which give Paz's *obra* its meaning and from which his work makes sense. This activity avoids more dubious and coarser discourse; from the biographical and the sociological to the psycho-analytical, where the disparity between critic and text reflects the rigidity of ideology. Poetry loosens the tongue; it is Ezra Pound's 'brief gasp between clichés'. Pas is a poet whose reading of surrealism enabled him to revalue and affirm the role of poetry in the twentieth century in terms of a liberating, quasi-religious vocation.

Octavio Paz's *place* is not only Mexico with its intangible conditionings and visible survivals; he must also be placed as a body of work reverberating between his masters, T. S. Eliot and André Breton. If we concentrate in our reading on Breton, space is our excuse. Further, these readings must be seen as critical, counter-readings. Within the wider context of history, Mexican post-revolutionary nationalism, the absence of a world image, the dead weight of ideologies, a sweetened Romantic tradition (and so on), they are liberating. The secret 'fathers' (cf. H. Bloom) who relate Breton to Eliot (their awkward placing together is symbolic, a simplification of hesitant, darker and more complex readings) are the Mexican poet Xavier Villaurrutia (1903–50) and his Castillian twin Luis Cernuda (1902–63), both poets whose readings of surrealism *initiated* Paz into an awareness that led him to become one of surrealism's foremost apologists, 'Breton's most brilliant disciple outside the French-speaking world' (H. Gersham). Villaurrutia and Cernuda are the 'Spanish' strands in our fabric.[1]

This study will explore Paz's poetics, 'poetics' being taken as a body of thought, morality, a life-attitude and metaphysic. We will deal with intention. This circumvents the problem of evaluating the poetry; it avoids excessive description, thematic summaries and what we might call the tautological trap, since many of Paz's poems are about the poem, the creative act, self-reflection and so on. The experience of one poem generates another. The responses to Paz's poems are determined by a chaos of factors that defies rationalisation and linearisation; from deep emotional responses and unconscious phonic associations to cultural conditioning (this critic is not Mexican; learned Spanish at sixteen, etc.). It would be presumptuous to attempt evaluation other than orally or privately. Our reading of Paz offers specialised insights, fitting the pieces into a version of literary history. However, what this critic 'hides' seeps through, in his selections, his use of adjectives, his desire to write this study and his irritation with the crudity of a medium ill-fitted to participate in the poetry.

3. Some quotations

'El pensamiento del surrealismo, crítico y utópico, fue tan importante como las creaciones de sus poetas y pintores' (*CA* 169; The thought of surrealism, critical and utopian, was as important as the creations of its poets and painters). This affirmation underpins our study: it points to a lucid awareness that the poem itself, severed from its matrix, fails as an act of communication in a time when there are no shared world views. Surrealism offers an alternative that is critical and utopian. This posits an extra-literary intent – the utopian surrealist dream that the poem will incarnate in society; Lautréamont's dictum that one day poetry will be *spoken* by all and that it will be lived, no longer *written in books*. The reverse of this vision is the desperation of the solitary poet. All Paz's writings envisage some *act* of communion beyond words, a faith that poetry *changes* the poet and the reader, ushering in the poetic society based on love, liberty and desire, the waking dream lived in broad daylight. The tension of Paz's writing stems from this utopian intention, for actual history is a 'nightmare', is reductive and repressive. Paz's insight about utopian surrealism is shared by others, for example Jorge Guillén: 'La poétique était peut-être supérieure à la poésie' (The poetic was perhaps superior to the poetry).[2]

'La obra de Cernuda es una biografía espiritual...todo presidido por una conciencia que desea transformar la experiencia vivida en saber espiritual' (*CA* 12; Cernuda's work is a spiritual biography...presided over by a consciousness that desires to transform lived experience into spiritual knowledge). Poetry for Paz is not a formal, aesthetic exercise, but it is his very being manifesting itself in the space of desire. The act of writing–reading is a metaphor of liberation from conditioning, from role, and the societal self; the pen runs beyond intention and the 'other' crystallises as desire; just as reading is to enter the 'other' and transcend the 'self'. (The 'other' is Paz's metaphor for the reality of those elements of the totality of the self that are ignored or repressed.) This is life (accidental and conditioned) transmuted into spirit, *saber espiritual*. 'Spirit', 'mind', 'self', 'being', 'desire' are all congealed terms for this elusive, denied truth. Heidegger, Norman O. Brown, Mallarmé and Buddhism would be supporting voices.

'Ser un gran pintor quiere decir ser un gran poeta: alguien que trasciende los límites de su lenguaje' (*A* 23; To be a great painter means to be a great poet: someone who transcends the limits of his language). Literary styles, generational tics and mannerisms fade away; genuine art overflows, raids the inarticulate, sings absence, voices silence. Art is an experience irreducible to its language, and experience is the only artistic truth. An analogy with mysticism forces itself upon us: experience renders *form* insignificant and absurd, but is its support and foundation. This is an ecstatic view of art; art is judged by its intensity as privileged moment, timeless *instante poético* (poetic moment), communion, fusion. Yeats (1917) speaks for all poets: 'for the awakening, for the vision, for the revelation of reality, tradition offers us a different word – ecstasy'.

'El surrealismo no es una poesía sino una poética y aún más, y más decisivamente, una visión del mundo' (*A* 172; Surrealism is not a poetry but a poetics and even more, and more decisively, a world vision). The gradation – poetry, poetics, vision – is crucial; Paz embodies twentieth-century man's anguished quest for meaning, for relating himself to a whole, *re-ligare* – to be tied back to matter. Life and death are re-interpreted; time, the fall, innocence, redemption are his concerns. Paz inherits the painful cries of the 'surrealists', the 'existentialists' – all who suffer *orfandad* (orphanhood). The centre has fallen apart and its absence justifies Paz's much criticised eclectic approach, sieving through marxism, surrealism, structuralism, Buddhism, Tantra and other things for 'nuggets'. Paz pursues an elusive salvation.

4. A parenthesis

We are not necessarily dealing with influences. Surrealism did not influence Octavio Paz in the sense that it suddenly transformed his poetry and life-stance, for Paz was seeking what he found. Writing of Agustín Yañez (1904–), the Mexican novelist, Paz employs the word 'example' rather than influence; for what determined his art was not stylistic borrowings but an attitude towards reality (*Pu* 144). Looking beyond technical borrowings, Paz, as a critic, is concerned to unravel and locate a writer's 'vital attitude' (*Pe* 91), for it is this energy that motivates the style; in other words style is a morality, the fibre in the patterned texture. Writing about Braque's supposed influence on the Mexican painter Rufino Tamayo, Paz claimed that such an influence could not be found in Tamayo's actual works but 'en su actitud frente a la pintura' (*Pe* 254; in his attitude towards painting). Inverting the process, I argue that Paz's 'vital attitude' manifests itself through the poetry, but that we must go beyond the poetry to understand it. I return to *intention*. It is here that surrealism clarifies.

Chapter 1

1 Octavio Paz and surrealism:
attitude versus activity

To write about surrealism is, above all, a problem of definitions, and this task itself has become a commonplace. Rather than repeat the familiar points of view – 'surrealism is dead', 'surrealism is a phenomenon of the inter-war years', 'surrealism still lives but in another form' – we shall approach it through Octavio Paz's friendship with André Breton. This defines surrealism as a historical and theoretical phenomenon tied to Breton's magnetic personality. With his death (1966) surrealism evaporated. This, of course, could be a limiting view (for those who never knew him, for those who still call themselves surrealists) and we use it only as a model, not as the truth.

In a series of interviews on the radio, published as *Entretiens* (1952), André Breton warmly alluded to Octavio Paz as the poet of the Spanish language 'qui me touche le plus' (who touches me the most), including him in post-second-world-war surrealist orthodoxy because his work/life-attitude/style, that grouping together of preoccupations so passionately sought by the surrealists, closely paralleled Breton's own 'esprit surréaliste' (surrealist spirit). Later (1956), Breton praised Paz for being a revolutionary theoretician conveying 'une image saisissante du Mexique' (a striking poetic image of Mexico) and singling out his 'ferveur' and his 'avidité spirituelle' (fervour; spiritual avidity). However, Breton confessed that he did not know Spanish poetry. He quotes Antonio Porchia (1886–1968, Argentinian author of *Voces* (1943; Voices), an odd collection of aphorisms and paradoxes translated into French by Roger Caillois in 1949) and discusses Pablo Neruda's political attitude as disqualifying him from being a surrealist. But he never knew Neruda's poetry. Rather, Breton talks of Spanish painters such as Miró, Dalí and others. Surrealistically, Breton confused works with authors; as he did not read Spanish, he had to speak of 'friends'. Jorge Guillén was correct when he wrote that 'l'unique ami hispanique d'André Breton sans doute fut Octavio Paz' (André Breton's one Spanish friend was Octavio Paz); we would underline *ami*.[1]

Thus Paz's surrealist qualities reached Breton through friendship, the spoken word, and gestures, and only later through translations by Lambert, Péret, and Mandiargues. That later critics include Paz in surrealist anthologies (César Moro (1903–55) and Paz are the only Latin Americans in Bédouin's anthology *La poésie surréaliste*) merely shows how faithfully the critics follow Breton's attitude, confusing works and lives to the point where the one stands for the other.[2]

This by no means implies that Paz failed to understand surrealism. For years before his actual meeting with Breton he had been assimilating ideas and images from his reading, perhaps even sharing a life-style (though that remains outside his texts) that would eventually pull him towards Breton. Without this previous internal evolution, Breton would not have interested himself in Paz, one of many Latin American 'poets' in post-war Paris.

This slow evolution towards the possibility of becoming Breton's friend and joining the Paris group blurs sharp divisions like the notion of a 'surrealist epoch' in Paz's poetry. He was not converted to surrealism. The notion of influence is too simplistic, for it is the 'vital attitude' that conditions the work. The real 'meetings' affect one's life first, and only later the poetry. It is not a matter of stylistic mimicry but life-style. Paz did not adopt a surrealist pose but shared the spirit and still does.

Paz assimilated surrealism long before meeting Breton personally, and he did this on many levels, some biographical, and impossible to unravel. We will outline two possible approaches. The first traces the repercussions of surrealism in Mexico, following my criterion of relating the movement to Breton's own personality as it developed out of his separation from Dada, from the first practical manifestation of automatic writing and from the manifestos – all this up to the meeting with

Paz. The second approach would be through what Paz himself has written about his discovery of surrealism. This would confirm that there was no 'surrealism' in Mexico before Paz returned from Paris in the 1950s with the good news. Further, Paz went directly to the sources, sometimes through translations, or through Spanish poets close to surrealism like Cernuda and Villaurrutia, or through others in a similar position like Saint-John Perse, and also through the precursors such as Rimbaud, Lautréamont, Blake.

Surrealism in Mexico

The first vibrations of the European avant-garde in Mexico were picked up by the seismograph-like poet José Juan Tablada (1871–1943), who experimented with Apollinarian *calligrammes* (in 1920), with certain 'imagistic' devices and with the Japanese haiku. His contemporary Ramón López Velarde (1888–1921) imitated Jules Laforgue's irony and burlesque (probably through the Argentinian Leopoldo Lugones), and completed the dismantling of *modernista* rhetoric, opening poetry to the 'nouveau'. In a melange of futurism, Dada and political anarchy, the *estridentistas* (strident ones) noisily presented the first *isms*. The first notice about surrealism appears in what is known as the *Contemporáneos* (Contemporaries) group, friend-poets contributing to the magazine of that name. As spokesman for his generation, Paz thanked these *Contemporáneos* poets for discovering precursors such as Baudelaire, Nerval and Blake, the poetics of the dream, and the theory of correspondences and analogy; but he criticised them for their insensibility 'a la fascinatión de la noche de místicos y románticos' (*Pe* 106; to the fascination for night of mystics and romantics). Paz guesses that literary curiosity was their motivating force, for the name of their magazine implies that they sought to be *modern*. They were fighting a stubborn spirit of post-revolutionary nationalism best expressed in its pictorial-political aspect (the Mexican murals of Rivera, Siqueiros, Orozco etc.) and they clutched on to all that was *new*, critical and European. They dabbled with different styles in a sort of dilettante experimentalism and, according to Paz, they did not *embody* poetically what they had learned through Nerval or Blake. Paz demanded more of the poet; he was an absolutist. Poetry had to be lived; it was a recuperation of man's lost half, his nostalgic wholeness.

The *Contemporáneos* group's literary curiosity did not lead to empathy with surrealism as surrealism demanded (that is, it did not lead to an alternative life-style). Jaime Torres Bodet (1902–), an articulate spokesman for this group, claimed in his autobiography *Tiempo de arena* (1951; Time of Sand) that his group introduced Proust, Joyce, Apollinaire and 'la confrontación con el superrealismo' (the confrontation with surrealism). But above all he praised their 'actitud de consciente alerta y de vigilancia frente a sí mismos' (attitude of conscious alert and vigilance vis-à-vis themselves). However, this lucid eclecticism belies his boast that he introduced surrealism, for surrealism to Torres Bodet meant little more than a reading of Breton's *Nadja* (1927), which he reviewed in 1928 as a work that lacked 'elaboration', based on that 'false' liberty that characterised all surrealism. He was bored by the coincidences, the miracles, the 'monotony' of the marvellous. Yet this book symbolised a moment: 'así es como vivía una parte de la literatura europea de 1929' (that is how a part of European literature in 1929 was lived). However, apart from a few Eluard and Desnos translations, some Man Ray and Miró illustrations, there is little else to back his assertion. It is more likely that the surrealists were read in that critical spirit of alertness and vigilance described by Bodet.[3]

Of this group, the poet Xavier Villaurrutia (1903–50) awoke in Paz more than a 'professional' interest in surrealism. Paz has recognised this debt, but admitted being unable to write anything on Villaurrutia, save two uncollected pieces (in *Letras de México*, 1938 and *Sur*, 1943). This 'block' is revealing; we will touch on crucial similarities between them in their attitudes to surrealism.[4]

Writing of Villaurrutia's poetry, Paz seemingly criticises a limitation:

A pesar de la influencia de los poetas franceses, de Chirico y de los surrealistas, Villaurrutia tampoco cerró los ojos, y sus poemas, aún los del período automático, son siempre reflexivos.

In spite of the influence of the French poets, of Chirico and the surrealists, Villaurrutia did not shut his eyes; and his poems, even those of the automatic period, are always reflective.

This mistrust of blind automatism in favour of *reflection* is to Paz's liking: 'No me parece una limitación: amo el lenguaje sonámbulo pero desconfío de los poetas sonámbulos' (It does not seem to me to be a limitation: I love somnambulistic language but I mistrust somnambulistic poets). This separation between *language* and *poet* is central; Paz was writing about Villaurrutia, but identified with him and slipped in his own values (Paz also rejected automatic writing, years afterwards, yet for similar reasons). Villaurrutia's real debt to surrealism came later through his intimate friend the Peruvian surrealist poet César Moro (the only Latin American contributor to Breton's *Le Surréalisme au service de la révolution*, 1926), when both contributed to the magazine *El hijo pródigo* (1943–6). Villaurrutia translated Breton and Eluard, practised automatic writing, exploited the dream as source of poetry, and reviewed surrealist books and films. But in spite of this activity he remained deaf to its seduction:

El irracionalismo, el automatismo de las nuevas escuelas poéticas, no ha entrado con la fuerza invasora que ha entrado en otras cosas, por la razón de que el mexicano es un ser reducido cuya embriaguez mayor consiste precisamente en mantenerse lúcido y que, aun a la hora de soñar, gusta de mantenerse despierto.

Irrationalism, the automatism of the new poetic schools, has not entered with the invading strength with which it has entered other things, for the reason that the Mexican is a reduced being whose greatest rapture consists precisely in remaining lucid and who, even at the hour of dreaming, likes to remain awake.

Like Paz, he stayed awake and lucid; for both of them it was a Mexican characteristic. Villaurrutia praised surrealism's revaluation of Romanticism, but found it unoriginal, merely a *systematising* of a tradition that appealed more to Villaurrutia than the act of systematising itself. His broader literary tastes

included Anatole France and Cocteau, both despised by the
sectarian surrealists. Villaurrutia was outside orthodoxy,
merely sympathising with certain strands of surrealist thought.
This 'delicacy' is also evident in Paz. Only recently has Paz
admitted that 'Villaurrutia me abrió las puertas de la poesía
francesa moderna, de Supervielle a la poesía de Eluard y de los
surrealistas' (Villaurrutia opened for me the doors of modern
French poetry, from Supervielle to the poetry of Eluard and the
surrealists). Paz confirms our view of *Contemporáneos* eclecticism.[5]

The editor of *Contemporáneos*, Bernardo Ortiz de Montellano
(1899–1949), though exploring narcotic and anaesthetic experiences in his poetry, explicitly dissociated himself from the
surrealists' 'recipes'; he valued their insights into the 'mechanism of poetic creativity' but defined real poetry as beyond
'schools'; for him poetry was 'un camino de personalidad; una
poética más que una retórica, dentro de la más completa
libertad sin reglas aparentes' (a path towards personality; a
poetics more than a rhetoric, within the most complete liberty
without apparent rules). Though aware of the surrealist intention, he too viewed surrealism suspiciously.[6]

Jorge Cuesta (1903–42), the group's 'intellectual', embodies
his generation's tepid attitude to surrealism. He translated
Eluard and Desnos; he lauded Breton's *Nadja*, 'ese bello libro'
(that beautiful book). He met Desnos and Breton in Paris. But
he too rejected surrealism. Whether poetry could be cultivated
or artificially induced – this was the question that separated him
from surrealism; as for all the *Contemporáneos*, automatic writing
was the stumbling-block. He was drawn to Breton's charisma-
tic personality and approved the intention of trying to 'live
poetry'. But he disapproved of Breton's flirtations with com-
munism – surrealism was too 'poetic' – and he was proved right
by circumstances. Later (1940) Cuesta wrote that no young
poet could 'ignorar ni desaprovechar las conquistas del
sobrerealismo' (be ignorant of nor waste surrealism's con-
quests). This neutral tone reinforces his group's disinterested
curiosity towards surrealism.[7]

More important than this group in my evaluation of the

spread of surrealism were Artaud's and Breton's visits to Mexico. With Peru, Mexico is the only Latin American country to
figure in the surrealists' map of the world. Mexico fascinated
because it embodied those occult forces sterilised by an over-
rationalised, predictable (Western) civilisation. Below the
touristic surface view lay obscure areas of violence, surprise,
weird contrasts – a dark, anachronistic 'primitiveness' which
made Mexico the 'other' or secret face of the 'great Western
tradition'. It was a place where the much-sought-after 'marvellous' flourished *naturally*. Paz endorses this myth: Mexico is
'un país que nunca ha podido vestir con entera corrección el
traje de la civilización racionalista' (*Pe* 57; a country that has
never been able to wear with complete correctness the suit of
rationalist civilisation). But if Mexico is 'surreal' it is only so for
the surrealists and those who have 'universalised' their view.[8]

Antonin Artaud, a leading member of the surrealist group
until his expulsion by Breton in 1926, visited Mexico between
February and November 1936. His declared purpose was to
rediscover the 'truth' repressed and ignored by Western
rationalism since the Renaissance. For Artaud, Mexico was
still in contact with those 'magic sources' that would enable
him to regenerate himself and become 'whole' again. He wrote:
'Je suis donc venu au Mexique chercher la force, et les forces, de
passer à ce changement' (I have thus come to Mexico to seek
force and the forces to pass to this change). He realised that this
change lay through participating in the *shaman peyotl* rites of the
Tarahumaran Indians; his record of this experience, of his
failure, is painful and unforgettable. While in Mexico he ran
out of money and subsisted by writing articles, translated into
Spanish for local newspapers. Luis Cardoza y Aragón collected
these, but the French originals have disappeared. Artaud gave
three talks at the university, and though he had no intention of
talking directly about surrealism he did convey its spirit. His
idiosyncratic, confused vision is hard to share; it differed radi-
cally from accepted, more literary versions, and though it is
difficult to gauge his effect on Mexican intellectual life, our
guess is that it went in one ear and out the other. Paz, for
example, did not hear or read him then.[9]

In 1938 André Breton arranged to be sent to Mexico. In return he had to give some talks on French culture, which he duly carried out, as well as showing Buñuel's and Dalí's film *Un Chien andalou* (1928) for the first time in Mexico. As with Artaud, public response was minimal: in Ida Rodríguez Prampolini's words 'tampoco causó la resonancia que se esperaba' (neither did he arouse the interest that he expected). He never published his lecture notes and, again, Paz was not present.[10]

In fact Breton went to Mexico for 'deeper' reasons. From his childhood Mexico had obsessed him. 'Eternal Mexico' with its aura of mystery was embodied for Breton in many experiences from the 'magic' of Mexican jumping beans (an anecdote concerning Breton's wilful magical view cruelly told by Roger Caillois) to a visit to a half ruined palace in Guadalajara and a meeting with a dawn 'nymph' who bewitched Breton with her beauty and mystery. For in Mexico, wrote Breton, 'man had remained in contact with nature's forces'. In an uncollected interview (only the Spanish version is known) Breton told Rafael Valle (1938) that Mexico was a surreal country. Thus years before meeting Octavio Paz, who perhaps incarnated this eternal, mythic Mexico, Breton sought in Mexico an antidote to jaded European culture (in the tradition of Rousseau and Chateaubriand).[11]

In Mexico Breton also discovered the paintings of Frida Kahlo, Diego Rivera's wife and Breton's hostess in Mexico. He called her art 'faithfully surrealist' in spite of her 'ignorance' of Parisian surrealism. Breton had found a *natural* surrealist in Mexico and was excited to have his view confirmed that surrealism tapped a natural, universal part of the human psyche. However, according to Prampolini, Frida Kahlo had been in Paris the year before (1937); and that was the reason why Breton stayed with her and her husband. This incident, true or not, shows clearly that Breton *wanted* to find *his* (surrealistic) Mexico; and nothing would change that.[12]

His other reason for choosing Mexico (Breton hated travelling) was Trotsky's presence. They had long chats, drew up an important manifesto uniting revolutionary art with revolutionary politics, and above all agreed warmly on many matters, despite Trotsky's prophetic remark that Breton's poetry 'kept a window open on to the absolute'. Later, Paz made much of this 'opening'.[13]

Between 1938 and 1940 more interest was shown in surrealism in Mexico, Agustín Lazo (1910–), Villaurrutia's close painter friend, wrote a long, sympathetic study of surrealist art (1938). The May issue of *Letras de México* (1938) dedicated a special number to André Breton which included a basic anthology, with translations and bibliography of surrealism, and was genuinely informative. However, this mood was short-lived. Adolfo Samara, in the June number of *Letras de México*, claimed that few Mexicans really understood surrealism; for him, by 1938, surrealism had grown 'frivolous' and 'rootless', and had nothing to offer Mexicans. This jingoistic tone was to become the norm. The *estridentista* poet Arqueles Vela attacked surrealism for being 'liberal', and 'capitalism's growth'. He mocked Breton, belittling him in comparison with the communist Aragon, and ending arrogantly: 'Breton no pudo influir en nuestro concepto estético' (Breton could not influence our aesthetic concepts).[14]

And this was so. Octavio Paz's magazine *Taller* included no surrealist contributors. Paz, the effective editor, opened the doors of the magazine to exiled Republican Spaniards; to such an extent that Rafael Solana called it a 'Spanish magazine published in Mexico'. The only vaguely surrealist note was José Ferrel's translation of Rimbaud. Later (1969), Paz stated that although the actual surrealists were not read, surrealism's precursors were (Rimbaud, Lautréamont). And it is only when Paz writes with hindsight that the aims of his magazine and group seem strangely close to surrealism: 'Los poetas de este grupo [*Taller*] intentaron reunir en una sola corriente poesía, erotismo y rebelión' (The poets of this group tried to reunite in one single current poetry, eroticism and rebellion). This trinity of values is clearly Bretonian. Is Paz superimposing his later awarenesses back onto his youth? Or had he and his generation reached similar conclusions to Breton's? However that may be, it is clear that the surrealists were not conscious or explicit models.[15]

In 1940 the Third International Surrealist Exhibition was held in Mexico City, organised by Breton, César Moro and Wolfgang Paalen, then resident in Mexico. The criticism of the time was unanimous. We quote from Cardoza y Aragón and Ramón Gaya: it was 'puerile', 'out of date', 'provincial', 'conventional', 'in good taste' and so on; in all, a 'parody' of surrealism. And the Mexican imitators were particularly criticised. Cardoza y Aragón wrote his hostile review in Paz's *Taller*; and even if he did not reflect editorial policy, he voiced a generalised aversion to surrealism. An anonymous editorial in *Romance* argued that surrealism was betrayed 'en esta cola pesada del movimiento que hoy no hace más que repetirse' (in this heavy tail of the movement that does little else but repeat itself). According to Miss Prampolini, the show 'cayó en el vacío' (fell into emptiness). Oddly, Rivera and Siqueiros contributed to the show; they were hardly, even on a generous estimate, surrealists.[16]

Surrealism took on a new lease of life with the second world war. Several painters and poets sought exile in Mexico. Among these was the painter Wolfgang Paalen, who edited a quasi-surrealist magazine *Dyn* (1942–4), and also Leonora Carrington, Remedios Varo and Benjamin Péret. The latter was in Mexico from 1941–8. He too explored with fascination the 'primitive-poetic' roots still visible in Mexico. He praised Mexico's 'primitive freshness'. He also knew Spanish and was less of a tourist than Artaud and Breton. He translated into French the *Livre de Chilam Balam de Chumayel* (1955) as well as Octavio Paz's *Pierre de soleil* (1962).[17]

Octavio Paz was one of the editors of *El hijo pródigo* from 1943 to 1945, another magazine that reflected a broad spectrum of interest, but was not seminal like *Contemporáneos*. Interest in surrealism was kept alive by Moro, Lazo and Villaurrutia through reviews and translations.

The Spanish poet Juan Larrea (1895–), most of whose poems were written in French, also settled in Mexico. This eccentric friend of Vicente Huidobro and César Vallejo expounded his personal brand of surrealism in the magazine *Cuadernos americanos* (1944–). The decline of surrealism in Paris, coupled with the second world war, led him to prophesy the end of European civilisation with its 'transplanting' and future flowering in Latin America, the promised land.[18]

However, by this date (1944), Paz was out of Mexico; even if he had been interested, the moment of surrealist 'influence' had passed. My point is that surrealism never took root in Mexico and that Paz was 'formed' outside the claustrophobic national culture. The only exceptions to the Mexican xenophobic rejection of surrealism were Villaurrutia, Moro and their group. It is more important to keep in mind that Breton was predisposed to view all that came from Mexico with sympathy.

Octavio Paz returned from his years in Paris in 1952. He was now an 'orthodox' surrealist; he had lived at the source, befriending Breton. In 1954 he gave a lecture on surrealism at the university. He ended this by saying that it was too early to take a critical, balanced view of surrealism. Surrealism still *lived* – that was the message of his lecture: and he, Paz, was its embodiment. Further, surrealism corresponded to a vital and eternal part of Western culture and was not a school: 'El surrealismo – en lo que tiene de mejor y más valioso – seguirá siendo una invitación y un signo; una invitación a la aventura interior y al redescubrimiento de nosotros' (*Pe* 183; 'surrealism – or what is best and most valuable in it – will continue to be an invitation and a sign; an invitation to inner adventure and to the rediscovery of ourselves). Later (1960), to Carlos Monsiváis, Paz repeated this view of surrealism as Western society's dissident, secret voice, the 'sacred disease of Western civilisation'.[19]

Paz's passionate, polemical tone still provoked hostility. An example is given by the magazine *Estaciones* (1956–60). Elías Nandino, the editor, repeated the attacks of the late thirties. He wrote: 'Hace más de cuatro lustros que el surrealismo falleció' (surrealism died more than forty years ago); thus it is 'passé', worthless as a model, 'porque queremos o no, todo el que actualmente ejerza el surrealismo, es un retrógrado' (because whether we like it or not, all who still cultivate surrealism are reactionary). In 1956 surrealism was still the enemy of *mexicanidad* (the essence of being Mexican).[20]

Salvador Echevarría echoed Nandino's attacks. The surrealist manifesto is 'una apoteosis del disparate', and surrealist poetry 'un malabrismo baladí' (an apothesis of stupidity; a cheap conjuring trick). The best surrealists (Eluard, Aleixandre) had left the group years before. Surrealism is 'una cosa venenosa y trágica' (a poisonous and tragic thing), especially in Mexico where it is 'unpardonable' to be a surrealist; surrealism is out of historical context, an 'aimless course'. He does not name Paz, but it is clear that Paz is his target. Salvador Reyes Nevares does name Paz. He deems that surrealism is antithetical to Mexican culture because the historical moment demanded a new 'realism', and in spite of Mexico's historically proved tendency to adopt foreign models, he thinks it 'very unlikely that surrealism might "take" in Mexico'. That he should dream that a 'surrealismo criollo' (creole (local) surrealism) could take roots in 1956 is itself significant.[21]

A change in mood can be discerned in two 'incidents'. The first concerns Paz's publication of *Semillas para un himno* (Seeds for a Hymn; 1954), a collection of poems that infuriated the critics mainly because Paz was one of Mexico's foremost practising surrealists. Margarita Michelena (1956) describes this:

A Octavio Paz, con preferencia sobre los demás, se le agrava a cada instante con tal calificación [de surrealista] que...por desconocimiento total de lo que realmente representa el surrealismo, resulta francamente peyorativa.

Octavio Paz, as a matter of preference and before all others, is insulted all the time and so branded with the name [surrealist] that...out of total ignorance about what surrealism really represents, it becomes a mere insult.

As an example, the poet Raúl Leiva writes off Paz's surrealism as 'hermetic', with consequent loss of 'feeling' and 'humanity'. Silva Villalobos (1955) repeats this criticism and adds: 'su lírica no pertenece a nuestra tierra. Está contaminada por experiencias en otras literaturas' (his lyrics do not belong to our land. They are contaminated by experiences in other literatures). Surrealism is alien to Mexican 'purity'. The tone evokes that ancient fear of 'conquest' and 'colonisation' that echoes the history of Western European expansion.[22]

In 1966 the poet José Emilio Pacheco (1939–) publicly declared his debt to Octavio Paz as 'endless' and 'growing with each new book'. As an unpublished poet of eighteen he reflected all the prejudices of the moment. He too saw surrealism as a 'contamination'; he laments the 'twisted' poems in Paz's *Semillas para un himno* compared with Paz's earlier 'good taste' and 'sensibility'. But by 1961 Pacheco is defending that same surrealism. For him, Paz's surrealism is the only viable form, and produces the best poetry that Paz has ever written, as if Paz had changed surrealism by making it his. By 1971 the whole issue had cooled off; Pacheco himself summarised that earlier moment by articulating the myth of the two Pazs: one was the gifted, committed young poet of the thirties, the other the 'corrupted' one of the fifties; corrupted by the 'surrealist infection'. Pacheco ends: 'El término "surrealista" se convirtió en la palabra prohibida' (the term 'surrealist' was converted into a taboo word), as Paz's case confirms.[23]

Since those days, then, surrealism has become respectable. Behind this 'history' my intention has been to show that Paz's surrealism was not 'idealistic' but 'polemical', or 'critical' of Mexico's endemic xenophobia; a fragment of that continuing antagonism between Mexico and Paris (or Latin America and Europe).

Octavio Paz and surrealism

Surrealism never took root in Mexico. In trying to trace Paz's development through surrealism I started with Paz and the literary atmosphere of his country, Mexico. However, Paz's first contact with surrealism, naturally, was 'bookish'. Through reading Luis Cernuda Paz discovered his poetic vocation. He has written much on this, pointing out his affinities with the 'surrealist' phases of Cernuda's work, whose 'true poetic voice' could be heard between 1929 and 1934, only to 'lose its tension' (*CA* 15). Like Cernuda, Paz 'discovers the modern spirit through surrealism' (*C* 174), or in Paz's case through Cernuda's version of surrealism. Like Cernuda, Paz intuited that surrealism was a mental attitude, a way of being, and not a poetic style (*C* 175). Later, reading André Breton's

L'Amour fou in Spanish (a fragment published in Victoria Ocampo's *Sur*, 1936) and reading William Blake's *The Marriage of Heaven and Hell*, again in Spanish (translated by Xavier Villaurrutia in *Contemporáneos*, 1928) 'opened the doors of modern poetry' to him (*CA* 58). Further readings, such as D. H. Lawrence and Saint-John Perse as well as Rimbaud and Lautréamont, prepared the ground. These are the formative years when he edited *Taller* (1938–41). Paz recalls them: 'A todos nos interesaba la poesía como experiencia' (*Pe* 15; We were all interested in poetry as experience), where poetry was *lived* as a moral option; this was the decisive difference with the *Contemporáneos* generation (according to Paz, perhaps exaggerating in order to define himself). Recalling what he felt about surrealism, he writes: 'pero no nos interesaba el lenguaje del surrealismo, ni sus teorías sobre la "escritura automática", nos seducía su afirmación intransigente de ciertos valores' (*Pe* 76; but we were not interested in the language of surrealism, nor in its theories about automatic writing, we were seduced by its intransigent affirmation of certain values). 'Intransigent' and 'values': here lay the moral core of Breton's surrealism.

Paz's second contact with surrealism proper was pictorial. In New York, he saw a Max Ernst painting, 'Europe after a rain storm' (1942), which, Paz wrote, was 'una de las primeras obras que me abrieron la vía hacia el surrealismo' (*Pu* 190; one of the first works that opened for me the way towards surrealism). Surrealism's universal language (painting) continues to occupy Paz; he has written on Tamayo, Remedios Varo, Marcel Duchamp and others.

The third level of contact is the most potent, that of friendship and personal contact. In 1937, on his way home from Spain, Paz met Robert Desnos, Luis Buñuel (later resident in Mexico) and Benjamin Péret. His friendship with Péret led him to meet Breton in 1945, when Paz went to Paris as cultural attaché to the Mexican government. His debts to Breton are deep, as can be seen in his warm obituary (*CA* 52–64). Not much can be added to this, other than Paz's avowed fear of Breton's disapproval – 'Confieso que durante mucho tiempo me desveló la idea de hacer o decir algo que pudiese provocar su reprobación' (*CA* 57; I confess that for a long time the idea of doing or saying anything that might arouse his disapproval kept me from sleep) – as well as Breton's survival in Paz's mind: 'en muchas ocasiones escribo como si sostuviese un diálogo silencioso con Breton' (*CA* 58; very often I write as if I was continuing a silent dialogue with Breton).

Later (1967), Paz decided that his activities within the surrealist group were 'tangential' (*CA* 58). In spite of his intimate friendship with Breton, he never felt that he was a 'surrealist'; he avoided the label, played down the associations. At the same time he elevated surrealist 'principles' to a high level, what F. Alquié has called a 'philosophy of surrealism'. In 1959 Paz said to Claude Couffon:

Para mi su influencia ha sido decisiva, pero más como mentalidad, como actitud...He encontrado en el surrealismo la idea de la rebelión, la idea del amor, y de la libertad, en relación con el hombre.

For me its influence has been decisive, but more as mentality, as attitude...I have found in surrealism the idea of rebellion, the idea of love, and of liberty, in relation to man.

This 'decisive' influence affected Paz mentally, as *ideas*. For Paz, surrealism is an attitude of mind based on the possibility of using poetry to transcend life's inherent contradictions; to make man whole again, communing with his fellows, participating and reintegrated in experiences that defy time; a poetics of the timeless moment, the *instante poético*. Earlier (1954) Paz said to Roberto Vernegro that what interested and moved him in surrealism was

el movimiento en sí: su carácter de aventura espiritual colectiva; su desesperada tentativa por encarnar en los tiempos y hacer de la poesía el alimento propio de la sociedad; su afirmación del deseo y del amor; su continuo proyectarse de la imaginación.

the movement in itself: its character of a collective, spiritual adventure; its desperate attempt to incarnate poetry in its time and make it the proper nourishment of society; its affirmation of desire and love; its continuous projection of the imagination.

Again, more than the poetry of surrealism, Paz selects the programme, the utopian poetics.[24]

Throughout Paz's writings there are many references to

surrealism, especially in his *El arco y la lira* (1956). But all that he writes falls within the opposition between attitude and activity. What Paz accepts and rejects follows a clear pattern of values based on that opposition. For Paz, surrealism as a historical movement degenerated into style and convention. All that is tainted with history, all that is subject to time's corrosion, is rejected by Paz.

Paz has lifted surrealism out of time and social context, elevating it into an attitude of mind. This was possible because he arrived late at the surrealists' table. Sifting theory from practice also enabled Paz to view surrealism as eternal, a universal constant impervious to time and change. Circumstantial involvement did not blur these clear distinctions.

First, Paz, like Villaurrutia and most of surrealism's detractors, rejected automatic writing, one of the theoretical and practical pillars of surrealism. That he, again like Villaurrutia, also attempted this method of writing confirms his criticism. The impossibility of making oneself passive, made automatic writing too *difficult* for its practitioner. Paz compared it to Buddhist meditation in the demands it made on the poet; automatic writing was not a way of writing but a 'psychic exercise' (*CA* 54). This latent, spiritual purpose brings us back to principles; the *idea* that automatic writing was the 'systematic destruction of the ego', or the 'objectifying of the subject' earned Paz's deep approval. Paz saw clearly through Breton's life-long dilemma and confusion; especially his swings between saying that automatism was the only surrealist criterion and saying that its history was a 'continuous calamity'. Paz managed this by simply separating the principle from its practice.

In Paz's version of surrealism, all the techniques became commonplaces, or inevitable conventions because forming part of history. His attitude towards automatism became his attitude to hypnosis, dream *récits*, the mode of poem-objects, the collective games and so on.

On another level, Paz criticised Breton for his dependence on Freud. Surrealism had fallen into 'psychologism'; Freud's pseudo-scientific vocabulary contaminated Breton ('subconscious', 'repression', 'pleasure principle' etc.). Many surrealist

texts were, he said, no more than 'psychological texts' (*Pe* 132).
Opposed to this, Paz sought lucidity. Faithful to his anti-
historical bias, Paz criticised as pointless Breton's dream-
fusion of Marx and Rimbaud; poetry for Paz will always be
dissident, antagonistic to any society. Paz also regretted that
Breton did not turn to Eastern thought as confirmation of many
of his insights; but that was 'historically' unlikely – instead
Breton 'used' Freud to undermine literature and stayed well
within the Western intellectual tradition.

However, most of Paz's criticisms affect the Breton of the
first manifesto (1924), the Breton universalised by most literary
historians, not the Breton Paz knew in the late forties. As Paz
said in an interview: 'No creo que Breton actualmente [1953]
haga suyas muchas de las afirmaciones de la primera época,
fundadas en una interpretación puramente psicológica del
hombre' (I do not believe that Breton at the present time offers
as still his the affirmations of the first epoch, founded on a purely
psychological interpretation of man). Accordingly Paz was
relatively indifferent to surrealism's explorations of madness,
or of black humour, and he did not hold '*chance*' in Breton's high
(early) esteem; Paz did not share the passion for coincidences,
chance meetings, *trouvailles*. Yet, because he was so close to
Breton, he did hold that erotic love was regenerative; that
woman was the answer to the riddle or mediatrix, and poetry
was the key to life's problems. He prized surrealism's explorations of 'inspiration', related to the concept of the 'other' as
against the dominant ego, the false persona and its various
roles. He singled out the notions of utopia, of analogy and the
instante poético as the constants that universalised surrealism
beyond mere literary style. *Arcane 17* was therefore the most
seminal of Breton's books for Paz; it and *Ode à Charles Fourier* are
'dos de las obras más intensas y poderosas de André Breton'
(two of André Breton's most intense and powerful works). As
Anna Balakian rightly states, 'the surrealism of *Arcane 17*, of an
older Breton, is quite different from his early *coup de revolver*
attitude'.[25]

René Daumal, in an open letter to André Breton (1930),
argued a similar case:

Les neuf dixièmes de ceux qui se réclament ou se sont réclamés du
titre de surréaliste n'ont fait qu'appliquer une technique que vous
aviez trouvée; ce faisant, ils n'ont su que créer des poncifs qui la
rendent inutilisable.

Nine-tenths of those who have laid claim to the title of surrealist have
done nothing but apply a technique that you discovered; having done
so, they have only been able to create stereotypes which make it
unusable.

Like Paz, Daumal dismissed the surrealism of 'empty' or literary technique that soon dissolves into cliché in favour of surrealism as 'spiritual' adventure, giving poetry as 'revelation' of
'truth'.[26]

However, in spite of this sieving of circumstance, Paz did
participate in the surrealist 'orthodoxy'. In 1950 his prose
poem 'Mariposa de obsidiana' (Obsidian butterfly; from his
collection ¿Aguila o sol?, 1951) was included in the Almanach
surréaliste du demi-siècle, an anthology representing all the post-
war surrealists. In 1951 he signed a surrealist manifesto drawn
up by Breton and Péret, denouncing the catholics Pastoureau
and Michel Carrouges. The same year he signed the manifesto
Haute fréquence, redefining surrealism as 'adventure'. At the
Cannes film festival of 1951 he defended Buñuel's film Los
Olvidados, parading outside the cinema with a placard; his
written defence of Buñuel's cinema (Pe 229–34) reads like a
surrealist manifesto. In 1955 Paz contributed to Breton's L'Art
magique (Pe 184–92). In 1957 he published 'Travaux forcés' (a
prose poem from ¿Aguila o sol?) in Breton's magazine Le Surréalisme, même (no. 3). In 1959 Paz included 'Lettre à une incon-
nue' (from ¿Aguila o sol?) in the catalogue for the International
Surrealist Exhibition. Included in this catalogue was a Lexique
succinct de l'érotisme where Paz wrote three entries, 'odeur',
'palper' (to touch), and 'plaisir' (a word which means more
than 'pleasure', implying orgasm). 'Palper' appeared as a
poem in Salamandra (1962). In the same year 'Soleil sans âge'
(Sun without age, a fragment of Piedra de sol), translated by
Péret, appeared in Le Surréalisme, même (no. 5). Symbolically, in
1960 Paz participated in a B.B.C. programme called 'In
Defence of Surrealism', partially published in Breton's Bief:

jonction surréaliste. André Pieyre de Mandiargues translated
Paz's only play 'La fille de Rappacini' (1960; Rappacini's
daughter); in 1962 Péret published his translation of *Pierre de
soleil* (Sunstone), though Breton was unable to write his promised prologue. By 1964 Paz was listed as an official surrealist in
Bédouin's *La poésie surréaliste*. By 1965 the wheel had turned full
circle and Paz is quoted by Breton in the catalogue for the
Eleventh Surrealist International Exhibition, *L'écart absolu*; a
consecration of Breton's esteem and Paz's 'surrealism'.[27]

Paz has written about those years in post-war Paris. He
describes a time of despair and depression, with no shared
ideals and nothing to believe in. Only the surrealists sought a
way out. Paz talks of the group (Péret, Breton, Lambert) by
their Christian names, and defines their aims:

No creíamos en el arte. Pero creíamos en la eficacia de la palabra, en el
poder del signo. El poema o el cuadro eran exorcismos, conjuros
contra el desierto...escribir era defenderse, defender a la vida. La
poesía era un acto de legítima defensa. (*Pu* 117).

We did not believe in art. But we believed in the efficacy of the word,
in the power of the sign. The poem or painting were exorcisms, spells
against the desert...to write was to defend ourselves, to defend life.
Poetry was an act of self-defence.

Poetry as self-defence, as exorcism, as life-enhancing in a
moment when life had been cheapened; this is the centre of
Paz's Bretonian surrealism, and it echoes an earlier epoch
when Breton also defined poetry as 'self-defence'. That Paz
played down his actual activity only strengthens the claim of
his 'principles'. But Paz did not start from ideas, but experiences.

'Mariposa de obsidiana', Paz's first surrealist contribution,
reiterates on another level Paz's family ties with Breton. The
prose poem's surface is 'decorative' Mexican pre-columbian
exotica (as Brotherston says) and the poem functions both as a
gloss on Paz's researches into the mythic substrata of Mexican
culture in his *El laberinto de la soledad*, and as (another) poetics
involving the fertile 'eternal feminine' where the ancient goddess Itzpapálotl ('our mother') is transformed into Tonantzin
and the Virgin of Guadalupe (thus defying historical change).

But over and above this, the poem invokes a nostalgic utopian poetics shared with Breton. The sense oscillates between the evocation of a sensual, rich past with its *meaningful* plenitude of sun, dance and bared breasts, and a present of arid sterility. This conflict (found in T. S. Eliot?) is overcome by the poet, who reaffirms a recuperation of the lost natural vitality: 'Te espero en ese lado del tiempo en donde la luz inaugura un reinado dichoso: el pacto de los gemelos...' (*L* 195; I wait for you in that side of time where light inaugurates a happy kingdom: the pact of the hostile twins). The poet is the visionary who penetrates the body, penetrates the *wound*, drinks the *water* and the images bubble out. This is a poem about the place of inspiration (a poetics) and depends on the reader's prior enthusiasm for utopian poetics. It also reveals why Breton liked it so; for it corresponds to that natural, Mexican surrealism that lies under the skin of the world: 'si me rozas, el mundo se incendia' (*L* 195; if you brush me, the world catches fire), where the fire of passion (Breton's terminology, borrowed by Paz) awakens the numbed mind.[28]

Surrealism as moral example

If we accept Paz's identification of surrealism as primarily an attitude or a 'spiritual orientation' based on categories like the overcoming of opposites, the timeless moment and so on, then to search for surrealist influences in his poetic style would not reveal the essential vision. This is extra-literary, the source of all his poetry. This attitude to life can be glimpsed through what Paz writes about his fellow surrealist and close friend Benjamin Péret. It was Péret who enabled Paz to fuse life and art as life-style; the heart of surrealism's programme. To Couffon (1959) Paz said that Péret had been a 'moral example' to all those who took poetry seriously. This exemplariness – like that of Breton – came from an intransigence in living out one's desire, whatever the circumstances. This implied a perpetual disconformity with society's values, or those of literature. In an uncollected article in French, an obituary of Péret, Paz admitted that Péret had revealed to him 'une direction de l'esprit' (a direction of the spirit) which attempted to reconcile (a key word for Paz) action and expression, 'poetry and life'. Through Péret Paz saw how poetry intensified life; a form of self-defence. Paz ends by saying that his meeting with Péret and Breton (the source of the poem 'Noche en claro' (Sleepless night) in *Salamandra*) made his personal and the universal 'night' 'plus claires' (more bright). This way of evaluating poetry (as life-style, as wisdom) helped Paz to come to terms with death. That Breton broke out of the temporal prison for a 'timeless moment', 'me reconcilia con su muerte de ahora y con todo morir' (*CA* 64; reconciles me with his death now and with all dying). Their example clarifies man's dread of death by positing presence, the 'now' with body and soul intensely unified through poetry as *vivencia* (life-style). This is what Paz meant when he said to María Embeita (1968) that surrealism 'me reveló una moral poética' (revealed to me a poetic morality).[29]

Paz turned to surrealism as part of his rejection of post-revolutionary Mexican nationalism, Stalinism, or official ideologies of any sort. He wrote:

Desde hace años sostengo una pequeña e interminable polémica, no contra este o aquel artista sino contra dos actitudes que me parecen gemelas: el nacionalismo y el espíritu de sistema. (*Pu* 271)

For years I have been sustaining a small and interminable polemic, not against this or that artist but against two attitudes that seem to be identical to me: nationalism and the spirit of system.

He seeks a critical stance, hostile to and free from official, repressive culture. This is where surrealism, first within the Mexican context, then more universally, offered him a way out. He wrote: 'A medida que pasa el tiempo me parece más cierto que la creación artística requiere un temple moral' (*Pu* 280; As time passes it seems to me more certain that artistic creation requires a moral temper). This is what Breton and Péret revealed, both personally and poetically.

Poetry as wisdom

Surrealist poetics is an answer to the enigma and stigma of death. After the failure of the sciences, the collapse of organised religions and philosophy and metaphysics, twentieth-century man 'buscará una Poética' (*CA* 125; will seek a Poetics). This '*poetics*' (surrealist lived poetry, utopian dream) is the new wisdom. Paz explicitly predicts:

La *sagesse* moderna no viene de la filosofía sino del arte. No es una sagesse sino una locura, una poética [Breton's *L'amour fou*?]. En el siglo pasado se llamó romanticismo y en la primera mitad del nuestro surrealismo. (*CA* 126)

Modern *wisdom* does not come from philosophy but art. It is not a wisdom but a madness, a poetics. In the last century it was called Romanticism and in the first half of ours surrealism.

Surrealist poetry, for which Breton coined the term *comportement lyrique*, solves the problem of how to live in a godless world. It was a question of *practising* poetry, Breton insisted.

Paz affirmed that poetry is a life-style and not a mode of writing as early as 1939. In an uncollected article on Emilio Prados (1889–1962) Paz wrote that 'la poesía, la mejor poesía, es una conducta: se expresa en hechos. Es una imagen viviente' (poetry, the best poetry, is conduct: it is expressed in deeds. It is a living image). Paz's programmatic poem 'Himno entre ruinas' (1948; Hymn among the ruins) ends on the line 'palabras que son flores que son frutos que son actos' (*L* 213; words that are flowers that are fruits that are acts). *Conducta* and *actos*: poetry affects life.[30]

Paz correctly intuited surrealism's quasi-religious function. According to him, modern poetry is the 'new sacred', especially the surrealism that seeks 'un nuevo sagrado extrareligioso, fundado en el triple eje de la libertad, el amor y la poesía' (*Pe* 182; a new extra-religious sacred, founded on the triple axis of liberty, love and poetry.). Paz repeats this same notion to Vernegro (1954), saying, if there is a 'new sacred', it 'is surreal-ist', composed of liberty, love and poetry. Here too Paz is faithful to Breton, who also articulated surrealism's 'certain sacré extra-religieux' (a certain extra-religious sacred). The notion has a long tradition, but Paz's wording goes back to Breton. For Breton was, in Paz's eyes, a 'religious' man, whose surrealism was based on an act of 'faith' (*CA* 53). This 'sacred outside the religions' worried Trotsky, who had criticised Breton for his 'little window giving onto the beyond'. Audoin called this Breton's task of 'resacralisation'; a cause that united Breton and Paz in a 'recherche du sacré dans la vie quotidienne' (Alexandrian; quest for the sacred in everyday life); for both of them surrealism was/is the sacred disease of Western culture.[31]

The incandescent triangle

The surrealist attitude is grounded in a series of 'rotating signs' or analogies, a chain of metaphors where each stands for the other. Sartre's complaint that surrealism is hard to pin down, that it is 'Protean', rings true, in that to speak of desire is to speak of love, to speak of erotic love is to speak of woman, poetry, liberty, the word and so on. This chain of analogies can be reduced to three notions that Paz called the 'incandescent triangle' or 'burning synonyms': love, poetry, liberty. It is the nucleus of Paz's poetics. He articulates it many times: in 1954 to Vernegro; in writing about his generation in *Taller* (*Pe* 78); in his lecture on surrealism (*Pe* 168), to Claude Couffon in 1959; again in 1966 in his prologue to *Poesía en movimiento;* and in 1969 (*CD* 139). To Julián Ríos (1973) Paz defined surrealism as a fusion of 'las vías de la imaginación poética con las del amor y con las de la revuelta social' (the ways of the poetic imagination with those of love and those of social revolt). However, this trinity is Bretonian; in *Arcane 17* (1947) Breton three times articulates that vision as three stars, three ways: 'C'est la révolte même, la révolte seule qui est créatrice de lumière. Et cette lumière ne peut se connaître que trois voies: la poésie, la liberté et l'amour' (It is revolt itself, only revolt that creates light. And this light can only know three ways: poetry, liberty and love). As J. H. Matthews says: 'Poetry, love, liberty: these lead us to the core of Breton's work and define the area of surrealism.'[32]

Stylistic affinities

In 1959 Paz said to Luis Suarez that there could be no Spanish surrealist poetry, then added, 'pero quiero precisar que mi poesía ha atravesado el surrealismo como espíritu y forma' (but I want to insist that my poetry has passed through surrealism as spirit and form). Although Paz stresses the mental aspect, there are also 'stylistic' surrealist influences. Though this book concentrates on poetics in the succeeding chapters, some of these affinities are noted here.

There are traces of Péret:

mon avion en flammes mon château rondé de vin du Rhin
(*Je sublime*, 1936)
my plane in flames, my castle surrounded by Rhine wine

Como cae el avión en llamas y el bosque se incendia
('En la calzada', 1946)
Like the plane in flames falls and the wood catches fire

Péret's poem 'Clin d'oeil' (Wink) has links with Paz's *Piedra de sol* (lines 41–80): 'et je m'éveille par tes yeux...et je pense par tes seins d'explosion...et je dors dans ton nombril de mer Caspienne...et je m'égare entre tes épaules' (and I awake through your eyes...and I think through your breasts of explosion...and I sleep in your Caspian sea navel...and I get lost between your shoulders), where in both poems there is the same exploration of the woman as image of the world, of the body as '*path*' to revelation. There are innumerable similarities with Breton; for instance:

El mundo nace cuando dos se besan (*Piedra de sol*)
The world is born when two kiss

Monde dans un baiser monde (*L'air l'eau*)
World in a kiss world

la vida es otra, siempre allá (*Piedra de sol*)
life is other, always beyond

L'existence est ailleurs (*Manifeste*, 1924)
Existence is beyond

Madrid 1937 . . .
los dos se desnudaron y se amaron

por defender nuestra porción eterna . . .
porque las desnudeces enlazadas
saltan el tiempo y son invulnerables   (*Piedra de sol*)
Madrid 1937...the two stripped and made love to defend our
eternal portion...because nakednesses entwined leap time and are
invulnerable.

L'étreinte poétique comme l'étreinte de chair
tant qu'elle dure
défend toute échappée sur la misère du monde
                    ('Sur les routes de San Romano', 1948)
The poetic embrace, like the flesh embrace, as long as it lasts forbids
all escape on the world's misery.

Yo vi tu atroz escama
Melusina, brillar verdosa al alba...
nada quedó de ti sino tu grito   (*Piedra de sol*)
I saw your atrocious scales, Mélusine, shine greenish at dawn...
nothing remained of you but your scream.

Mélusine après le cri, Mélusine au-dessus du
buste, je vois miroiter ses écailles dans le
ciel d'automne   (*Arcane 17*)
Mélusine after your scream, Mélusine above your bust, I see your
scales flash in the autumn sky.[33]

Paul Eluard leaves clear traces, particularly references to
eyes and women, as does Henri Michaux in Paz's ¿*Aguila o sol?*;
there are surprising coincidences between Paz and Yves Bonnefoy, and so on. But then, poetry is nothing but a tissue of
'other voices' and we are proving nothing except that style and
attitude are *vases communicants* and that Paz plays down the close
relation between the two.

Conclusion

Paz consciously separated attitude from activity, raising surrealism to the category of *idea*, thought, spiritual orientation; but
only because he could reject the historical and anecdotal side:
he had lived it with Breton in Paris and not through 'books',
and so he transcended it. Surrealism answered many of Paz's
problems; it was a 'desesperada tentativa por encontrar la vía

de salida' (*Pe* 165; desperate attempt to find the way out). Surrealism was, then, the new *wisdom* based on a system of values personified and embodied in Péret's and Breton's moral examples. It was an extra-religious religion that answered the question in the poem '¿No hay salida?' (Is there no way out?). Yes, there is – through poetry: 'Damos vueltas y vueltas en el vientre animal, en el vientre mineral, en el vientre temporal. Encontrar la salida: el poema' (*L* 205; We turn and turn in the animal belly, in the mineral belly, in the temporal belly. To find the way out: the poem). It is a poetry that is both written and lived. Surrealism is thus a quest for the 'true life' so desperately sought by Breton and still sought by Paz. As Breton foresaw: 'un jour viendra . . . où l'homme sortira du labyrinthe, ayant à tâtons retrouvé dans la nuit le fil perdu. Ce fil est celui de la poésie' (a day will come...when man will leave the labyrinth having gropingly found at night the lost thread. This thread is that of poetry). Both a faith and a promise, this religiously oriented surrealism expresses and articulates itself as the very structure that allowed and still allows Paz the possibility of organising and integrating and giving meaning to his experiences, even those in India (as will be shown). In this sense, the word 'surrealist' reveals itself as fiction and loses its sense.[34]

To jump back to 1954, Augusto Lunel, a Mexican critic, equated the attacks on Paz's surrealism as simple ignorance on the part of those critics as to what surrealism really was: 'Así llamamos...surrealista a todo poeta contemporáneo, cuando hay peligro de que se nos escapa de las manos' (Thus we call...every contemporary poet surrealist when there is danger that he will escape from our hands). Paz's mission has been that of a lucid *interpreter* recuperating the best in surrealism. In 1973, in an open letter published in *Plural*, Paz disassociated himself from a surrealist exhibition held in Mexico City because he felt that surrealism had been 'swindled' and 'deformed'. In 1974, in a review, he described surrealism as '*osmotic*'; eluding all castrating classification, 'una actitud vital, total – ética y estética – que se expresó en la acción y la participación' (a vital attitude, total – ethic and aesthetic – that expressed itself in action and participation).[35]

II The Marquis de Sade, surrealism and Paz's 'El prisionero'

The poem 'El prisionero' was written in 1948 while Paz was in Paris serving his country as cultural attaché. It perfectly formulates his adhesion to surrealist concerns. The poem is intentional, a poetics dealing with a reputation (Sade's). It diverges from orthodoxy by re-interpreting André Breton's poetics, and borrowing from Maurice Blanchot's lucid *Lautréamont et Sade* (1949). The poem has a prose counterpart in Paz's uncollected piece on Sade.[36]

The poem is more than a document. An early reviewer, Raúl Leiva, referred to it as one of Paz's most beautiful poems, underlining its 'desatado impulso pasional' (wild, passionate impulse). More revealing, Paz himself thinks highly of this poem; it survived cuts and changes through its three editions; it was chosen by Paz for Muriel Rukeyser's translations (1963) as well as for his first Spanish anthology, *La centena* (1969; Hundred).[37]

The poem is subtitled 'Homage to D. A. F. de Sade'. In it Paz suggests that Sade, who was against the world, has become a 'name', a 'leader' and a 'flag' for a whole group of people, from erudites to madmen and poets, who 'disputan como perros sobre los restos de tu obra' (*L* 108; fight like dogs over the scraps of your work). Paz separates himself from these 'dogs'.

Those who particularly invoked Sade were the surrealists; Sade's position in their hierarchy was unequivocal. Maurice Nadeau writes: 'Le marquis de Sade est la figure centrale de son [le surréalisme] panthéon' (The Marquis de Sade is the central figure of its pantheon), and no critics disagree. However, the surrealists' relationship with Sade was ambiguous, especially in Breton's case; and this is what Paz siezes on.[38]

The surrealists find little interest in Sade's literary style or his aesthetics; he is not a literary influence. He is not a 'pornographer' for them either – they do not evoke his mathematical combinations; nor do they explore the political aspect of his work. Hence Geoffrey Gorer decides that they 'completely caricature him'. This is true in the sense that the surrealists' Sade is not touched by historians or moralists.[39]

Octavio Paz clearly sensed this paradox. He was puzzled by Breton's admiration for Sade, feeling that Rousseau was closer. Paz doubts that Breton and Sade come from the same 'spiritual' family. We quote:

> Sade es un ejemplo de la derechura moral y Rousseau no lo es. Aunque Breton también fue íntegro e incorruptible, sus pasiones no fueron las de Sade sino las de Rousseau. Otro tanto ocurre con sus ideas. Unas y otras giran en torno a una realidad que Sade ignoró con ceñuda obstinación: el corazón.   (*CA* 65)

> Sade is an example of moral straightness and Rousseau is not. Although Breton was also honest and incorruptible, his passions were not those of Sade but of Rousseau. The same is true of his ideas. Both revolve around a reality that Sade ignored with grim obstinacy: the heart.

Their passions divide them: Paz's emblem for Breton is the *heart,* palpitating life, love.

Paz's point is valid. Breton placed great redemptive value on love: but love must be erotic and concretely love of and with woman. Love, like poetry, is a means of self-transcendence. Breton fused love, poetry and liberty. But his erotic love was not that of the libertine; for the core of his view was his recognition of woman as the 'other'. She is mediatrix, opening communication between man and himself and nature. Breton fought for 'free choice' and fidelity to this on the moral level, while extolling eroticism and woman as promise.

Sade's views are diametrically opposed. Maurice Blanchot (cited by Paz as the source of his divergence) shows that the basis of Sade's philosophy is 'total egoism', with only one rule : that 'each one do what he wants to do, his only law being his own pleasure'. Total egoism goes with a despotic liberty, and Sade's liberty is the 'power to submit people to your wishes'. Woman, therefore, is mere instrument, an object for the libertine's selfish pleasure; every relationship is the struggle for supremacy of an elite who mercilessly crush the rest. This seemingly contradicts Breton's views on love and woman.[40]

André Parinaud put the same paradox to Breton, who interestingly answered as a surrealist by claiming that the surrealist 'courtly love' attitude recognised in Sade a weapon against 'sexual taboos'; that surrealism aimed at breaking all those sexual barriers that limited man's free love. Breton admired Sade for destroying moral barriers.[41]

However, Breton is more explicit in a poem that answers Paz's doubts. This poem is the 'secret' text behind Paz's poem; both are explicit and intentional, in both lucidity triumphs over automatism. Breton's poem, from *L'Air de l'eau* (1934), opens by coupling Sade and a volcano in eruption; symbol of destructive passion. The poem continues:

> Il n'a cessé de jeter les ordres mystérieux
> Qui ouvrent une brèche dans la nuit morale
> C'est par cette brèche que je vois
> Les grandes ombres craquantes la vieille écorce minée

He has not ceased to throw out mysterious orders that open a breach in the moral night. It is through this breach that I see the great crackling shadows, the old eroded bark.

Sade opened a *breach*, undermining the hardened crust of bourgeois morality; further, Sade still issues these orders. But, more crucial, Sade has enabled Breton to 'see', to love:

> Pour me permettre de t'aimer
> Comme le premier homme aima la première femme
> En toute liberté
> Cette liberté
> Pour laquelle le feu même s'est fait homme
> Pour laquelle le marquis de Sade défia les siècles de ses grands
>   arbres abstraits
> D'acrobats tragiques
> Cramponnés au fil de la Vierge du désir[42]

To allow me to love you as the first man loved the first woman, in all liberty; this liberty for which fire itself became man, for which the Marquis de Sade defied the centuries of its great abstract trees of tragic acrobats, clutched onto the thread of the Virgin of desire.

Sade's example restored to Breton the possibility of a love washed clean of sin and guilt, and regenerated through passion:

a love that liberates *desire*. The poem offers a gradation from the breach of Sade's moral revolt to love, liberty and desire. And desire's liberation is the surrealist dream, utopia.

Sade's influence on Breton is rooted in the notion of desire. J. H. Matthews has read Sade through Breton, casting aside the surrealists' 'distorted' view, in favour of the surrealists' 'unshakable confidence in the validity of desire as motivating force of all human activity. For them the world Sade depicts is one in which desire is placed before moral and social constraint.' Sade may be caricatured, but his defence of the 'free expression of desire' marks him as a 'surrealist' progenitor. The volcanic Sade freed love by restoring *instincts* and *passion*, as Paul Eluard wrote.[43]

In his uncollected prose piece on Sade (1961), Paz repeats the surrealist case. Sade's originality is seen as a breaking down of taboos concerning our natural instincts, for morality has nothing to do with passion; erotic acts are 'desvaríos' (extravagancies), 'desarreglos' (disorders). Sade's philosophical rigour is praised; his destruction of limits, of the modes in which words distort the reality of sensations; pain and pleasure melt together. Paz ends: 'Sade abrirá puertas condenadas hace muchos siglos' (Sade will open doors sealed centuries back). For Paz, Sade opened sealed doors, for Breton he made a breach. Up to this point in his piece, Paz is 'orthodox'. Then his reading of Blanchot allows him to diverge from Breton's 'blind' admiration. Sade's negation of God, morality, man, and nature lead to a negation of self. Thus Sade's thinking is circular. Further, by elevating the libertine as his only model of conduct, Sade condemns himself to total isolation, for people are but objects; there is no communication and Sade cannot escape himself.[44]

This leads to Paz's poem, which conveys a similar 'reading', but imagistically and passionately; the intention is identical. The title 'El prisionero' (The prisoner) relates to this divergence; it conjures up not just the physical prison of history (Sade spent some twenty-seven years in eleven prisons), but a 'mental' prison, the ego-prison, the libertine prisoner in himself, imprisoned by his system.

The poem opens with Paz's counterclaim that Sade had not disappeared, as he had boasted in his will. The will was made famous by Breton who included its last paragraph (the part cited by Paz) as an example of black humour in his *Anthologie de l'humour noir* (1940). Rather, Sade's very name is an open scar, a tattoo visible on those who vainly tried to suppress him. Sade is seen as a 'comet' exploding in the twentieth century:

> atraviesas el siglo diecinueve con una granada de verdad en la mano
>   y estallas al llegar a nuestra época   (*L* 108)
> you cross the nineteenth century with a grenade of truth in your
> hand and explode when you reach our epoch.

In prose Paz explains his meaning: 'Desde una prisión o asilo de locos [Sade] puede lanzar sus armas explosivas, aunque estallen a un siglo de distancia' (From a prison or lunatic asylum he can throw his explosive weapons, although they explode a century later). This 'explosive truth' is recreated in images of passion, though the truth is associated with a person, with a 'máscara que sonríe bajo un antifaz rosa' (mask that smiles under a pink veil) – lines that powerfully picture Sade's insensitivity and inhumanity. He has no identity; no portraits exist of him; under the pink skin-veil smiles the hardened monster. Here Paz slips into 'poetry': the images speak for themselves.[45]

Paz then wants to know what Sade means to this age; he asks the meaning of:

> esa manada de icebergs que zarpan de tu pluma y en alta mar
>   enfilan hacia costas sin nombre,
> esos delicados instrumentos de cirurgía para extirpar el chancro de
>   Dios,
> esos aullidos que interrumpen tus majestuosos razonamientos de
>   elefante,
> esas repeticiones atroces de relojería descompuesta,
> toda esa oxidada herramienta de tortura?   (*L* 108)
> that pack of icebergs that set sail from your pen and on the high sea
> bear towards nameless coasts, those delicate surgical instruments to
> extirpate the chancre of God, those screams that interrupt your

majestic elephantine reasonings, those atrocious repetitions of broken down clockwork, all those rusty tools of torture?

Behind the flow of images, the thick, long lines that mirror Sade's physical presence, there is a tension between passion and reason. Sade's excess is cold and calculating, not sensuous and soft, but exact: icebergs, instruments of surgery and torture, reason, the 'mad' clock. Paz calls this 'la imaginación más violenta y libre al servicio de un silogismo cortante como un cuchillo' (CA 116; the most violent and free imagination at the service of a syllogism cutting like a knife). Sade is elephantine, treading down all before him. Yet, for all this, his calculating power, his mathematical precision and obsessions – 'furor geométrico' (geometric furor) – lead nowhere, are 'rusty', 'broken down' and perpetually repetitive.

Sade is compared to Saturn looking lovingly down at his children; dissolving culture and barriers: 'Los surcos calcinados que dejan el semen, la sangre y la lava' (L 108; the calcined furrows left by semen, blood and lava).

Sade's traces ('surcos') passionately trail the destruction of moral, fear-created limits. Semen and lava, man and nature, creation and destruction, violence and truth; Paz's emblem for Sade is 'lava enfriada' (CD 15, 117; cooled lava). But this also is a hidden homage to Breton; Breton took the connection between lava and sperm from Sade's La nouvelle Justine as an example of (and we quote Paz) 'un homenaje de amor a la naturaleza, "une façon, des plus folles...de l'aimer"' (CA 63; a homage of love to nature, 'a way, the most crazy one...of loving it').

Sade fused natural phenomena with human passions; love, death, liberty and destiny:

¿no se llama catástrofe, no se llama hecatombe?
¿Dónde están las fronteras entre espasmo y terremoto,
entre erupción y cohabitación?   (L 108–9)
isn't it called catastrophe, isn't it called hecatomb? Where are the frontiers between spasm and earthquake, between eruption and cohabitation?

There are no 'frontiers' between things and passions; only

verbal traps. The poem then progresses, logically in its intention, from admiration and confessed homage to a reckoning of Sade's serious limitations, and the title of the poem is invoked:

Prisionero en tu castillo de cristal de roca
cruzas galerías, cámaras, mazmorras,
vastos patios donde la vid se enrosca a columnas solares,
graciosos cementerios donde danzan los chopos inmóviles. (*L* 109)
Prisoner in your castle of rock crystal, you cross galleries, halls, dungeons, vast patios where the vine coils round solar columns, elegant cemeteries where the immobile poplars dance.

Sade becomes a prisoner in transparent rock crystal; the central image of the poem. Rock crystal's hard transparency, its natural time-defying solidity, visually portray Paz's ambiguous view of Sade. Admirable (crystal) yet static (rock), trapped, imprisoned. Rock crystal's transparency also conveys lucidity and rationality, a *personal* association for Paz: 'el castillo de cristal de roca de la dialéctica' (*A* 101; the rock crystal of dialectics), 'la cárcel de cristal de roca del yo cartesiano' (*Pe* 210; the rock crystal prison of the cartesian ego). The image spreads beyond this poem, for Sade becomes rationality taken to the extreme of insanity, 'broken down', the end of a long tradition. Mineral, as Paz noted, is inhuman, the absence of life. Life flows, moves like running water, while Sade is congealed in eternity, trapped within himself.

'Mineral' has further resonances; Breton deemed it the perfect analogy of that work of art that naturally hardens, spontaneously crystallises. Paz's admiration for crystal (rock crystal is common in Mexico) does not endorse Breton's; Cirlot says that 'mystic and surrealist share the same veneration for crystal'; but this is where Paz diverges. He points out the moral flaw in Sade's suspicious clarity:[46]

¡Todo es espejo!
Tu imagen te persigue. (*L* 109)
All is mirror! Your image chases you.

The libertine's total egoism turns the other into an object; and denies his humanity. Only the libertine survives, and he only sees himself, in a *mirror*, trapped in his ego, behind its wall. The libertine's pleasure is solitary, 'rabia fría' (cold hate), without human communication, each one alone in his hell (*A* 126). Here is the flaw; Paz now moves to his prescription, yoking Rousseau, not Sade, with Breton.

Paz plainly states: 'El hombre está habitado por silencio y vacío' (Man is inhabited by silence and emptiness); his premiss is that man's meaning is the *act* of communicating (poetry). Paz asks the question ' ¿[cómo] acallar este silencio y poblar su vacío?' (how to quieten this silence and populate its emptiness?). Paz is a humanist in a godless world where relationships are what humanise; the human voice fills the silence; poetry relates, links and unites. For Paz there is a way out, a breach:

> Sólo en mi semejante me trasciendo,
> sólo su sangre da fe de otra existencia.   (*L* 109)

Only in my fellow do I transcend myself, only his blood bears witness to another existence.

Self-transcendence through awareness of the 'other'; passionate, erotic love solves the problem of solitude, for love is a relationship. It would not be forcing the metaphor to include writing and reading as an act of communication made out of emptiness and loneliness.

The final stanza passionately enlarges upon this ethic; it is a surrealist manifesto defending poetry as the answer to life's limitations. Behind the 'seeming' chaos and heat, the fusions of lava and sperm, nature and man continue to function and dictate their tensions. Imagination, desire and boredom, death, pleasure, flooding, vomit – all overflow their categories and melt into each other; desire, madness and dreams soften the rigidities which fence life in. Paz's list ends on the word 'desmesuras' (excesses): that excess that Sade exploited, that surrealism preached in order to become human again:

> desmesuras: tu medida de hombre.
> Atrévete:
> la libertad es la elección de la necesidad.   (*L* 109–10)

excesses: your measure of man. Dare yourself: liberty is the choice of necessity.

Only extreme states cleanse and purge; purifying man of his cultural conditioning. Man's 'hunger for being', his need for

'momentary eternities' are only quenched by destroying measure; by *desmesura*. For Paz the very history of modern poetry is
that of *desmesura* (*A* 253). Here Sade is exemplary; he *dared*. The
you of the poem becomes the reader, no longer refers to Sade.
Paz dares the reader (and himself?) to follow Sade and the
surrealists. Only through risk can liberty be won, that 'liberté
couleur d'homme' (liberty the colour of man) that Breton
sought. Liberty is the choice of necessity; liberty is not accepting destiny but fighting; it is a necessity because man is the only
free being (*A* 207).

From taunting the reader to follow, Paz moves to the first
person and articulates his skill, his poetic and faith:

> Sé el arco y la flecha, la cuerda y el ay.   (*L* 110)
> I know the bow and the arrow, the string and the *ay*.

But this *sé* is equivocal; it is both 'I know' and 'be it'. Paz tells
the reader to assume all his opposites, his tensions. It is a
Heraclitean image, a balancing of opposing tensions in the
continuous war of opposites; more, it has Zen resonances: be
the archer, the arrow, the string and the target, shoot, hit
yourself. The *ay*, the scream (both of pleasure and pain in
Spanish) of the perfect hit. The bow is what shoots man out of
himself, beyond his ego (*SR* 69–70). Here is Paz's refutation of
Sade. Poetry enables man to transcend himself and time, if only
momentarily in extreme experiences; it is his only liberty. *La
cuerda, la lira;* poetry is salvation because it transcends the ego,
both of the poet (the poem is the poet's 'tomb') and of the
reader, who becomes another through language. Language
devours both poet and reader.

The stanza ends:

> El sueño es explosivo. Estalla. Vuelve a ser sol.   (*L* 110)
> The dream is explosive. It bursts. Becomes a sun again.

This is the second use of 'explosive'; Sade explodes and shatters
conventional morality, and dreams explode, dissolve rationalised reality and release repressed desire: another surrealist
constant. As Paz said: 'el sueño es pasional' (*CA* 53; the dream
is passionate), for the dream is where desire is active. Paz's

dream must be lived in the day-time, a waking dream. It must rule man's life, like the sun; it gives health, warmth and light. Man should worship the dream sun as the Aztecs the 'real' sun.

The poem ends by repeating its central image:

En tu castillo de diamante tu imagen se destroza y se rehace, infatig-
    able.   (*L* 110)
In your castle of diamond, your image destroys and remakes itself
indefatigably.

Sade laid bare the mechanism that prevented the true man from discovering himself; on that level he is admirable like rock crystal or diamond, and there he still remains (his work), indestructible and absolute (no one can replace his excess). But Sade himself found no way out; his philosophy was a 'callejón sin salida' (*CD* 17; blind alley); he was trapped in his own magnificence, a prisoner in his own splendour. But because the world has not changed or has not incorporated his discoveries, Sade is still explosive, destroying and re-making himself in each generation.

Read this way, Paz's poem affirms a poetic by proposing an alternative. Paz diverges from surrealist orthodoxy in favour of a hidden Bretonian vein that leads back to Rousseau, utopia and love. Sade ignored poetry; and poetry is communion, an erotic relationship that results in the *ay* of self-transcendence. Paz yokes poetry to intention.

The real poem begins where this one ends; it is the reader's own life that is the real poem. This poem merely proposes and affirms its own intention intensely. It says what prose cannot say, because the whole reader responds with his visual and aural senses to the rhythms, images, symbols. The centre is that magnificent image of Sade crystallised into rock crystal, congealed into eternity. Years later Paz admitted that Sade's followers provoked 'en mí ganas de blasfemar contra el gran blasfemo' (*CD* 21; in me an urge to blaspheme against the great blasphemer). Paz's blasphemy is a provocation which only the reader can answer.

Chapter 2

Mentalist poetics, the quest, 'fiesta' and other motifs

I have commented on Paz's use of the word *espiritual*; it could be translated as 'mental with a spiritual glow'. This points to Paz's intention: poetry is not for him the mere writing of a poem, but an event, a faith that borders on the religious experience. Poetry involves salvation and grants meaning. This is a mentalist concept in that the activity of mind in language, especially the writing and reading of poetry, is a symbolic process that opens out a symbolising consciousness. The aim is the activating of the full potentialities of the mind: poetry is faithful to this process. In 1924 André Breton defined surrealism as revelation of 'le fonctionnement réel de la pensée' (the real functioning of thought). This revelation must start from a critical and analytical act, for what we normally isolate as thought is a mere parody, a disguise, a crust over the immensities of human potential. To let language 'live' would be to recover its symbolic resonances. In surrealism the poet's role is to 'ressaisir la vitalité concrète, que les habitudes logiques de la pensée sont pour lui faire perdre' (to recapture the concrete vitality, that the logical habits of thought have almost made him lose). This justifies surrealism's attacks on 'reason', 'logic' and 'common sense' as reductive and sterilising.[1]

This mentalist poetics can be traced to Breton's oft-quoted 'certain point de l'esprit' (certain point of the mind) where contradictions cease, a 'mental' (ideal?) place, that 'monde mental à la Genèse' (mental world in Genesis) at the heart of the surrealist concern.[2]

To have liberty is to *experience* this release from a language dead to the whole person, with his body, and his dreams. Paz criticises Lévi-Strauss for not allowing a liberty 'deeper' than economic, material or sexual conditionings, 'hay que penetrar en una esfera en que el espíritu opera con mayor libertad' (we must penetrate into a sphere in which the spirit operates with greater freedom). But to penetrate so far, conventional reality, morality and language-use must be rejected. Paz accepts the concept of the 'Romantic outsider', a position glimpsed in Luis Cernuda's poetry. Paz describes:

el descubrimiento de un espíritu que se conoce a sí mismo y se afronta, el rigor de una pasión lúcida, una libertad que es simultáneamente rebelión contra el mundo y aceptación de su fatalidad personal.   (*CA* 16)

the discovery of a mind that knows itself and faces itself, the rigour of a lucid passion, a liberty that is simultaneously rebellion against the world and acceptance of personal fatality.[3]

Spiritual liberty is the name for the celestial vision at the centre of Paz's poetics: 'la imagen celeste es visión de libertad: levitación, disolución del yo. La luz frente a la piedra' (*CA* 97; The celestial image is a vision of liberty; levitation, dissolution of the ego. Light confronts stone). The antinomy of light and stone expresses that of liberty and its limitations; light and life against insensitivity, gravity and death. All of Paz's poetry spreads out in waves from this tension; for 'spirit' only exists in terms of its repression, as a relationship. Any other word, like 'being' or 'desire' (for the same area) would also imply this dynamic concept of truth.

In the relationship between liberty and poetry, the perception and experience of the spirit is liberty, is language purged and washed of its fixed associations, freed from dead metaphor. As early as 1939 Paz experienced poetry as liberating: 'El milagro poético, la única creación del hombre, la única operación que, en verdad, lo libera' (The poetic miracle, man's only creation, the only operation that in truth liberates him). The title of Paz's collection *Libertad bajo palabra* expresses a dual act: first, the word in the poem liberates language (*A* 22); second, language in the poem liberates the reader. The poem writes 'innocence' where there was 'sin', and 'liberty' where there was 'authority'. Paz's faith is that 'El hombre es libre, deseo e imaginación son sus alas, el cielo está al alcance de la mano' (*A* 238; Man is free, desire and imagination are his wings, the sky [heaven] is within reach). 'Within reach'; poetry is a liberating, sensuous experience, for it liberates desire. Thus poetry's inner, spiritual and experiential liberty is extra-aesthetic; it affects the whole man. Liberty is an elusive possibility given epiphanic reality through the poem. Here also is the seed of utopian poetics; the momentary glimpse of this liberty is projected into a society living this liberty as daily experience.[4]

So art is not 'artistic' but 'inner liberation'. Writing about Marcel Duchamp, Paz defines this:

Para los antiguos como para Duchamp y los surrealistas el arte es un medio de liberación, contemplación o conocimiento, una aventura o una pasión. El arte no es una categoría aparte de la vida.

For the ancients as for Duchamp and the surrealists art is a means of liberation, contemplation or knowledge, an adventure or a passion. Art is not a category separate from life.

Real art alters consciousness and modifies life. *Corazón* (Heart), Paz's emblem for Breton, symbolises his own poetics: the heart is passion, life, experience, temporality and mystery. It is a fragile hope. Paz's poem 'El desconocido' relates the poet's bitter search after his meaning, like 'un fantasma que buscara un cuerpo' (a ghost that seeks a body) but finds nothing. Written in 1942, the poem embodies Paz's quest and anticipates that vision promised (codified) by surrealism:

> Pero su corazón aún abre las alas
> como un águila roja en el desierto.   (*L* 98)
> But his heart still opens its wings like a red eagle in the desert.

The heart is hope in the spiritual desert.[5]

The quest

One way of identifying Paz's attitude and surrealist poetics is through a latent metaphor underpinning all his writing. André Breton alchemically called himself a 'chercheur d'or' (seeker of gold), where base matter (life) is transformed into spirit (gold). Life becomes enriched by the action of poetry.[6]

This quest for intensified life never ends, is never satisfied. Man finds nothing, there is no gold (only fool's gold?). For Paz, life is not static, and we live in time. He emphasises the open, the flowing.

With the notion of quest, we also articulate that of journey; poetry is a process of discovery, an adventure, an exploration. These notions have been common currency at least since Baudelaire. The poet seeks (*buscar*) the unknown; he rarely finds (*encontrar*). Because the voyage is perpetual motion (only death is rest), verbs like *entrar* (enter), *ir* (go), *penetrar* (penetrate), *descender* (descend), *seguir* (follow), *avanzar* (advance), *cruzar* (cross), *atravesar* (cross), *andar* (walk), *caminar* (walk), *correr* (run), *internar* (penetrate), *hundirse* (sink), *perforar* (perforate), condition the poetry. It would be tedious to list the occurrences.

Because poetry is a quest, verbs like *nombrar* (name) and especially *inventar* (invent) mirror the intention. The whole process is an adventure. In 1952 Breton defined surrealism as 'aventure spirituelle' (spiritual adventure); also in 1952 Paz called poetry 'aventura espiritual' (*Pe* 26). In 1951 Paz signed Breton's manifesto claiming surrealism as an 'adventure'.[7]

The sense of the quest is utopian, based on the intuition that man is more than he seems to be or has been historically. Breton sought 'la récupération des pouvoirs originels de l'esprit' (recuperation of the original powers of the spirit) or a wholeness that had once existed. 'Recuperation' posits a Golden Age and a fall. Paz siezed on this and entitled his passionate obituary 'André Breton o la búsqueda del comienzo' (André Breton or the search for the beginning); surrealism attempted to return to the 'beginnings' to find out 'where it all went wrong'. Surrealism's 'passionate quest' is awareness of a universal nostalgia, and it became a 'método de búsqueda interior' (*A* 249; method of interior search) where each man had to penetrate inside himself to his lost or forgotten or repressed self.[8]

Paz wrote that Breton's quest was 'la reconquista de un reino perdido: la palabra del principio, el hombre anterior a los hombres y las civilizaciones' (*CA* 52; the reconquest of a lost kingdom: the word of the beginning, man before men and civilisations). Earlier (1956), Paz had defined poetry as 'búsqueda del hombre perdido' (*A* 244; search for lost man); as early as 1942 he wrote that 'buscamos en vano al hombre perdido, al hombre inocente' (*Pe* 131; we seek in vain the lost man, innocent man). Paz roots this nostalgia in the tradition of rebellion of the Romantic poets, a 'búsqueda de la mitad perdida, descenso a esa región que nos comunica con lo otro' (*SR* 38; search for the lost half, descent to that region that links us with the other). Paz and Breton belong to the same family.

'Encuentro' (Encounter), a long tripartite poem written in 1940, and excised in the 1968 edition of *Libertad bajo palabra*, deals with a fleeting 'encounter'. The poem opens with the poet in everyday reality; he hears 'music' and is transposed to another plane of experience:

> En la estancia contigua sonó la música...
> Y me quedé desnudo y sin pasado.   (*LBP 60* 243)

In the room next door the music sounded...and I remained naked and without past.

Naked, without past or name, the poet communes with his real self; this is not union with God, but an experience beyond attributes, beyond 'words and signs'. He descends to the rock where he finds a 'new Adam dreaming', born among his ruins. Here is pre-lapsarian man, Adam asleep and immanent in twentieth-century man. *Ruins* are Paz's name for culture and history. The poet senses a possibility of 'rebirth':

> Toco tu destrucción,
> tu verde renacer entre mis ruinas: (*LBP 60* 245)

I touch your destruction, your green rebirth between my ruins.

The poet touches this lost self, but there is no permanence in this region, the rebirth is momentary only: 'Oh fugitivo encuentro, mortal beso' (*LBP 60* 245; Oh fugitive encounter, mortal kiss). The kiss, sensual union, is the kiss of death. In spite of nature's 'invading, daily innocence', in spite of the new Adam, there is evil; and evil is time, Chronos, death. Man communes briefly; otherwise he is outside, an indifferent, unalterable nature. In 1940, the problem of time and death has not been resolved: there are experiences, but no meaningful pattern, no timeless aesthetic moment.

A later prose poem (1951) is also entitled 'Encuentro'; but the mood is contemporary, assured; sentimentality and naivety are cast aside. The text allegorises the impossibility of a real encounter. The narrator watches himself 'leave' himself; sees his real self desert him. He realises that it is impossible to grasp this other self, so elusive is it: 'Quise alcanzarlo, pero él apresuraba su marcha exactamente con el mismo ritmo con que yo aceleraba la mía, de modo que la distancia que nos separaba permanecía inalterable' (*L* 183; I wanted to reach him, but he hurried his steps with exactly the same rhythm with which I accelerated mine, such that the distance that separated us remained the same). The quest for self never ends. There is no certainty for man is a temporal being; the (other) self maintains its distance. This text, with its dynamic, ironic view of illumination, with a savage sense of humour rare in Paz, *plays* with the philosophical problem of identity ('who am I?', 'How many I's are there?'). It ends on a note of confusion: 'En el camino, tuve esta duda que todavía me desvela: ¿si no fuera él, sino yo...?' (*L* 183; On the road, I had this doubt that still keeps me awake: and if it were not him, but myself?). By 1951 Paz is the 'hardened' Romantic; irony has replaced naivety; but, as in many of Paz's poems, this poem articulates 'ideas' (allegory) not experiences; it deals with mental life. Between the two poems lies surrealism; the first is a yearning in weak language, soft with cliché; the second a 'cautionary tale' about the elusiveness of self.

The failure to 'encounter' is redeemed by the timeless moment; by ecstasy. Paz's much praised *Piedra de sol* fuses the *buscar/encontrar* antinomy; it is a clear quest poem, a groping through the world-as-woman's-body for points or moments of contact where the phrases 'busco a tientas' (I search gropingly) and 'busco un instante' (I seek a moment) reveal the intention and structure. This has been noted by most critics. We shall return to this 'synthesis' poem.[9]

Because the journey–quest is an inner one, undertaken by the imagination in symbols and exteriorised into poems, the poet does not see, but *invents*. To 'in-vent' (with distant associations of wind, breath and inspiration) is not to coin neologisms

but to drag up to light; to restore language's original purity
through the critical, selective and surgical act of writing where
language is released from the 'chains' of convention, its *karma*,
and allowed to be. *Inventar* occurs seven times in the poem
'Libertad bajo palabra' which ends on this note of faith: 'Contra el silencio y el bullicio invento la Palabra, libertad que se
inventa y me inventa cada día' (*L* 10; Against silence and bustle
I invent the Word, a liberty that invents itself and invents me
every day). Poetry, which is freed language, speaks the real
'me'. Words, made autonomous, living beings freed by the
poet, create the poet by releasing his being, dulled and made
opaque by cliché and culture.

True reality is desire, is invention:

> Deseada
> La realidad se desea
> Se inventa un cuerpo de centella   (*S* 27)
> Desired, reality desires itself, it invents for itself a body of sparks.

This 'body of sparks' is the poem, which transforms abject
conventional reality by releasing desire (how crucial Cernuda
seems here). Desire is the only truth: 'Sólo se completa cuando
sale de sí y se inventa' (*C* 190; It only becomes complete when it
goes out of itself and invents itself).

We fall back on the surrealist apologist and critic J. H.
Matthews who affirms: 'Paz is faithful to surrealism in consid-
ering poetry as a means to enlarge self-knowledge, to advance
persistently man's search for true identity.'[10]

'Fiesta' poetics

I will show how subtly Paz infuses a Mexican custom with
metaphysical resonances central to his poetics. An obvious
reality of Mexican cultural-social life, the *fiesta*, in the middle
forties assumed symbolic proportions for Paz. In *El laberinto de
la soledad*, written during his 'surrealist' days in Paris, Paz
describes the *fiesta*. It is a popular art-form (*LS* 39); an explosion of energy in an otherwise repressed ('masked') people (*LS*
40). The cyclical recurrence of the *fiesta* implies things sacred

where time 'deja de ser sucesión y vuelve a ser lo que fue, y es, originariamente: un presente en donde pasado y futuro al fin se reconcilian' (*LS* 39; stops being succession and becomes what it is again and is originally: a present in which past and future at last are reconciled). The *fiesta* is another name for the timeless moment. Through the *fiesta* Mexican man breaks down his wall of solitude and communicates with others and himself. Then Paz shifts from description to poetics. The *fiesta* inaugurates an enchanted world ruled by 'surprise', that central aesthetic element underlined by Apollinaire and taken up by the surrealists (*LS* 42). Anything can happen: what does is poetry, spontaneously lived. The *fiesta* demotes authority, 'gobiernan los niños y los locos' (*LS* 42; children and madmen govern), surrealism's moral models. During the *fiesta* 'nos aligeramos de nuestra carga de tiempo y razón' (*LS* 42; we lighten our load of time and reason). Reason, common sense, morality, convention are all discarded; poetry rules: 'A través de la fiesta la sociedad se libera de las normas que se ha impuesto' (*LS* 42; Through the *fiesta* society liberates itself from the norms which it has imposed on itself). *Fiesta* is liberation. It is 'revolt', a sudden immersion in 'pure life', a 'return', a 'recreation' and a 'participation' (*LS* 42–3).

For a moment repressive society is revoked, in a return to those dionysiac orgies where desire, not law, ruled. Paz reads the Mexican *fiesta* as a survival of a life-attitude embodied in poetics, in surrealism, in living poetry. In 1969 he defined man's inner needs as 'nostalgia for *fiestas*' (*CD* 139); a nostalgia for myth, for the eternal return of the present, for ritual and ceremonies (*CD* 77, 126). The *fiesta* is the reincorporation of the pleasure principle. The same nostalgia haunted Rimbaud, who sought the key to the 'ancien festin' (ancient feast) where he might regain his appetite; Rubén Darío was 'triste de fiestas' (sad of *fiestas*); and surrealism's optimistic vision tended towards the *fête*, a perennial utopian dream. Most tellingly, Breton laments that there 'se perd de plus en plus le sens de la fête' (the sense of the feast is increasingly lost to us).[11]

The notion of *fiesta* spills into that of the poem. Paz suggests

that 'el poema es fiesta' (*Pe* 37; the poem is a feast); the poem is
a participatory ceremony, a rite (*A* 282). If art is the new *sagesse*,
then it will be both spiritual and communal, like a *fiesta* (*CA* 24).
This new spiritual art heralds the end of the *obra* through its
momentary 'incarnation' (*CA* 73). In the lived poem –*fiesta*: 'La
época que comienza acabará por fin con las "obras" y disolverá
la contemplación en el acto' (*CA* 73; The epoch that begins will
end with 'works' and will dissolve contemplation in the act).
This is the West's only hope, art as sacred happening, as
collective act: 'la encarnación del poema en la vida colectiva: la
fiesta' (*CA* 217; the incarnation of the poem in collective life: the
fiesta). Here again is the dream: 'la poesía puede ser vivida por
todos: el arte de la fiesta aguarda su resurrección' (*A* 281;
poetry can be lived by all: the art of the feast awaits its resurrection). It was restated in 1972: 'our time suffers from hunger and
thirst – for *fiestas* and rites', a spiritual hunger. The *fiesta* is
decidedly a spiritual, mental art. Paz's shift from Mexican rite
to metaphysic is self-evident. [12]

The Mexican revolution failed, for example, through being
too narrowly 'political'. No 'vital order' was created which
might coordinate a world vision of a just, free society (*LS* 144).
But Paz is utopian, in that his 'society' would be rooted in
myth, outside evil and history, obeying a poetic wisdom. In
1954 Paz writes: 'El mundo se ordenará conforme a los valores
de la poesía – libertad y comunión, o caerá' (*PE* 78–9; The
world will order itself according to the values of poetry, liberty
and communion, or it will fall). As N. O. Brown states: 'To be
awake is to participate carnally and not in fantasy, in the feast,
the great communion.'[13]

Another prototypical utopia for Paz was the Spain of 1937.
This vision stood for more than the writer's congress, more
than his poems (mostly uncollected), more than his work for
the exiles in Mexico. Paz said in an interview about the Spanish
civil war, 'descubrí entonces una posibilidad para el hombre y
advertí que allí se perdía algo cuya reconquista quizá exigiría
siglos: la tradición revolucionaria no marxista' (I discovered
then a possibility for man, and perceived that there something
was being lost whose reconquest would perhaps demand cen-

turies: the non-marxist revolutionary tradition). Paz had glimpsed a society which was not gripped in a life-denying ideology.[14]

He saw a 'new man', a society open to 'transcendence'. He saw faces expressing a 'hopeful desperation' which he never forgot – 'su recuerdo no me abandona' (its memory never leaves me). The dream of hope at the source of Paz's poetics was here rooted in concrete, historical experience (*LS* 23–4). Writing about the poet Antonio Machado, Paz recreates this vision in terms of a *we* where contradictions ceased and 'liberty [was] incarnate' (*Pe* 212). Above all, it was a concrete experience, like lived poetry: 'Casi podíamos palpar el contenido, hoy inasible, de palabras como libertad y pueblo, esperanza y revolución... el sabor de la palabra fraternidad' (*Pe* 278; we could almost touch the content, today ingraspable, of words like liberty and people, hope and revolution...the taste of the word fraternity). Dead and numbed concepts lived again; against the forces of repression rose spontaneity, naturalness, something that 'will not die' (*Pe* 283). The failure of this dream, rather than embittering him, rather than making hope a cynical joke, allowed Paz to internalise this experience, to incorporate it into his poetic dream and to sense a similar vision in the 'brotherhood' of poetry and surrealism.

For Paz, politics and power are the enemy ('la lengua hinchada de política' (*L* 199; tongue swollen with politics)), for they are abstract: 'la benévola jeta de piedra de cartón del Jefe, del Conductor, fetiche del siglo . . . las divinidades sin rostro, abstractas' (*L* 205; the benevolent papier mâché face of the Chief, the Leader, the century's fetish, the faceless abstract divinities). In 1938 Paz wrote a eulogistic, almost euphoric 'defence' of Pablo Neruda's 'experiential' marxism. By 1942 he was accusing Neruda of being contaminated with politics, and attacking political poetry as otiose; Paz argued that he preferred a good speech by Lenin to a 'dead' poem by Mayakovsky. Neruda's 'vanity' sickened Paz and symbolized his deviance from traditional revolutionary theory in favour of a 'visionary' poetics.[15]

At the same time, Paz doubts the value of merely writing

poetry. He asks the crucial question: 'No sería mejor transformar la vida en poesía que hacer poesía con la vida?' (*A* 7;
Wouldn't it be better to transform life into poetry than to make
poetry with life?); and he reiterates the vision of a universal,
live poetry with man freed of gods and masters. He cites Blake
and Lautréamont in support, and awaits the day when 'la
poesía entra en acción' (*A* 238; poetry enters into action). By
1965 he accepts this vision as a chimera, but a necessary
ambition, and repeats that it is the question of all questions (*A*
257). This ideal, frustrated by actuality, is based on the inner
organisation of the poem in relation to the 'communing' reader.
This is surrealism. Breton's 'comportement lyrique' heralds
the end of the poem, where the reader is transformed into the
poet, and where the dream is of opening the door out of the
poet's shaky house to find oneself 'on his feet in life'. For Paz
this dream too is surrealism: 'le surréalisme est la tentative
désespérée de la poésie pour s'incarner dans l'histoire. C'est
pour cela que son sort est lié à celui de l'homme même' (surrealism is poetry's desperate attempt to incarnate itself in history.
That is why its lot is tied to that of man himself). Paz's disillu-
sion with politics only temporarily blurred his vision; his contact with the surrealists, that brotherhood who lived a utopia of
open friendship, enabled him to 'believe' again.[16].

In 1939, reviewing Emilio Prados' poetry, Paz wrote that the
best poetry was a 'life-style'. By 1944 the desire to incorporate
poetry into life, to live poetry, becomes his central dream:

> soñé en un mundo en donde la palabra engendraría
> y el mismo sueño habría sido abolido
> porque querer y obrar serían como la flor y el fruto. (*L* 101)
> I dreamed of a world where the word will engender and the very
> dream would have been abolished, because wanting and doing
> would be like a flower and fruit.

But this early poem remains pessimistic; 'communion' is a
vain desire, and the poem ends with the poet's despair at the
atrocities of history (*L* 102). Like all despair, it stems from a
frustrated vision: that the word could take root and flower. By
1948, in his celebrated (and possibly over-rated) 'Himno entre

ruinas', the vision overpowers the 'nightmares' of history and ends on the utopian hope of 'palabras que son flores que son frutos que son actos' (L 213; words that are flowers that are fruits that are acts). This would be the process that would restore meaning and truth; a poem-act that ushers in a change in consciousness. Paz's text 'Eralabán' (1949) describes how man could live the intensities of the poem; where language would consist of beautiful objects, conversations would be exchanges of gifts, life would be 'un insólito brotar de imágenes que cristalizan en actos' (L 189; a strange sprouting of images that crystallise in acts) and poetry would be 'al alcance de todos los paseantes' (L 189; within reach of all who pass). Again the poet is unable to sustain the vision and falls back into 'this' reality.

The tension between this reality and the vision is formally evoked again, as in 'Himno entre ruinas', through italics and lower case in the poem 'Un poeta' (a poet). This 'poet' posits a perfect society where knowledge, dreaming and action are one (L 198–9). He writes: 'La poesía ha puesto fuego a todos los poemas. Se acabaron las palabras, se acabaron las imágenes. Abolida la distancia entre el hombre y la cosa, nombrar es crear, e imaginar, nacer' (L 199; Poetry has set fire to all poems. Words have finished, images have finished. Abolished the distance between man and thing, to name is to create and to imagine is to be born). This is the millennial dream where the poem gives birth to 'real' language in which the word is the thing it names and not mere arbitrary convention. The text 'Hacia el poema' (Towards the poem) symbolises this 'future' poem that actual written poetry prophesies. It is the same vision, with the same tensions. When history sleeps, it talks in our nightmares; when history 'awakes' it stops being a nightmare and 'la imagen se hace acto, acontece el poema: la poesía entra en acción' (L 207; the image becomes act, the poem happens: poetry enters into action). Real poetry for Paz is a lived act. This is the dreamed-of Golden Age again 'en la que pensamiento y palabra, fruto y labio, deseo y acto son sinónimos' (A 247; in which thought and word, fruit and lips, desire and act are synonymous). Roland Barthes calls this the

'dreamed-of language whose freshness, by a kind of ideal anti-
cipation, might portray the perfection of some Adamic world
where language would no longer be alienated'. Northrop Frye
sees this 'vision' as the central myth of art, 'the end of social
effort, the innocent world of fulfilled desires, the free human
society'. Behind these lines lies William Blake; a Blake recup-
erated by the surrealists and Paz.[17]

Adamic man, innocence, nostalgia and unity: these are the
Romantic-surrealist constants veining Paz's *obra*. The Golden
Age for Paz is an immutable model that lies between nature and
history, deep in every man. And this golden-age quality must
be restored:

> los dos se desnudaron y se amaron
> por defender nuestra porción eterna
> nuestra ración de tiempo y paraíso,
> tocar nuestra raíz y recobrarnos,
> recobrar nuestra herencia arrebatada
> por ladrones de vida hace mil siglos   (L 246)

the two stripped naked and made love to defend our eternal portion,
our ration of time and paradise, to touch our root and recover ourselves, to recover our heritage snatched by thieves of life a thousand
years ago.

This is a clear poetics; life has been *stolen*, and at the dawn of
time man lost his roots. Paz wants to start again; wants to
return to the 'beginning' (L 223). This can be related to Breton's cry that 'Tout paradis n'est pas perdu' (All paradise has
not been lost) and his paradoxical awareness of this 'croyance
irraisonnée' (unreasonable belief) which mocks his belief in an
Edenic future even as he pursues it. For Breton and Paz, it is
woman who leads man back:

> Derrière toi
> Lançant ses derniers feux sombres entre tes jambes
> Le sol du paradis perdu

Behind you throwing its last dark fires between your legs the ground
of lost paradise.[18]

The myth of purity and innocence is confronted with the
anguish of contamination. Breton's fanatical anti-Christianity
is grounded in this conflict. For Paz, man's way back to inno-

cence is through poetry which is innocent (where language is 'purified'): 'con la poesía el poeta recobra la inocencia, recuerda el paraíso perdido' (with poetry the poet recovers innocence, remembers lost paradise). This is also Paul Eluard's dream: 'La force absolue de la poésie purifiera les hommes' (The absolute force of poetry will purify men). It leads us to Paz's serious pun: 'Inocencia y no ciencia' (*S* 32; Innocence and not science). This innocence is natural wisdom and is antithetical to culture and learning. Paz lauds 'noble ignorance' (*L* 19); he boasts that

> No sé nada
> Sé lo que sobra No lo que basta
> La ignorancia es ardua como la belleza
> un día sabré menos y abriré los ojos　　　　(*S* 43–4)

I don't know anything. I know what is superfluous, not what suffices. Ignorance is arduous like beauty; one day I will know less and will open my eyes.

Poetry de-schools, unlearns, teaches innocence and re-writes language; it is a 'fiesta de ignorancia' (*S* 55; a feast of ignorance).[19]

The child is the archetype for this 'song of innocence'. The child is a *natural* poet, a discoverer, free and open to ventures into the unexpected and the unknown; he embodies a magical attitude to reality. Childhood is another name for paradise lost, with poetry as 'childhood recovered at will' (Baudelaire).

In Paz's poem 'Soliloquio de medianoche' (1944; Midnight soliloquy), the insomniac poet reflects on his 'buried infancy', irremediably lost:

> Inocencia salvaje domesticada con palabras, preceptos con anteojos,
> agua pura, espejo para el árbol y la nube,
> que tantas virtuosas almas enturbiaron.　　　　(*L* 99)

Wild innocence domesticated with words, precepts with glasses, pure water, mirror for tree and cloud, that so many virtuous souls have muddied.

The adults' 'dirty' language with their abstract concepts, cultural artificialities and castrating morality: these are the weapons that an 'unpoetic' society employs against the poet (the child). To the child, reality is not 'fixed' and 'dead', but in a perpetual state of metamorphosis where 'las cosas cambiaban su figura por otra' (things changed their figure for something else), where nature *talks*:

> Sobre su verde tallo una flor roja me hablaba
> y sólo yo entendía su cifrado lenguaje;   (L 100)
> On its green stem a red flower talked to me and only I understood its cyphered language;

The 'magic word of childhood' opens all doors and reality obeys the child's inner desires. But inevitably and painfully the adult world triumphs:

> Infancia, fruto comido por los años,
> barca de papel abandonada en el légamo una tarde de lluvia
> Infancy, fruit eaten by the years, paper boat abandoned in the mud one rainy afternoon.

Mud and corruption symbolise the way the adult's world alienates the child from the poet. There is an echo of Rimbaud's farewell to childhood; the sad child launching a frail boat in a cold black puddle. But for a litany of memories, nothing remains of that magic, a 'sepulcro tapiado' (L 101; a covered tomb). Prudence, the summa of adult values, condemns the poet to sterility and loneliness (L 101).

A symbol for Paz of childhood's natural wisdom and spiritual permanence is the fig tree. Paz's emotional identification with the *higuera* in the Mixcoac garden of his childhood found a strange correspondence and confirmation in that Buddha sat under a *ficus religiosa* when he was illumined. As a symbol, it spreads across his *obra*; we note that same process from experiential reality to spiritual emblem typical of Paz.

The prose poem 'La higuera' describes the fig tree as the child's only comfort; it called him and he penetrated its centre, experiencing an intense 'plentitude'. But his special pleasure was to climb this tree, 'mi cabeza sobresalía entre las grandes hojas, picoteada de pájaros, coronada de vaticinios' (L 195; my head stuck out among the great leaves, pecked at by birds, crowned with prophecies). From up there the child envisioned the world as a promise; and though the same tree still invites him, the poet is unsure whether to chop it down with an axe or to dance with it (*L* 196). This fig tree is a mental event: 'La higuera aquella volverá esta noche' (*S* 44; That fig tree will return tonight). It is a religious, maternal, sexual and natural symbol, but its richness is rooted in experience.

Another analogy for the magic of childhood and paradise is the garden, Baudelaire's 'vert paradis des amours enfantins' (green paradise of childhood loves). The garden is the magical enclosed space of childhood. Paz's suppressed poem 'El jardín' is a projection of the poet's mind and his luxuriant inner world, with its 'alta delicia inmóvil' and its 'quieto universo' and its 'parada hermosura sin orillas' (*LBP 60* 58; its high immobile delight, its quiet universe, its still beauty without shores). The poet 'drinks from this source' and it survives in him (*LBP 60* 58).

The later text 'Jardín con niño' (Garden with child) evokes, during a bout of insomnia, a green intact garden that defies time and that, like the pines, is 'siempre de pie, sin cambiar nunca de postura' (*L* 187; always standing, without ever changing posture). The poet lists its natural delights and calls it a 'sacred site', the 'gloria entrevista, compartida' (glimpsed, shared glory) of childhood. He relives its moments of discovery; the purity of his vision made all the more bitter by the present moment of the adult poet writing 'estos cuantos adioses al borde del precipicio' (*L* 188; these few goodbyes at the edge of the precipice). The precipice is the fall into adulthood. Only poetry leads back.

In the poem 'Cuento de dos jardines' (Tale of two gardens), the poet remembers his Mixcoac garden, and sees the 'other side of being' only to realise that 'después no hubo jardines' (after there were no gardens). Yet his garden is always there in his mind: 'No hay más jardines que los que llevamos dentro' (*LE* 139; There are no more gardens other than those we carry inside). The same process from physical reality to mental symbol is inherent in the very nature of the word.

The dream is the emblem of the poetic society; for during the dream desire is released. This is a constant in surrealism, the attempt to integrate waking and dreaming into a liberating synthesis. Dreams must be lived.

Tracing the role of the dream chronologically in Paz's poetry leads to the problem of expression and meaning. His early poem 'Monólogo' (Monologue) poses a technical problem. The 'dark current of dreams' rises up from a 'mar sonámbulo, ciego' (*L* 13; a blind, somnambulist sea). This 'blind' source points to a split between lucidity and what the dream is saying. The poem 'Nocturno' (1931; Nocturn) predicates the same split: '¿Cómo decir, oh sueño, tu silencio en voces?' (*L* 53; How to say, O dream, your silence in voices?). The poet finds no words adequately to evoke the dream; it slips through. The poet complains 'Quedo distante de los sueños' (*L* 54; I remain distant from the dreams); and there is no balance between dreaming as escapism and compensation, and dreaming as nightmare.

By 1937 he glimpses, in the suppressed poem 'Al sueño' (To the dream), written while in Madrid, that the dream is also a liberation:

> El sueño nos penetra,
> rompe todos los lazos,   (*LBP 60* 235)
> The dream penetrates us, breaks all the bonds.

The dream strips away appearances and reveals the real person by revealing desire: 'somos nuestros deseos' (*LBP 60* 236; we are our desires). And through the dream the new man is born out of the annihilated self. The poem ends on a paradox about truth's experiential thrill, for the dream gives a 'death' that is more life than life, where 'death' is only the death of the social or false self. The dream becomes a manifestation of the spirit, an archetype of the perfect society, for it undermines the ego.

The poem 'Noche de resurrecciones' (1939; Night of resurrections), severely abridged in its later versions, hints in its title at a dream-salvation. The dream 'grows' inside man and raises its fiery 'maravilla' (marvel) where the body's resurrection is glimpsed. The dream leads man back to his origins, his 'remote baptism' where his true self is born.

But the tension between empirical reality and the dream continued. In the poem 'El muro' (The wall), the wall represents the final and real limitations of man's nature, as opposed to the dream's promise of 'eternity'. The dream's

> dichas, goces, bahías de hermosuras, eternidades
> sustraídas, fluir vivo de imágenes, delicias desatadas, pleamar
> (L 67)
> happinesses, joys, bays of beauties, eternities removed, living flow of images, released delights, high tide

are but a 'blind' paradise because the dream has not been incorporated into waking life. This is also a poetic problem, for the dream is *mute* (L 91), and the poet's sterility and incapacity to express the dream's visions are the source of the anguish, the wall or block in his work. Until the 1940s the dreams are no more than 'brief paradises' (L 78); that they are 'henchidos de presagios' (L 95; swollen with portents) is all the more painful.

'Soliloquio de medianoche' (1944) expresses this dissatisfaction. Mere dreaming divorced from the act of living is frustrating, for there is no pattern, no synthesis. Paz seeks a more real dream, real vision:

> Soñé en un mundo en donde la palabra engendraría
> y el mismo sueño habría sido abolido   (L 101)
> I dreamed of a world where the word would engender and the very dream would have been abolished

but this greater dream that foretells the end of daily dreaming is a chimera; trapped in history, man's only escape is random dreaming.

If dreams must be lived, then liberty is to become one's dream (L 70). However, by 1948, Paz has overcome this problem of 'context' of meaning; he has found a metaphysic, an integrating poetic: 'El sueño es explosivo. Estalla. Vuelve a ser sol' (L 110; The dream is explosive. It bursts. Becomes a sun again). The dream becomes daylight, the new sun. Surrealism's poetics illumined Paz's confusion and darkness.

The true life is the lived dream:

> Ni el sueño y su pueblo de imágenes rotas
> ...Más allá de nosotros
> ...una vida más vida nos reclama.   (L 119)
> Not the dream and its people of broken images...Beyond us...a life, more life, reclaims us.

Paz envisions the poetics of the waking dream. His dreams urge the dreamer to 'live them in broad daylight' (*Pe* 132). For the dream expresses man's inner truth: 'somos ese sueño y sólo nacimos para realizarlo' (*Pe* 132; we are this dream and we are only born to realise it); not to be the dreamer but the dream itself. This dissatisfaction with the dream's gratuitous imagery reflects Paz's quest for lucidity, 'a tener conciencia de su delirio' (*Pe* 133; to be conscious of his delirium); also his (and Villaurrutia's) rejection of 'blind' automatism.

His crucial poem 'El cántaro roto' (1955; The broken jug) contrasts the fecundity of the dreamscape with the aridity of the Mexican landscape. There seems no way of uniting vision with this empirical reality, except through the notion of the waking dream:

> Hay que dormir con los ojos abiertos, hay que soñar con las manos, soñemos sueños activos de río buscando su cauce, sueños de sol soñando sus mundos,
> hay que soñar en voz alta . . .
> cantar hasta que el sueño engendre y brote del costado del dormido
>   la espiga roja de la resurrección,   (*L* 235–6)
> We must sleep with our eyes open, we must sleep with our hands, let us dream active dreams of a river seeking its bed, dreams of a sun dreaming its worlds, we must dream aloud...sing until the dream engenders and spouts from the side of the sleeper the red wheat-ear of resurrection.

Dreams must be lived, must become part of our daily activity (with our hands) and must speak out aloud (the dream is the real language of communication). But this is prescriptive, a *must*, and not an actual experience; Paz's is a poetry of intentions, a poetics. Between 1939 and 1955 we can trace how subtly Paz has embodied an integrative poetics (of surrealism) through the notion of the lived dream (utopia) despite similar imagery (resurrection, wheat). Paz conforms to Paul Eluard's definition of the poet as the 'rêveur éveillé' drawing his poetry up from the 'sommeil vivant' (the awakened dreamer, living sleep).[20]

Open and closed eyes

Paz's vision is articulated in a recurrent motif cutting across all his work. It is rooted in a dialectic – the open and the closed – crucial to Paz. It runs through *El laberinto de la soledad*, a critique of the 'closed' Mexican, trapped in himself and scared of opening out and revealing himself. But it also looks back to surrealism. Breton's exploration of the 'subconscious' and the dream led him to define surrealism as 'la descente vertigineuse en nous, l'illumination systématique des lieux cachés' (the vertiginous descent into ourselves, the systematic illumination of hidden places). Paul Eluard posits a utopian future when man will only have to close his eyes 'pour que s'ouvrent les portes du merveilleux' (so that the doors of the marvellous open). Many other poets exploit this closed-eye vision, from Pedro Salinas and Robert Desnos to Luis Cernuda and others. It is a visionary tradition rooted in a verbal expression.[21]

When Paz the poet opens his eyes, he sees empirical reality as shadowy, ungraspable and empty: 'bosteza lo real sus naderías' (*L* 214; reality yawns its nothingnesses). When the poet looks down at Mexico in 'El cántaro roto' he sees a moonscape of bones, dust, rags and insects. The perceptive and reflective eye, pure retina without faith or vision and unable to grant sense to 'abject' reality, sees a wasteland.

Thus the poet *shuts* his eyes and looks inside himself; the surrealist proposition. He shuts his 'outer' eyes and 'opens' them inside himself (his mind's eye). Inside he sees the real midday, the real light, and hears the real song of his ancient, buried nakedness. This is real seeing, the poet's mental lucidity. Poetry is light, and when the poet invents he sees his own creation 'que renace lentamente bajo la dominación de mis ojos' (*L* 10; that is reborn slowly under the domination of my eyes). The poet sees the 'evidencias del mundo / para los ojos puros' (*LBP 60* 49; evidences of the world for my pure eyes), for poetry purifies and restores vision, not mere sight. This is linked to Eluard's claim: 'Je devins esclave de la faculté pure de voir' (I became a slave to the pure faculty of seeing). Poetry makes the poet's eyes 'prophetic' (*L* 91) and reveal the real self 'me vi al cerrar los ojos' (I saw myself when I closed my eyes), the self beyond reductions:[22]

> Y los sentidos palpan
> la forma presentida
> y ven los ojos lo que inventan   (*L* 33)

And the senses touch the intuited form, and the eyes see what they invent.

The inner eye that sees is a device in many poems: 'tu espalda fluye tranquila bajo mis ojos' (*L* 114; your back flows tranquilly under my eyes); this is not retinal art but desire-art, vision. Paz writes:

> La presencia sin más
> ...Con nuestros ojos ven lo que no ven los ojos   (*S* 44)

Nothing but presence . . . with our eyes see what our eyes do not see.

The paradox, seeing what cannot be seen, is illusory; with desire 'liberated' we see and we experience.

Woman is closer to this truth or insight. She is in touch with herself; her eyes are 'puertas del más allá' (*L* 113; doors of the beyond). Paz unequivocally states: 'abre los ojos el Poeta, los cierra la Mujer. Todo es' (*L* 200; the poet opens his eyes, woman closes them. Everything is). She grants reality, for the act and experience of love is the truth.

And this truth is beyond words and eyes: 'Toma mis ojos y reviéntalos' (*L* 90; Take my eyes and burst them); and the truth of presence is described thus:

> Mis ojos han de ver lo nunca visto
> Lo que miraron sin mirarlo nunca
> El revés de lo visto y de la vista   (*S* 53)

My eyes have to see what has never been seen, what they looked at without ever looking, the reverse of what is seen and sight.

Paz the poet sees beyond what man has earmarked as reality; but this is done only through desire, liberating the self from this marking, this deformation. Poetry helps because it 'cleans the doors of perception' by stripping language of its dead, dirty 'skins'. That sight is the prime sense in Paz is clear; from his interest in the visual arts to his visionary poetics, his aim is to *see*. His intention is to 'dream again with his eyes closed' and, living that dream, to become himself.

Urban wasteland

The open mind, the surrealists' 'disponibility', always open to chance and arbitrary experiences, responding to whatever stimuli it received without imposing any deforming schema or grid; this corresponds to Paz's poetics, to his dialectic of 'loneliness' and 'communion'. André Breton was obsessed by the 'Ouvert' (Alexandrian; Open), always striving to 'ouvrir, toujours ouvrir, à tout prix' (Jaccottet; to open, always open, at all costs). To write, for Paz, is to 'abrir las puertas condenadas' (to open sealed doors); to prise open the hardened, encapsulated ego and let fresh air and life in.[23]

Soledad (Loneliness) shows that the root of man is his essential loneliness; the fact that only he himself can die and that his profoundest experiences are solitary and incommunicable. On another level, meditating, thinking, reading and writing are solitary acts. Each poem begins in an act of *soledad* and only from this inner laboratory of loneliness will the new poetry spring: 'Por todas partes los solitarios forzados empiezan a crear las palabras del nuevo diálogo' (*L* 206; Everywhere the forced solitaries begin to create the words of a new dialogue). The centre of Paz's psychology is man's *soledad*: 'Soledad / Única madre de los hombres' (*S* 27; Loneliness, man's only mother). It is this real *soledad* that forces man to communicate, talk, write, make love and transcend his solitary self.

The poet suffers this *soledad* more intensely because of his values, his insights, his lucidities, that isolate him from the mass of society and place him to one side of the time-sanctioned securities. Paz writes: 'Condenado a vivir en el subsuelo de la historia, la soledad define al poeta moderno' (*A* 242; Condemned to live in the subsoil of history, loneliness defines the modern poet). The poet reflects the fragmented and divided culture in his over-sensitised self. For *soledad* is being divided in two: 'Todos estamos solos, porque todos somos dos' (*A* 134; We are all alone, because we are all two).

The critic Ramón Xirau has shown how this theme of isolation characterises an epoch (1938–42), without suggesting that 'surrealism' offered Paz a way out, a poetic. Both in *El laberinto de la soledad* and in 'Himno entre ruinas' there is a solution to loneliness, and both were written in Paris.

Two central, recurrent symbols convey the restricting and alienating sense of *soledad*: *muro* (wall) and *espejo* (mirror). Both are poetic commonplaces and reflect the poet's inability to convey the real sense of isolation. Deeper than the *theme* of *soledad* is the feeling that the poet was divorced from his capacity to write poetry; repeating other men's symbols; dead, literary symbols: the 'wall' that blocks the exit, the 'mirror' that reflects the surface self. And the 'wall' is closer to what psychologists call the 'block'; rather than accept this block nostalgically Paz seeks a poetics of self-knowledge. For only self-knowledge will reveal the wall and smash the mirror; and surrealism gave Paz the clue in its utopian dream of a poetic society that would 'echar abajo las paredes entre el hombre y el hombre' (*L* 236; knock down the walls between man and man).

A deeper meaning underlying Paz's use of the 'wall' is that it is *artificial*, a man-made barrier. The sense is that man has lost contact with his *natural* sources and has universalised reason, worshipped science and numbers and what is quantifiable. To Paz this is a mutilation: 'mas él cierra los poros de su alma al infinito que lo tienta ensimismado en su árida pelea' (*L* 98; but he shuts the pores of his soul to the infinite that tempts him, absorbed in his arid struggle).

Paz senses that the things we label reality – social, urban, 'objective' reality – are all grotesque parodies of what *is*. Paz sympathises with the Romantic rebellion against 'wasteland' culture. For culture has lost contact with its 'spiritual' roots.

Mexican reality, part of universal reality, is a deformed parody of what it should be. This is the theme of *El laberinto de la soledad* and central poems like 'Himno entre ruinas' and 'El cántaro roto'. 'Ruins' is Paz's word for contemporary culture; a 'broken' absent wholeness. Mexican culture is damned; its 'guitarras roncas', its songs that end in a curse, its shadowy substance that 'nos cierra las puertas del contacto' (*L* 212; hoarse guitars; close the doors of contact). This is the wasteland of 'El cántaro roto'; there are no living people, no crickets singing, only cold volcanoes, dry gulches and cacti and stones, and a vague smell of burnt seed: 'He aquí a la piedra rota, al hombre roto, a la luz rota' (*L* 235; Here is the broken stone, the broken man and the broken light).

But Mexican man is contemporary with all men; the grey uniform of the twentieth century is worn by all (*Pe* 56); New York, London and Moscow are no different to Mexico City; all are peopled by a 'crowd of rats', by 'domestic bipeds'. And Paz includes himself, trapped in his own inner, sunless mental labyrinth; he is sterile and empty: 'Y todo ha de parar en este chapoteo de aguas muertas' (*L* 212; And everything has to stop in this splashing of dead waters).

Paz rejects conventional, societal values and morality; he identifies with a surrealist *topos*. He senses the stranglehold of 'shoes', 'family ties', 'false smiles and hopes' (*L* 54); he satirises 'money, glory, justice, power, god'; the capitalistic system is unacceptable. 'Magic money' builds its dreams on human bones; 'porque el dinero es infinito y crea desiertos infinitos' (*L* 86; because money is infinite and creates infinite deserts). The grand ideals are 'elocuentes vejigas ya sin nada: Dios, Cielo, Amistad, Revolución o Patria' (*L* 99; eloquent bladders now without anything: God, Heaven, Friendship, Revolution or Fatherland). Businessmen, politicians, *caudillos* and urban man in general have renounced the quest for a 'better' life and go to the cinema, Mass, the office and death (*L* 106).

All that divides man from man – laws, banks, prisons, the army, the church, teachers – must be rejected:

> mejor el crimen,
> los amantes suicidas, el incesto
> ...
> el adulterio en lechos de ceniza,
> ...
>   mejor ser lapidado
> en las plazas que dar vuelta a la noria
> que exprime la sustancia de la vida,
> cambia la eternidad en horas huecas,   (*L* 248–9)

better crime, suicidal lovers, incest...adultery in beds of ash... better to be stoned in the squares than to turn the waterwheel that squeezes out the substance of life, changes eternity into hollow hours.

The rebellion is in terms of a richer *life*, not 'abstract shit' nor 'copper coins'; it is any rebellion that is against convention, anything that restores despised 'spirituality' rather than tread round and round the wheel.

The only imperative is 'pisotear las reglas' (*L* 150; to trample on the rules); to step on literature, morality, reasonable women, novels, psychology, friends (*L* 150). The imperative is to negate: 'No: renuncio a la tarjeta de racionamiento, a la cédula de identidad, al certificado de supervivencia' (*L* 175; No: I renounce the ration book, the identity card, the survival certificate). Paz defines modern poetry as an experience that implies 'a negation of the exterior world' (*CA* 7). He seeks *desmesuras* (excess), extreme actions.

The artificiality and abstractness of urban reality nauseate Paz. The city is a sterile labyrinth, hostile to poetry; it is both very real, out there, and *mental*; the city as symbol of rational consciousness. Again the outer city reflects the inner and vice versa.

Other city symbols repeat this sterility: in the poem 'La calle' (The street) it is the street that alienates:

> Es una calle larga y silenciosa.
> Ando en tinieblas y tropiezo y caigo
> ...
> Todo está oscuro y sin salida,
> y doy vueltas y vueltas en esquinas
> que dan siempre a la calle   (*L* 73–4)

It is a long and silent street. I walk in darkness and stumble and fall ...All is dark and without exit, and I turn and turn at corners that always give on to the same street.

Other images of sterile repetition include 'corridors', 'galleries', 'halls', 'alleyways', all leading nowhere.

Another set of symbols of *soledad* in the city clusters around the hotel room; expressive of what is anonymous and transient. 'Room', bedroom, door and *puerta condenada* amplify these connotations. These last are both outer doors and inner doors; the doors to being that are opened by poetry.

There are many other wasteland symbols and most are conventionally literary; some are also obvious allusions to the

Mexican landscape and convey the fusion between inner mental sterility and the outer, real deserts of most of Mexico; recurrent words such as sand, desert, wasteland, ash, dust, saltpetre, stone. This last – stone – is most frequent in Paz; stone is dead matter which can also be resurrected through poetry, for stone is a word that can defy gravity and live, a symbol. There is a tension between 'las piedras mudas' (*L* 73; the mute stones) and the 'piedra [que] vive y se incorpora' (*L* 99; stone [that] lives and gets up), the 'piedra partida que mana inagotable' (*L* 125; cracked stone that flows inexhaustibly).

The poet negates the *'ruins'* and *'shadows'* of twentieth-century urban culture, symbolised in a set of images – the Mexican landscape, urban culture and its values, and the modern poetic tradition. As a cluster of images, it is derivative and stale because Paz is still in the shadow of other poets, unable to find his voice. The poems of this period (1938–42) antedate by a few years Paz's sought-after surrealist experience, and the *mood* is dominated by the crushing presence of T. S. Eliot's urban poetics. Paz has noted this conjunction:

El hombre moderno es el personaje de Eliot. Todo es ajeno a él y él en nada se reconoce. Es la excepción...El hombre no es árbol, ni planta, ni ave. Está solo en medio de la creación.   (*A* 79)

Modern man is Eliot's character. All is alien to him and he does not recognise himself in anything. He is the exception...Man is not a tree, nor plant, nor bird. He is alone in the middle of creation.

Paz rebels against this derivative, alienated voice. His use of negatives reveals his values. He seeks to belong (religion), to find his roots (tree), to overcome his loneliness.

The way through, life, epiphany

At this point (the early 1940s) we leave T. S. Eliot's shadow, and we leave Paz groping for a style, and go in search of a poetics. Paz believes in redemption. For him, as for Breton (in the poem to Sade) there is a *'breach'*, the door can be unlocked. Various recurrent images point to this sensing of a way through. Terms like *herida* (wound), *llaga* (wound), *cicatriz* (scar), and *tatuaje* (tattoo) reveal this. The wound is also woman's sexual organ, a reminder that we have an origin and that we have fallen. This wound sings; it is resonant. One day it will 'open' again; and man must scratch around these badly healed wounds (*L* 177). The ancient goddess (obsidian butterfly) reminds the poet: 'Yo soy la herida que no cicatriza' (*L* 198; I am the wound that never heals); for every wound is also a fountain. This is explicit in the poem 'Mutra' (1952):

> Tras la coraza de cristal de roca busqué al hombre, palpé a tientas la brecha imperceptible:
> nacemos y es un rasguño apenas la desgarradura y nunca cicatriza y arde y es una estrella de luz propia,
> nunca se apaga la diminuta llaga, nunca se borra la señal de sangre, por esa puerta nos vamos a lo oscuro. (*L* 224)

Behind the rock-crystal cuirass I looked for man, I gropingly touched the imperceptible breach: we are born and it is hardly a scratch, the tear, and it never heals up and it burns and it is a star of its own light, the diminutive wound never goes out, the sign of blood is never wiped out, through that door we go to the dark.

The rich sonorous lines lead the reader like an umbilical cord back to the dark origins: woman's sexual organs, breach, scratch, unhealed scar, the 'life door' which is the site of separation. Paz's metaphysics of union is very literal and symbolic, for this 'oscuro' is none other than Rimbaud's 'bouche d'ombre', the very source of life. Back through woman lies 'real life': 'una herida en la que bebo la sustancia perdida de la creación' (a wound in which I drink the lost substance of creation).[24]

Other terms prevalent in his poetry, such as the conventional symbols of *llave* (key) and *puente* (bridge) – the key to the sealed door, the bridge over to the 'other' – also underscore the process from breach through to communion. Expressions of and variations on *frontera* (frontier) and *orilla* (shore) substantiate this 'journey' through limitation and restrictions. But above all, poetry will be the poet's *weapon* to break down the wall; this is a violent aggressive activity (the Romantic outsider) and the poet invokes *daga* (dagger), *puñal* (dagger), *cuchillo* (knife), *navaja* (razor), *hacha* (axe), *lanza* (lance), *espada* (sword), *flecha* (arrow) as well as *garra* (claw), *uñas* (nails). Faced with the numbed body of culture, the act of writing a poem is at first a destructive act, in that its starting point is critical. This is clearly reflected in these listed terms.

But all this is only in search of a richer, more intense life. The poet despairs that 'la vraie vie est absente' (Rimbaud; the true life is absent) and he cries out 'qué sonido remoto tiene la palabra vida' (*L* 229; what a remote sound the word 'life' has). The poet wants to sense that he is living, and that life has a meaning.

Above all, this means facing death by stripping away false illusions, by rejecting the comforting gods and the diverse religions and ideologies, and incorporating the fact of death into life. Paz affirms 'el culto a la vida, si de verdad es profundo y total, es también culto a la muerte' (*LS* 50; the cult to life, if it is truly profound and total, is also a cult to death). Poetry becomes this cult to life, the 'poétique vécue' is the answer: 'el decir poético, chorro de tiempo, es afirmación simultánea de la muerte y la vida' (*A* 148; poetic saying, stream of time, is a simultaneous affirmation of death and life). Poetry, like music, is an art in time (we read along the lines, each word effacing the next) and yet the whole act is repeatable and defies time by charging the timeless moment with presence: where desire, being and language are one: 'Nacer y morir: un instante. En ese instante somos vida y muerte, esto y aquello' (*A* 155; To be born and die: an instant. In this instant we are life and death, this and that). Poetry fixes the *vertiges* (as Rimbaud put it) and redeems time by recreating it.

However, nothing can be said about death except

> Todos vamos a morir
> ¿Sabemos algo más?   (*S* 39)
> We are all going to die. Do we know anything else?

and a living life is what we have and are. Yet to sense this living intensely is not easy, for life has been numbed and dulled. Paz can write lines like 'Yo estaba vivo, en busca de la vida' (*S* 100; I was alive, in search of life). Straightforward living is given (i.e. that we are breathing) but to experience real life, 'asir la vida' (*L* 78; to grab life), is arduous. The poet wants to 'give [more] life to life' (L 79), for to him living should mean living the full intensity of the present (ecstasy) as a 'lúcida embriaguez' (L 227; lucid rapture), as a 'vivacidad instantánea' (instantaneous vivacity). Paz seeks an elixir: 'Qué agua de vida ha de darnos la vida' (L 211; What water of life has to give us life?).

The actual situation is that life is alienated from man, as if life 'unlives' man (L 252); Paz (deliberately?) echoes Breton in his cry 'la vida es otra, siempre allá, más lejos' (L 252; life is other, always over there, farther away). Something is very wrong with what we call life and it is the poet who suffers this 'absence'. Paz ends his prose poem 'Carta a dos desconocidas' (Letter to two unknowns; life and death are the two unknowns, both feminine in Spanish) thus: 'A la verdadera vida, a la que no es noche ni día, ni tiempo ni destiempo, a la vivacidad pura' (L 173; To true life, that which is not night or day, nor time nor untime, to pure vivacity); real life is 'pure vivacity', the centre of Paz's poetics, as the excellent critic Guillermo Sucre has shown in another context.[25]

Vivacity, presence, the present moment: these notions point to the ontological centre of Paz's poetics, the intense experience that transcends language (culture and history) to reveal desire and being and man's inner truth in the epiphanic moment, or *instante poético*. This is Paz's answer to man's pressing, ever-present temporal limitations; what Breton called 'eternity' in the 'instant'.[26]

As an experience that transcends Chronos the most apt analogy with the timeless moment would be the orgasm (*Pe* 125); the basic metaphor in Paz's body–spirit poetic. Erotic love is the link, the 'absolute' experience shared by poet and reader, the cypher of eternity. This orgasmic *instante* reveals desire–being, where the poet becomes the poem he has written, an *image* of what he can be, his desire temporarily liberated (A 180). However, behind the uniqueness of this 'now' or poetic presence lies a paradox: for man the arrival of a successive 'now' is trapped in time. Once again poetry points to a solution; for it redeems time and fixes the temporal flux by creating a *retour éternel*, an ever-renewable experience based on cyclical or natural time. Paz ends his book *El arco y la lira*: 'En el poema, el ser y el deseo de ser pactan por un instante, como el fruto y los labios. Poesía, momentánea reconciliación' (*A* 284; In the poem, being and desire for being agree for a moment, like fruit and lips. Poetry, momentary reconciliation). Hence poetics (surrealism) replaces religion and metaphysics.

The centre of Paz's poetics is *experience*: not coherence, nor even originality of thought; experience is the sensuous apprehension of the present moment intensified, and this is a common heritage, a commonplace.

Here poetics ends and the problem of writing begins, much as in 'mystical' verse where the crux is how to recreate (or invent) in language the intense experience. Many of Paz's poems deal with negative moments – also moments that elude the word – as well as dealing with the positive, ecstatic ones. These latter sustain many poems. The long 'Piedra de sol' is structured about these negative and positive *instantes* of successive time. Paz describes this as

el tema central [el] de la recuperación del instante amoroso como recuperación de la verdadera libertad, 'puerta del ser' que nos lleva a la comunicación con otro cuerpo, con los demás hombres, con la naturaleza.

the central theme is that of the recuperation of the moment of love as a recuperation of true liberty, 'door of being' which leads us to communication with another body, with other men, with nature.

This poem 'recuperates' the epiphany where the moment of erotic union gives life its meaning in terms of experiential knowledge:

> se derrumban
> por un instante inmenso y vislumbramos
> nuestra unidad perdida, el desamparo
> que es ser hombres, la gloria que es ser hombres
> y compartir el pan, el sol, la muerte,
> el olvidado asombro de estar vivos;   (*L* 248)

they collapse for an immense instant and we glimpse our lost unity, the helplessness that is being men, the glory that is being men and sharing bread, sun and death, the forgotten amazement of being alive.

The experience of this momentary *amazement* at being alive is given through erotic love and poetry.

Paz conveys the *instante* through a series of terms such as *relámpago* (lightning) – that sudden, blinding flash of light – and *chispa* and *centella* (spark); or *ola* (wave), the wave of time, rising and falling; or *mediodía* (midday), the moment of revelation with the sun casting no shadows; and many others. We will restrict ourselves to one other imagistic vein.

Vertigo, the experience of dizziness and thrill glorified by André Breton, is a figure of the fusing of 'orgasm' and the *instante poético*. Vertigo is the experience of lovers: 'los amantes se asoman al balcón del vértigo' (*L* 201; the lovers show up on the balcony of vertigo); the climax of their union is 'en lo alto del vértigo' (*L* 168; in the height of vertigo), the trampoline of vertigo (*L* 203) where man is thrown out of himself. To sense that one is alive is a 'vertiginosa y lúcida embriaguez' (*L* 227; vertiginous and lucid rapture). Vertigo can be ascribed to the inner world of the dream: 'y un mundo de vértigo y llama nace bajo la frente del que sueña' (*L* 232; and a world of vertigo and flame is born under the brow of him who sleeps), a variation on Breton's 'descente vertigineuse en nous'. Vertigo can also be predicated of the experience of the poem itself (*S* 95): as it is the dissolution of reason, of form and language itself, 'el vértigo sin forma' (*LE* 90; formless vertigo), as in Rimbaud's poetics, 'fijar vértigos' (*LE* 90). Vertigo is the word that describes the experience of the absolute: 'luego el vértigo: caer, perderse, ser uno con lo Otro...Ser todo. Ser' (*A* 133; then vertigo: to fall, lose oneself, be one with the other...Be all. Be). To give in to vertigo might even change the world:

> el mundo cambia
> si dos, vertiginosos y enlazados,
> caen sobre la yerba...   (*L* 249–50)
> the world changes if two, vertiginous and entwined, fall on the grass
> ...

Vertigo is the source-experience of a new religion:

> Esculpimos un Dios instantáneo
> Tallamos el vértigo   (*S* 55)
> We sculpt an instantaneous God, we carve vertigo.

Vertigo is the centre of Breton's poetics as well: 'Ce que j'ai

connu de plus beau c'est le vertige' (What I have known that
was most beautiful is vertigo); he is only moved by nature and
events

> ...qu'en fonction de la part de vertige
> Faite à l'homme...

only as a function of the amount of vertigo dealt to man.[27]

A metaphor of vertigo and the vision granted by the *instante
poético* is provided by the notion of 'transparency'; according to
Rachel Phillips this is Paz's most personal motif. Transparency
is otherwise opaque matter penetrated by the vision, just as
crystal is stone metamorphosed. The state of transparency is
described as one of the most effective and beautiful conjunctions of opposites: a state sought by 'mystic and surrealist alike'
(Cirlot). The point here is that Paz is not being 'personal', but
consciously participating in a tradition. André Breton was
obsessed by the 'crystallisation' of thought into poetry, which
he deemed the 'total transparency' between the material and
the mental. His 'praise of crystal' derives from a sense of it as the
archetypal work of art, combining hardness, regularity, lustre
and transparency, but formed naturally and mysteriously. Breton's poetic ideal is 'transparence' (Alexandrian); he was
haunted by transparency (Audoin); this is also the basis of
Eluard's poetics, where the 'idea of transparence, of the penetration of surfaces, of passing the frontiers of the real' (Matthews) is the ideal. The crystal is the surrealists' emblem, and
their enemy 'c'est l'opacité' (Breton; is opacity).[28]

Paz inherits and shares this ideal: 'el arte aspira a la transparencia' (art aspires to transparency). Transparency is the
quality of all great poetry, and Paz applies it to Gorostiza,
Mallarmé and Michaux. Answering a questionnaire sent by
Breton and published in Breton's *L'Art magique*, Paz selects an
Uccello vase for its transparency, 'on peut voir l'autre côté' (one
can see the other side). Poetry transforms language's normal
opacity; it creates 'bosques de árboles transparentes' (*L* 228;
woods of transparent trees), rocks of 'entrañas transparentes'
(*L* 232; transparent cores); poetry is a 'dialogue of transparencies' (*L* 232). This is the essence of the mental and visionary

worlds where poetry is not a question of style or words but of vision:[29]

> el mundo ya es visible por tu cuerpo,
> es transparente por tu transparencia,   (L 238)

the world is already visible through your body, is transparent through your transparency.

This leads us to the central symbol of 'unity' in Paz's poetics; namely *light*. Paz is a poet who *looks*, lucidly seeking enlightenment. Light bathes his concerns; it is the light of creativity as well as mental light, and as well as the sun or the dawn revealing the world as it really is. This stress on light has its roots in Paz's ambiguous *mexicanidad* where the light of the high plateau is so 'crystal clear'. We will investigate some of these layers of meaning.

When the dream 'explodes' it becomes a 'sun'; here lies the link between light and spirit and being. The divine vision is one of light, of 'seas of light' (*CA* 89); for the original divinity was light. Paz recalls a quartz stone shown him by the surrealist painter Wolfgang Paalen, engraved with an image of the rain god Tlaloc: Paz wrote a short poem (haiku?) about this:

> Tocado por la luz
> el cuarzo ya es cascada.
> Sobre sus aguas flota, niño, el dios.   (L 140)

Touched by the light the quartz is already a cascade. On the waters floats, a child, the god.

The mineral quartz is brought to life by the light and *flows*. Light is the divine creative archetype (*CA* 97–8); and, as in this short poem, its antithetical image is that of inert matter, the opposition between 'la luz frente a la piedra' (*CA* 97; light confronts stone). Petrification is another metaphor for ego-limitation, as David Gallagher has pointed out, and as we saw in Paz's poem on Sade. Light is a traditional symbol of the spirit, and there is also an inner, mental sun, a 'soleil spirituel', Nerval's 'black sun'. The *word* 'sun' is not the sun that heats the earth, but the word shines.[30]

Gaston Bachelard makes this clear by quoting from Novalis: '"Dans les espaces infinis, la lumière ne fait donc *rien*. Elle attend l'oeil. Elle attend l'âme. Elle est donc la base de l'illumination spirituelle"' ('In the infinite spaces, light then does nothing. It awaits the eye. It awaits the soul. It is then the base of spiritual illumination'). Paz is rooted in this tradition of poets who give evidence of the sovereignty of light. He has his eyes open and sees the light that reveals, destroys, creates and gilds a world indifferent to man:[31]

> como la luz ligera y sin memoria
> que brilla en cada hoja, en cada piedra,
> dora la tumba y dora la colina
> y nada la detiene ni apresura.   (*L* 79)

Like the agile and memoryless light that shines in every leaf, in every stone, gilds the tomb and gilds the hill and nothing stops it nor hurries it.

Light is an image of Eden and infinity; it inaugurates 'un reinado dichoso' (*L* 195; a happy kingdom); it is formless perfection (*L* 20).

Paz's *Semillas para un himno* (1954) is a series of poems about the paradisal world before man, inundated with light; it explores a dual theme, linking this dawn of pre-history and myth with the creative act itself in the form of the *birth* of the solar, luminous world–word. Light leads the world out of the darkness of chaos, and the word out of the dark mass of language. Here light fuses inner and outer, poet and paradise:

> Al alba busca su nombre lo naciente
> Sobre los troncos soñolientos centellea la luz
> . . .
> La luz despliega su abanico de nombres   (*L* 121)

At dawn what is born seeks its name. On the dreamy trunks the light sparkles . . . The light unfolds its fan of names.

This 'light' creates (invents) a world of surface perfections:

> La luz corre por todas partes
> Canta por las terrazas
> Hace bailar las casas   (*L* 123)

Light runs everywhere, sings on the terraces, makes the houses dance.

Creative light makes reality tangible, 'luz que madura hasta ser cuerpo' (*L* 126; light that matures until it is a body), and this body–light is song or poetry:

Cierra los ojos y oye cantar la luz   (L 128)
Shut your eyes and hear the light sing.

The dawn of light is the dawn of the word in poetry, and the result is language perceived sensuously. Real man, buried under a civilised mask, is a fragment of this cosmic light. Through woman this light can be recovered in the *instante* of erotic love which leaves the poet dazzled: 'Gran vasija de luz hasta los bordes henchida de su propia y poderosa sustancia' (*L* 132; Great vessel of light filled to its edges with its own and powerful substance).

The inner light of being, *estrella interior* (interior star), the divine light of the beginning, daylight, the light in woman, and the light of creativity are all *analogues* linked by the celebration of the *instante* in the title poem of the collection, which ends:

La luz se abre en las diáfanas terrazas del mediodía
Se interna en el bosque como una sonámbula
Penetra en el cuerpo dormido del agua

Por un instante están los nombres habitados   (L 139)
The light opens out in the diaphanous terraces of midday. It penetrates the wood like a sleepwalker. It penetrates the sleeping body of the water. For an instant, names are inhabited.

The critic Ramón Xirau, in a review of the book, selected unity and 'luminosity' as the central motifs of the collection, labelling it a 'diurnal' or 'daylight' poetry.[32]

The main source of light is the sun, the heart of the sky. Paz's sun has associations with the Aztec cosmology as well as with the more mundane omnipresence of the sun in the Mexican sky. The sun 'reveals the reality of things' ambivalently, for it both regenerates and burns to destruction. Paz is well aware of the Aztec solar religion; the ancient dream was to be born again as a sun (*Pu* 161). Paz modifies this nostalgia for regeneration and incorporates it into his poetics. For Paz, behind the jade mask of the Mexicans shines a 'secret sun' (*Pe* 100); and Mexicans still dream of being suns again (*LS* 17–18).

To be a sun, in Paz's terms, is to live the dream and recover the spiritual centre, for 'el sol es la vida henchida de sí' (*C* 145;

the sun is life swollen with itself). Paz writes of the painter
Rufino Tamayo: 'le bastaba descender al fondo de sí mismo
para encontrar el antiguo sol, surtidor de imágenes' (*Pe* 258; it
sufficed him to descend to the bottom of himself to find the
ancient sun, fountain of images). The link between inner sun
and descent inside returns us to the surrealist myths and
metaphors. Paz describes his poetics: 'preveo un hombre-sol'
(*L* 206; I foresee a man-sun). This man-sun will be the new
man, and the experience of regeneration is described in the
poem 'Piedra nativa':

> El sol lo cubre todo lo ve todo
> Y en su mirada fija nos bañamos
> Y en su pupila largamente nos quemamos
> Y en los abismos de su luz caemos
> Música despeñada
> Y ardemos y no dejamos huella   (*L* 129)

The sun covers all, sees all, and in its stare we bathe, and in its pupil
for a long time we burn, and in the abysses of its light we fall, hurled
down music, and we burn and leave no trace.

This sun burns away the false selves, and through its heat and
passion liberates desire; this act of liberation is music or poetry
or being.

The poem 'Himno entre ruinas' has the sun as its central
motif. The opening stanza describes the perfect, natural world
without man, a paradise lost. The sun's 'alto grito amarillo'
(high yellow shout) fecundates nature. Here the sun lays its
golden egg that spills over the sea (*L* 211); 'La luz crea templos
en el mar' (*L* 212; The light creates temples in the sea) where
the visual and symbolic meet in an image that expresses all
Paz's poetics – light penetrates the water, creating shafts or
columns that hint at some other, grander and natural 'sea-
temple'. This same sun becomes the luminous, sweet orange of
twenty-four segments through which man communes (tastes,
bites) with nature and his natural self. Compared to this
magnificent sun, the sun of twentieth-century man in his
labyrinthine civilisation is 'un sol anémico' (*L* 212; an anaemic

sun) and a 'sol sin crepúsculo' (*L* 213; a sun without twilight). Likewise the whole of the literally splendid *Semillas para un himno* is bathed in sunlight; the seed of the sun opens noiselessly; this sun is in all things as *seed*. It is a poetics of hope, of potential, a seminal poetics.

Chapter 3

The nature myth

Underlying all Paz's poetics is a myth about nature that can be conventionally schematised as seeing the natural (good) set against the artificial (evil). Paz sympathises with the Romantics' 'flight towards nature'; and painfully he suffers 'separation from nature' and yearns to be tied back, *ligado* (*Pe* 181). Paz shares Breton's enthusiasm for Charles Fourier: 'Toi qui ne parlais que de lier, vois tout s'est délié' (You who only spoke of binding, see all is unbound). Paz too feels *délié*, and seeks umbilically to return to nature, and also to his instincts and sensations as 'lo más antiguo' in him (the most ancient). This return or recuperation is conveyed imagistically as the poetic society and as the restoration of man's innocence, as the resurrection of the humiliated animal inside him, or as the kernel and all that grows 'a lo cual estamos más ligados de lo que se piensa' (to which we are more tied than to what is thought).[1]

Paz's claim is that man has severed himself from nature culturally, through excessive reliance on his intellect or his analytical reason, placing them above the voice of his feelings and experience. There is nothing very original about this view. In 1945 Paz affirmed that the word in poetry – liberated from its numbed, asymbolic contexts – is capable of 'reconciliating' man with the stars, the animals and his roots (*Pe* 88). In 1972 Paz is still concerned with the 'abolition of differences' (*SG* 95) between man and things; or man and monkey-cries, parrot-squeals and the wind. To know as much, he writes 'c'était se réconcilier avec le temps, réconcilier les temps' (*SG* 95; it was to reconcile oneself with time, to reconcile all times). Reconciliation is Paz's term for the return to nature.

We return, however, to André Breton. Paz has quoted one of Breton's favourite phrases (*Pe* 178) about the 'delirium of absolute presence' which is the act of love between a man and a woman 'au sein de la nature réconciliée' (in the bosom of reconciled nature). Breton dreamed of reconciling man and woman through passion; he exposed a 'terrestrial magnetism' with one magnetic pole in man (and woman) and another in nature, only activated or woken through passionate love.[2]

For Paz, the core of Breton's poetics is this notion of attraction; the notion that 'nature is language' (*CA* 55); and that to recover this language 'es volver a la naturaleza, antes de la caída y de la historia' (*CA* 55; is to return to nature, before the fall and history). Paz admitted to admiring *L'Amour fou*; for him as for Breton, real love is a *natural* passion. Paz traces this 'heresy' back to Rousseau, the nature-lover, who handed down some basic notions to Breton, such as the 'exaltation of passion' and 'faith' in man's limitless natural powers (*CA* 118). Rousseau's genius lay in discerning that 'las fronteras entre cultura y naturaleza son muy tenues' (the frontiers between culture and nature are very tenuous); consequently, to return to Rousseau is 'healthy' (*CA* 68). Two titles reveal this direction and explain the intention: Breton's *La Clé des champs* (1967; The key to the fields) and Paz's *Puertas al campo* (1966; Doors to the field). Both sought ways (key, door) back to the natural in man.

When describing Luis Cernuda's attitude to love, Paz silently evokes André Breton. According to Paz, Cernuda returns to 'ancient nature', mother and myth; discovering that love springs from the *energy* that moves all things (*C* 196). Nature is neither matter nor spirit but energy (*Pu* 105); a synonym for Breton's magnetism. Paz often echoes this: 'El universo está imantado. Una suerte de ritmo teje tiempo y espacio' (*A* 127; The universe is magnetised. A kind of rhythm weaves time and space). Paz's later acute reading of Claude Lévi-Strauss confirms this debt to Rousseau (and Breton). Lévi-Strauss reduced the plurality of societies to the dichotomy 'savage thought' and 'domesticated thought', or nature versus culture. But he then shows that the products of society, though 'essentially' different from the natural, obey the same laws. Paz summarises this argument: 'La cultura es una metáfora del espíritu humano y éste no es sino una metáfora de las células y sus reacciones químicas' (Culture is a metaphor of the human mind and this is but a metaphor of the cells and their chemical reactions). Paz reads Lévi-Strauss as a confirmation of his belief: 'Salimos de la naturaleza y volvemos a ella' (We come out from nature and we return to it). This is a tradition stretching back through Breton and Rousseau.[3]

Paz borrows the term 'revelation' to describe the ecstatic union with nature. To start with the natural world is alien; nature speaks a language that man does not understand, and he feels insignificant faced with so much existence closed to itself (A 153). But then, suddenly, he perceives that he belongs; that the rhythm of the sea is that of his blood, that 'arder entre las arenas es caminar por la extensión de nuestra conciencia, ilimitada como ellas', for in those moments of intense 'correspondence', in Paz's words, 'todos formamos parte de todo' (A 153; to burn in the sand is to walk along the extension of our consciousness, limitless like the sand; we all form part of everything). Man 'vibrates' in the universal rhythm, in the vital, magnetic energy underlying all possible natural forms.

Experience

Experience is at the source of Paz's response to poetry and what he feels poetry can do for twentieth-century man. Behind this lies a literary tradition that equates authenticity with the uniqueness of personal experience (best represented by Rimbaud) coupled with an existential drive to 'start again', to 'rethink'. For Paz, the only certainty is that of the senses, of the experiencing body. Philosophical coherence, logical clarity and all the claims of the Western intellectual tradition to answer man's spiritual hunger are meaningless if they do not correspond to feeling, emotions, sensations; in a word, experience.

Rimbaud's disenchantment with the literary, conventional qualities in the poetry of his time had its roots in the harassing problem of identity and the meaning of life. Rimbaud turned away from external disciplines and converted himself into his own 'experiment'.

In his famous (and over-quoted?) 'Lettre du voyant', the *calculated* derangement of all the senses was aimed at recovering the purity of direct sensual experience through sensual excess, like a purge. His later 'Alchimie du verbe' relates this activity to the art of poetry where the vision was to be directly conveyed, not described. The poet 'devra faire sentir, palper, écouter ses inventions...cette langue sera de l'âme sur l'âme, résumant tout, parfums, sons, couleurs' (should make his inventions felt, touched, heard...this language will be from soul to soul, comprehending everything, perfumes, sounds, colours). Rimbaud ends his *Une Saison en enfer* with a notion central to Paz's poetics: 'posséder la vérité dans une âme et un corps' (to possess the truth in soul and body); transcribed from the infinitive of utopia to run 'verdad de dos en sólo un cuerpo y alma' (*L* 246; truth of two in only one body and soul).[4]

If we have evoked Rimbaud again it is because he was such a formative example for Paz, one of whose earliest essays was dedicated to Rimbaud (in 1939). Following Rimbaud, Paz also views poetry as 'self-knowledge' (*CA* 80); as a 'saber experimental' (*CA* 81; experiential knowledge) where experiment and experience are the same word. Only the awakened senses can help man rediscover the numbed truth: 'oiré con la vista y con la piel, me cubriré de ojos. Todo...será tacto y oreja. Todo deberá sentir' (*Pu* 216; I will hear with my sight and my skin, I will cover myself with eyes. All will be touch and ear. All will be felt). Though it is described in the future tense, this conjunction of thought with feeling is the sought-after 'total experience'. As Paz warns, 'ninguna verdad se aprende, cada uno debe pensarla y experimentarla por sí mismo' (*CA* 110; no truth is learnt. Each one must think it and experience it for himself).[5]

By purifying his senses the poet sees the world as 'fresh', as washed and reborn. For the poet has his eyes in his hands (*Pu* 102) and writing (hands) leads to vision (eyes). This is the *marvellous* vision of the surrealists, where the poet's 'skin becomes a new consciousness' (*Pu* 126). This, for Paz, is the exciting truth underlying modern poetry: 'la eternidad y lo absoluto no están más allá de nuestros sentidos sino en ellos mismos' (*Pu* 127; eternity and the absolute are not beyond our senses but in them).

It is through his senses that the poet contacts the 'secret energy' of the world (*Pu* 126) and this leads to an 'erotic,

electric' relationship with nature, woman, the world (*Pu* 188).
In 1955 Paz defined his poetics of sensation in a questionnaire
sent out by André Breton as '*tocar con el pensamiento y pensar con el
cuerpo*' (*Pu* 188; to touch with thought and think with the body)
where again the intention (infinitive) is what counts. Through
passion (the excited senses) the poet experiences a 'magnetic
reality' (*CD* 137). Paz wrote that in 1969: he remains faithful to
his poetics. 'Heart' is Paz's emblem for this poetics (*CD* 137); as
it was for Rousseau and Breton (*CA* 65).

For Paz (and Breton) man is not essentially alienated. From
being separated, he can also belong, become and be a tree, a
plant and a bird (*A* 79). Man belongs to nature; his senses 'tell'
him so and poetry confirms this:

> Por ti, delicia, poesía
> ...
> el mundo sale de sí mismo
> ...
> Y los sentidos palpan
> la forma presentida
> y ven los ojos lo que inventan   (*L* 33)

For you, delight, poetry . . . the world comes out of its self . . . and the
senses caress the intuited form and the eyes see what they invent.

The word that links Paz back with Rimbaud is *palpar*, which
has not the neutrality of 'touch' (*tocar*), but means to fondle,
caress; it is the ecstasy of the lover's contact with the world.

In Paz's later 'Himno entre ruinas' (1948) the world of
surface appearances is described as beautiful: 'Todo es dios' (*L*
211; All is god), and man's relationship with this solar paradise
is through sensual participation; through touch and sight: 'los
ojos ven, las manos tocan' (*L* 212; the eyes see, the hands
touch), and man experiences the need for direct contact with
things:

> Ver, tocar formas hermosas, diarias
> ...
> extiendo mis sentidos en la hora viva: (*L* 212)

to see, to touch beautiful daily forms,...I extend my senses in the
living hour.

Only through the opened senses will intelligence become

alive and embodied, and man will experience integration, reconnected (*lié*) to nature, his ego-consciousness (the self in the mirror) dissolved. And he becomes a tree, a fruit, a flower, a living part of the natural, dynamic activity of nature.

In the poem 'Cerro de la estrella' (Hill of the Star) this dream is expressed in infinitives without punctuation: 'ver oír tocar oler gustar pensar' (*L* 123; to see hear touch smell taste think), suggesting the flow of the senses liberated from repression and combined with thought. This is real thinking, a *pensar* that is rooted in the senses; it is the *raison ardente* (burning reason) of Apollinaire that Paz places as epigraph to his *La estación violenta* (1958; The Violent Season).

The poem 'Lauda' (from *Salamandra*) advances the same poetic, quite different from a mindless hedonism or primitivism:

> Olfato gusto vista oído tacto
> El sentido anegado en lo sentido
> Los cuerpos abolidos en el cuerpo
> ...
> Antes después ahora nunca siempre   (*S* 55–6)

Smell sight hearing touch. The senses [what is sensed] drowned in all that is sensitive, bodies abolished in the body . . . before after now never always.

'Lo sentido' expresses that natural world, to which our senses and body send us back. Paz embodies Paul Eluard's 'multiplicity of appeal to the sensations of touch, hearing, sight, taste' (Louis Perche); and a sampling of some of Paz's key verbs would underline this: *mirar, tocar, palpar, rozar, saber, ver, morder, pulsar, oler, comer, asir, rasgar* (to look, touch, caress, brush, taste, see, bite, touch, smell, eat, grab, scratch).[6]

In a similar vein, but earlier than Paz, Paul Eluard wrote that 'ma raison se refuse à nier le témoignage de mes sens. L'objet de mes désirs est toujours réel, sensible' (my reason refuses to deny the witness of my senses. The object of my desires is always real, tangible). The poetry of these two is a poetics of *evidence*; where the language in a poem becomes a natural phenomenon, with love as the combustive force that restores man to natural, experiential time. Eluard wrote 'le présent est éternel' (the present is eternal) and Paz echoes him in 'El presente es perpetuo' (*LE* 104; The present is perpetual). This present is the time of the senses and instincts made aware, awake. From this point we can see surrealism as 'an effort to recuperate the natural rights that man has lost in an ever tightening structure of society' (Balakian).[7]

The four elements

To return to direct perceptions, to a consciousness of sensations, is to return to an earlier, neglected, pre-scientific way of thinking and feeling and classifying. Because reality can only be apprehended through the senses, only a schema that makes *sense* is acceptable. The ancient four elements serve as a model for this poetic consciousness, or what Gaston Bachelard called 'material imagination'. The primitive and the poet (so often linked by the surrealists) share a world view based on sensual or 'concrete' experience, a 'phenomenology of the feelings' (Bachelard). Bachelard showed how 'primitive' images still condition creative thought; expanding this, we could say that the senses are anachronistic, incapable of keeping abreast of scientific abstractions and progress. Hence Bachelard's claim that 'la physiologie de l'imagination...obéit à la loi des quatre éléments' (the physiology of the imagination...obeys the law of the four elements).[8]

André Breton's obsession with the four elements as symbols of integration is clear from titles alone – for instance *Claire de terre* (Light of Earth) and *L'Air de l'eau* (The Air of the Water). His celebrated love poem to his wife, *L'Union libre* (1931), ends 'Ma femme aux yeux...de niveau d'air de terre et de feu' (My wife with eyes...on a level with air earth and fire): for she, woman, is the way to unity. His poem 'Sur la route qui monte et descend' similarly ends: 'Flamme d'eau guide–moi jusqu'à la mer de feu' (Flame of water guide me to the sea of fire). Another poem, 'L'aigle sexuel', ends: 'Je prends l'empreinte de la mort et de la vie / A l'air liquide' (I take the imprint of death and life from the liquid air).[9]

But this adoption of the 'elements' is archetypal, a product of what Jung called the 'natural mind' that derives from natural sources and offers a natural wisdom. Paz's poetry is structured on basic, primordial images and symbols such as light, sun, river, woman, tree, sea. Paz has enumerated his own imagery in his evocation of the mescalin paradise in all of us as

grandes países *fluviales, árboles,* espesura verde y rojiza, *tierra* color de ámbar, todo bajo una *luz* ultraterrena. La sensación de *movimiento* – los largos *ríos,* el *viento,* el latido del *sol*...A veces, al borde del *agua* centelleante, surge una *mujer*...Edad auroral, mundo de signifi- caciones *paradisíacas.*   (*CA* 96)

great fluvial countries, trees, green and reddish thickets, amber col- oured earth, all under an ultraterrenial light. The sensation of move- ment – broad rivers, wind, the beat of the sun...At times at the edge of the sparkling water, emerges a woman...Auroral age, world of paradisical significations.

I have put into italics Paz's archetypal world, his recourse to elemental imagery. This 'sensation' of fluidity is the vertigo of ego-dissolution, and the reincorporation with nature. They are all images of 'paradise lost', but regainable through the senses; as Breton entitled a poem 'Tout paradis n'est pas perdu' (All paradise is not lost).[10]

Wholesome imagery

Paz's images refer to wholesome, natural archetypes dormant and unconscious in man. Jung writes that the 'religious need longs for wholeness, and therefore lays hold of the images of wholeness offered by the unconscious'. This 'laying hold' is the act of poetry; poetry is consciousness of this 'source'.[11]

I will now explore some of these, beginning with *aquatic* imagery. Paz links water symbolism with woman and pre-natal paradise; water is fertility and self-knowledge (*CA* 97), and is both creative and destructive. However, this symbolic world is not fixed in meanings, but based on powerful, emotive associa- tions; it is a world of analogies and correspondences. Water can be itself, felt by the senses; and it can metaphorically be woman, night, being and poetry. It lies dormant in woman (*L* 36) and it sings and *flows,* a key verb in Paz's poetic. Water is also inspiration: 'el agua que habla a solas en la noche y nos llama con nuestro nombre' (*L* 236; water that talks alone at night and calls us by our name); water is the dream: 'agua que con los párpados cerrados / mana toda la noche profecías (*L* 237; water that with closed eyelids flows with prophecies all night).

In woman's eyes there is a 'secret water', a 'dream water' (*L* 115); man drinks his 'health' through her, swims in her (*L* 122, 238). Water is a naked woman (*CA* 101) and naked woman is pure water (*L* 123); she is fresh water (*L* 134, 225). Woman is the water of creation, of regeneration:

> Dulzura del agua en la hierba dormida
> Agua clara vocales para beber   (*L* 124)

Sweetness of water in the sleeping grass, clear water vowels to drink.

Poetry is water outflowing: 'y brote al fin el agua' (*L* 235; and the water breaks out at last); it is the 'escritura del agua' (*L* 146; writing of water), the 'idioma de vocales de agua' (*L* 189; idiom of vowels of water). The aim of the poet is described as 'Ser al fin una Palabra...un poco de agua en unos labios ávidos' (*L* 158; To be at last a Word...a drop of water on some avid lips), for communion is given aquatic associations: 'Agua, agua al fin, palabra del hombre para el hombre' (*L* 205; water, water at last, word of man for man). The poem taps the waters of the dark, of night, of the unconscious: 'Allá la noche vestida de agua despliega sus jeroglíficos al alcance de la mano' (*L* 228; There the night dressed in water displays its hieroglyphs within reach of the hand).

According to Paz the critic, 'sea' is one of the basic polarities in Rubén Darío's poetry; what he calls Darío's 'aquatic space' (*CA* 45) with its analogies 'blood', 'heart', 'wine', 'women', 'the passions', 'the jungle' (*CA* 46). This system of 'rotatory signs', or this chain of analogies, defuses conceptual criticism; for the point of this poetics is its associative flow.

'River', for example, central *topos* in all ages of literature, becomes woman; she flows like a river (*L* 114); she contains a river inside her (*L* 115); her arms curve like a river, she moves like a river and walks like a river (*L* 117, 122, 249). She is a river that flows by man's side (*L* 200). The poem is also a river. The poem 'Arcos' (1947; Arches) describes the descent inwards as flowing down a river, a river of words and meandering lines. Man too is a river seeking his riverbed (*L* 235); and time is a river; thoughts are rivers.

Paz's poem 'El río' (The river) dramatises this flowing thought-river, the stream of consciousness. About this poem, Paz said that it was his attempt to transmute 'individual consciousness into poetic song'; if we are to experience consciously this river (of being, desire, time) it has to be fixed in language; the poet seeks the source of words and wants to reach the 'centre of water' (*L* 230) and to sing of this contact: 'decir lo que dice el río...larga palabra que no acaba nunca' (*L* 230; to say what the river says...long word that never ends). The poet intends to crystallise the flow of thought into song; this implies stopping the inner river of words and penetrating upstream to the heart, the 'crystal tree', but this poem does not lead there and records a failure. To 'deletrear la escritura...del río' (*L* 236; to spell out the writing...of the river) is an elusive task, because language congeals, straining to fix the flow while the real river just flows on.[12]

'Blood' is the inner river while *marea* (tide) describes its natural rhythm, the tides of being. Further aquatic terms that play across Paz's poetry include 'cascade' as conveying this inner fluidity; the poet's dream is to become 'la cascada de sílabas azules' (*L* 230; cascade of blue syllables). Paz uses *manantial* (source) quite literally as the source of poetry and being:

> el manantial para beber y mirarse y reconocerse y recobrarse,
> el manantial para saberse hombre,...
> el manantial de las palabras para decir yo, tú, él, nosotros...
> (L 235–6)

The source to drink and look at oneself and to recognise and recover oneself, the source to know one is man,...the source of words to say I, you, him, us...

This evokes the fresh source that dissolves the poet's (and reader's) false faces (*L* 254); only through this source does the poet discover himself: 'Estoy de nuevo, manantial de evidencias' (*LBP 60* 28; I am again, source of evidences). Paz's poem to Luis Cernuda ends:

> Verdad y error
> Una sola verdad
> Realidad y deseo
> Una sola substancia
> Resuelta en manantial de transparencias   (*S* 28)

Truth and error. Only one truth. Reality and desire. Only one substance resolved in a source of transparencies.

Paz's use of *fuente* (fountain) evokes similar associations: 'El hueco que somos se llena hasta rebasar, hasta volverse fuente' (*CA* 87; The hollow that we are fills until it overflows, until it becomes a fountain). This is the image of inspiration; and again woman is the agent of fertility; she too is a fountain, and the word is also a fountain. Given this possibility of regeneration (rebirth?), the poet is the new saviour. The poem 'Fuente' ends:

> En el centro de la plaza la rota cabeza del poeta es una fuente.
> La fuente canta para todos.   (*L* 218)

In the centre of the square the broken poet's head is a fountain. The fountain sings for all.

Chorro (jet) and *surtidor* (spout) are similar aquatic constants in Paz's work. And behind all of them is the transmutation from *natural* symbol to word-symbol in poetry, and literal analogies between the writing or reading of a poem and nature. For poetry is a natural activity; it restores man's fallen nature.

The next cluster is around *earth* imagery, with its associations of fecundity, passivity and femininity, where the crucial analogy is between woman and earth. She is the visible centre of the earth, and the poet seeks this earth–truth through her. The form of this contact is poetry: in the poem 'En la calzada' (On the highway) the poet is led to an inner paradise where 'la tierra madre siempre virgen' (mother earth always virgin) is the fertile soil in which the poem sprouts. This complementary feminine aspect of earth is man's real patrimony: 'Única tierra que conozco y me conoce' (*L* 115; Only earth that I know and knows me).

The earth is a fertile matter: 'tierra confusa inminencia de escultura' (*L* 121; confused earth imminence of sculpture). At the end of 'Piedra de sol' the poet pleads with the mother to be made fertile like earth: 'entiérrame en tu tierra' (*L* 253; bury me in your earth) is the way to experience truth.

A literal symbol of the way back is *raíz* (root). Man's 'roots' are in nature, but twentieth-century man is rootless – 'el sin raices' (*L* 225; the rootless) – or his roots have dried up. Root is the spiritual symbol of contact. Poetry is a song that grows *roots*; in the poem words become natural: 'como hablan entre sí el agua y las hojas y las raíces' (*L* 235; as water and leaves and roots talk among themselves). The aim (and we return to the premise that Paz's is a poetry of poetics, expressed in infinitives) is 'tocar nuestra raíz y recobrarnos' (*L* 246; to touch our root and recover ourselves): to retrace the lost steps (Breton, Carpentier), and find the lost roots.

Semilla (seed) is all that will grow and flower into a natural wisdom; it refers to the poem that 'seeds' itself in the reader, naturally integrating him: '*la semilla del canto se abre en la frente del poeta*' (*L* 220; the seed of the song opens in the poet's brow). The seed grows – into a tree; archetype of 'rooted' man, and an obsessive image in Paz's work. In woman's palm there grows a tree (*L* 121); she resembles a tree (*L* 240) and moves like a tree (*L* 249); words in the poem are trees (*L* 116). However, the real tree is inner and symbolic, what Paz calls his *árbol mental* (*L* 242; mental tree). This 'tree' is man's true body (*L* 23), for man is a tree of images (*L* 213). In his poems there are dancing trees, transparent trees, musical trees, trees of precious stones and sacred trees. It is another crucial symbol.

There are other 'archetypal' images frequent in Paz that relate to the tree and verticality. The central support between heaven and earth is like a *columna* (column), *tallo* (stalk), *flor* (flower), *espiga* (ear of grain), *bosque* (wood). The meanings are transparent and it would be tedious to list their use.

Another central earth symbol in Paz's poetics is *fruit*; this stands for earthly desires, the ripe word, inner being, woman, and all that is open to taste, touch, smell and sight. Paz, alluding to one of his titles *Las peras del olmo*, writes that man is the elm that gives incredible pears (*Pe* 15); this miraculous

process indicates that fatality and contingency can be transmuted through poetry into liberty. Poetry transforms determining reality by releasing the blocked flow, the repressed sap: 'la
palabra, al fin en libertad, muestra todas sus entrañas, todos
sus sentidos y alusiones, como un fruto maduro' (A 22; the
word, at last free, shows all its insides, all its senses and allusions, like a ripe fruit). Language in the poem is restored to its
natural, ripe self. And the poem allows man to bite the apple or
the fig, to live his desire, to live his poetics. To bite into the fruit
is to satiate desire momentarily; then the mundane world is
illumined by poetry and 'La alegría madura como un fruto / El
fruto madura hasta ser sol' (L 128; happiness matures like a
fruit, the fruit matures until it's a sun). Or again, 'al mediodía
las piedras se abren como frutos' (L 123; at midday the stones
open like fruit) for in this magical world there are jade-fruits
and dawn-fruits. Desire realised is the sought-after fusion:
'porque querer y obrar serían como la flor y el fruto' (L 101;
because to want and do would be like flower and fruit); where
'la flor es fruto, el fruto labios' (L 106; the flower is fruit, the
fruit lips). The image fruit–lips simultaneously expresses the
sensual nature of truth coupled with desire liberated, and the
speaking of the poem (word–fruit–lips).

Another bunch of images clusters around *air* imagery; this
relates to the 'creative breath of life', to a sense of freedom. The
wind hurls man out of himself and into himself (A 123); it is
inexplicable, shatters rationality. Wind is another form of the
natural language: 'Tal vez el viento dice algo que no es distinto
a lo que dice el agua al caer en la piedra. Por un instante
entrevemos el sentido de la palabra reconciliación' (A 68;
Perhaps the wind says something which is not different from
what the water says as it falls on a stone. For a moment we
glimpse the sense of the word reconciliation). The wind speaks,
sings and dances; it is a playful, creative element. It heralds the
cosmic language, the 'escritura del viento' (L 246; writing of the
wind); the original but forgotten language: 'Hay el viento y
nombres hermosos en el viento' (L 121). There is also an inner
wind – inspiration that uproots man.

The wind blows the clouds in the *cielo* (sky, heaven). 'Space' is the metaphor that indicates inner 'spirituality' where man at last sees and becomes transparent:

> La poesía
> Es la hendidura
> El espacio
> Entre una palabra y otra   (LE 92)
> Poetry is the crack, the space, between one word and another.

The notion of 'l'espace du dedans' (Henri Michaux), the symbolic mental sky, is central to Paz. Further airy symbols appear in his writings, such as *torbellino* (whirlwind), *huracán* (hurricane), and *tempestad* (tempest); natural symbols of spirit, poetry and liberation. The air elements lead to associations with birds, wings and flight, as well as with the key verbs *subir* (to rise) and *volar* (to fly). The act of writing the poem liberates the poet sensuously: 'Todo lo que mis manos tocan, vuela' (*L* 40; All that my hands touch, flies). Poetry releases words from gravity: 'todo se transfigura, todos vuelan' (*L* 247; all is transfigured, all fly). The archetypally entitled 'Fuente' (Fountain) describes a similar liberation:

> todo lo atado al suelo por amor de materia enamorada, rompe amarras
> y asciende radiante entre las manos intangibles de esta hora.
> El viejo mundo de las piedras se levanta y vuela.   (*L* 216–17)
> all that is tied to the ground by love of enamoured matter, breaks loose and ascends radiantly between the intangible hands of this hour. The old world of stones rises and flies.

The real 'new world' is the world projected by the poem. Again in the poem 'Piedra nativa' (Native stone) we have reality freed by the poem:

> Zarpan las casas la iglesia los tranvías
> El mundo emprende el vuelo   (*L* 129)
> Houses, the church, trams set sail, the world takes to flight.

Paz returns to the air element because of his experience that the poem lifts language out of its deadened contexts; poetry creates verticality and defies gravity; it is a *signe ascendant*, as Breton said.

Fire imagery brings us to the heart of Paz's passionate

poetics; fire relates to passionate energy and purification; to the
Buddhist's inner flame and many other conventional readings
restored by Paz. Lovers recreate this fire; passion is the 'return
of fire' (*L* 18). Poetry taps this original and inner fire:

> espíritu que no vive en ninguna forma,
> mas hace arder todas las formas
> con un secreto fuego indestructible   (*L* 90)

spirit that does not live in any form, but makes all forms burn with a
secret indestructible fire.

This is the fire that burns up the poem, for poetry is a spiritual,
extra-literary experience. It is the 'lenguaje de incendios' (*S* 62;
language of fires) spoken between poet and spirit, reader and
spirit.

This is the 'flame' of poetry that provokes the poet, the
'pensar en llamas' (*L* 251; to think in flames) that creates spirit:

> y sea todo como la llama que se esculpe y se hiela en la roca de
>   entrañas transparentes,
> duro fulgor resuelto ya en cristal y claridad pacífica.   (*L* 232)

and let it all be like the flame that sculpts itself and freezes itself in
the rock of transparent cores, hard glow already resolved into crystal
and pacific clarity.

Fire purifies, and man must burn before being reborn (like the
phoenix); Paz's obsessive use of the verbs *arder* and *quemar* (to
burn), related to the action of poetry, attests to this. *Incendio* (a
fire) and its verb *incendiar* point to similar releases and libera-
tions. André Breton's poem 'Sur la route qui monte et descend'
(1932) illustrates this flame found in flowers and in women's
eyes, everywhere, 'Et la flamme court toujours' (And the flame
runs always). This flame destroys false appearances; it is the
imagination, leading poets (the 'endangered travellers')
through passion to understanding. The poem ends with a plea:
'Flamme d'eau guide-moi jusqu'à la mer de feu' (Flame of
water guide me to the sea of fire).[13]

'Burning water' is a traditional mystic and 'metaphysical'
synthesis, found also in Nahual poetry. Paz often links fire and
water, echoing the elemental paradox: 'mi libertad golpea...
buscando el mar de fuego' (*LBP 60* 47; my liberty knocks...
seeking the sea of fire).

Paz's title poem 'Salamandra' explores the associations: fire, passion and poetry. The salamander survives fire; through the poem the salamander is transformed into *semilla* (seed), *grano* (grain), *niña* (girl), *fuente* (fountain), *espiga* (ear of grain), *herida* (wound); all regenerative symbols in Paz's poetics. The salamander is

> Hija del fuego
> Espíritu del fuego   (*S* 102)
> daughter of fire, spirit of fire

in other words, man's indestructible spirit. These analogies reveal the poet's intention: the 'eternal' salamander unites the ages (*S* 103) as the 'axis', the 'column', sun, sea and light. It could be called essence, desire or being. In terms of our 'elemental' structuring, it unites the four elements:

> Salamandra de tierra y de agua
> ...
> Salamandra de aire y de fuego   (*S* 105)
> Salamander of earth and water...Salamander of air and fire.

The salamander is the centre of all, the core of man and nature and language, the origin:

> Roja palabra del principio
> ...
> Es inasible Es indecible   (*S* 106)
> Red word of the beginning...is ungraspable, is unsayable.

It is the emblem for what lies beyond/behind/inside words, for words are its ever-changing forms. The salamander is the mother, the axial archetype; it is also water and salt sea through the serious puns *Salamadre* (Saltmother) and *Aguamadre* (Watermother). Salamander is the *eau-mère*, the alchemists' prime matter, the infra-language that continually flows up into our fallen, relative language, rejuvenating and recreating it. Paz said to María Luisa Mendoza that the salamander was above all an 'erotic symbol'. Poetry is a passion, it is erotic. Yves Bonnefoy's poem 'Lieu de la salamandre' (Salamander's place) evokes the same myth, quite explicitly in Pazian terms:

Le mythe le plus pur,
Un grand feu traversé, qui est esprit
The most pure myth, a great fire crossed, which is spirit.

This fire is not a cold, puritanical spirit, but passion, or heart, as Bonnefoy writes:

Mais je voyais son coeur battre éternel
...
La seule force de joie
But I saw its heart beat eternally...the only force of joy.

Both poets work with mythic associations, both seek to recuperate and reconnect man with a meaningful tradition (symbolised by the return to the four elements); and both transform the poem into a 'spiritual' act grounded in a *sagesse*, a vision of human nature and life.[14]

Through analogies with each of these four elements, Paz builds up a poetic universe of correspondences that is elusively hard to pin down, since each analogue refers to the next. Yet these analogies, taken from the natural world, are quite concrete, immediate and open to the senses; this is Paz's sensual truth. Yves Bonnefoy sees these elements as the centre of 'true' poetry: they are 'éléments concrets mais universels...Omniprésent, animés. On peut dire qu'ils sont la parole même de l'être, dégagée par la poésie' (Concrete but universal elements ...Omnipresent, animated. One could say that they are the word of being itself, redeemed by poetry). The four elements articulate the archetypes of all poetry, the sensual language of desire, of being.[15]

Poetry reveals the possibility of a total communion or reconciliation with 'reality' (whether self, nature or woman). Paz pictures Luis Cernuda writing a poem in some lost room. The page becomes reality because it reveals man to himself, because it crystallises desire:

Escribe el poeta las palabras prohibidas
Signos entrelazados en una página
Vasta de pronto como lecho de mar
Abrazo de los cuatro elementos
Constelación del deseo y de la muerte
Fija en en cielo cambiante del lenguaje   (S 26–7)

The poet writes the forbidden words, signs interlaced on a page suddenly vast like a sea bed, embrace of the four elements, constellation of desire and death fixed in the changing sky of language.

From chaos and the flux of language the poem binds erotically together man's inner being and the world, and it does this as a sensual experience, an *embrace* of the four elements. This erotic tone deals with woman as another analogical variant, as water, being, even poetry. In the poem 'Vaivén' (Oscillation) the poet 'falls' into 'her' (woman, the poem) and is reborn:

> El viento sopla afuera y reúne las aguas
> Todos los bosques son un solo árbol
> ...
> Tierra y cielo y marea que no cesa
> Los elementos enlazados tejen
> La vestidura de un día desconocido   (*S* 83)

The wind blows outside and reunites the waters, all the woods are one single tree...Earth and sky and tide that does not cease. The bound elements weave the clothing of an unknown day.

In poetry all is woven together by the elements (nature) and experienced by man in the body: 'Agua tierra y sol son un solo cuerpo' (*L* 129; Water earth and sun are one body). This is freedom, reunion, reconciliation with nature. The short poem 'Soltura' (Agility) ends:

> Las cosas se desataban de sus nombres
> Al borde de mi cuerpo
>   Yo fluía
> Entre los elementos desceñidos   (*LE* 85)

Things untied themselves from their names. At the edge of my body I flowed between the loosened elements.

Poetry lures man back to what is 'elementary'; the forgotten origin and true meaning where body and spirit are one. André Breton's affirmation that 'l'amour charnel ne fait qu'un avec l'amour spirituel' (carnal love makes but one with spiritual love) is shared by Paz. It falls to the poet to make a dialogue 'de la riña elemental' (*PU* 57; of the elemental fight), and in that way he creates meaning.[16]

Here we return to André Breton's revival of Charles Fourier (later taken up by Paz as well) and the notion of the 'harmonious' vision. Man has been severed from paradise; has been trapped in a labyrinth, in one of the worst *cloaques* (cesspools) of history, the twentieth century. Only poetry (a poetics) 'fleetingly' re-establishes contact with this lost vision. Breton writes: 'Tu as embrassé l'unité tu l'as montré non comme perdue mais comme intégralement réalisable' (You have embraced unity, you have shown it not lost but as integrally realisable). And this is unity with nature, the sap flowing from Fourier's fingertips; an integrated world view with no separation but a vital continuum. This is the necessary vision of a 'futur édenique' (Edenic future), the 'universal harmony...whereby the human mind and heart would be wholly in accord with the laws of nature' (Browder).[17]

The poet–critic Guillermo Sucre aptly defined Paz's poetry as 'el rescate del pensamiento utópico' (the recovery of utopian thought), but it is a desperate one, for the vision, the poetic, is always shimmering, mirage-like, on the horizon.[18]

Poetry and love

Paul Eluard's title *L'Amour la poésie* leads Paz to formulate his theory of correspondences, where everything 'rhymes' in a universe composed of opposites which separate and join to a 'secret' rhythm. This magnetic attraction and repulsion finds its mental equivalent in the notion of analogy, suggesting that all relationships whether of words in sentences or of man with woman or man with nature are but erotic analogues of each other. André Breton's 'la poésie se fait dans un lit comme l'amour' (poetry is made in a bed like love) is fundamental in surrealism's 'aventure mentale'. The *étreinte poétique* (poetic embrace) is as 'real' and as felt as the *étreinte de chair* (carnal embrace). Paz agrees; poetry and love are similar acts (*Pe* 179); love and poetry are the two faces of the same reality (*Pe* 76); both are attempts to recover Edenic man before the 'tearing away'.[19]

The poet is the lover of language and woman; the poem is the creation, the product. And this is still the classic view. However, within the poem, words 'copulate' and combine (embrace) erotically with the poet, with the reader and among themselves. Breton's lapidary 'les mots font l'amour' (words make love) is merely descriptive of the creative process, the copulative rhythm of writing, of words left to their own devices. Through this copulation language is restored to its 'destination pleine'. This is to 'open' language, to subvert its rigidity, to turn it away from its 'duty' of signifying. Poetry releases the potential of words; it grants them life; and words living on their own account are 'creatures of energy'; they participate in that terrestrial magnetism also sparked off by lovers.[20]

'Caress' singularises the love–poetry conjunction; one word caresses another as man caresses woman; poetry is 'un langage unique de caresses' (an unique language of caresses). For Eluard, all caresses are sacred, whether of the body or of language. Thus the poem becomes a physical body; it becomes palpable yet is still of words, a mental image. The poem is a body to which the reader makes love; he reads with his body as an experience that is pleasurable.[21]

For Paz, the poem is an emblem of the language of nature and of the body; and the 'heart' of the emblem is the verb, the word in motion (*Pu* 92). Language sets reality in motion and mirrors this movement; language is copulation, its essence is an 'erotismo verbal' (*CD* 92) where copulation is not only a sensation but the union of opposites: 'el amor, como la imagen poética, es un instante de reconciliación de los contrarios' (*Pe* 7; love, like the poetic image, is an instant of the reconciliation of opposites). Saúl Yurkievich has summarised this well: 'En Paz poética y erótica se abrazan y confunden como la pareja primordial' (In Paz poetics and eroticism embrace, fused like the primordial couple).[22]

Desire, being

In writing about desire, which is central to his own poetics, Paz acknowledges Cernuda's presence. He defines it as 'la imaginación amorosa que, lanzada hacia un objeto, no teme *incendiarlo* ni *incendiarse*, para renacer de nuevo' (*Pe* 6; the amorous imagination that, launched towards its object, does not fear to burn it or burn itself, to be reborn again) – the italics bring out the same elements in the same eternal drama of passion, fire and re-birth. Desire, then, both postulates man's 'condición desgarrada' (rent condition) and promises its end; in this ambivalence it taunts man's anguished temporality and pushes him toward the amorous vision of unity as joyful relief.

Desire is man's core-reality; his inner being is the theatre of desire's conflict with reality, where the meeting-point between the two is love; love posits the 'other' (*C* 191). Man's real identity, his real self, is desire: 'un ser de deseo, tanto como un deseo de ser' (*A* 136; a being of desire as much as a desire of being).

Two recurrent terms in Paz's writings testify to this drama; to desire's perpetual becoming and perpetual dissatisfaction: *sed* and *avidez* (thirst and avidity). Man is thirsty for truth in a wasteland, a spiritual desert. Paz has been called a 'chasseur de l'être' (hunter of being) by Julio Cortázar, and Breton saw avidity as Paz's salient characteristic. Desire, truth, self, being; all are 'words' for what moves man (in both senses). Man continually projects himself – invents himself, to use Paz's term – or makes himself, to fulfil the etymology of the word 'poet' (*Pe* 288). Desire is a *path towards* an ever elusive goal: 'El ser no se da; el ser no es: es un llegar a ser' (*Pe* 226; Being is not given; being is not, it is a reaching to being).[23]

The perfection of the non-human world is described through the verb *estar* (to be, stand). In the poem 'Paisaje' (Countryside) Paz lists insects, horses, donkeys, rocks and trees as a self-contained series of endless analogies:

> Todos están ahí, dichosos en su estar,
> frente a nosotros que no estamos,   (*L* 144)
> All are there, happy in their being, opposite us who are not.

Man is the odd one out, the outsider (not outside society but the natural world): 'el que voy a ser, y que no seré nunca, entra a saco en el que fui, *arrasa mi estar*, lo deshabita' (*L* 195; He I am to become, and will never be, plunders who I was, rases my being, leaves it empty). Man cannot settle, cannot stand still or be in the present; he always moves forward, and only death stops him as an *estar*. The tragic flaw is his consciousness of his own temporality; this agonises him, and Paz makes it the seed of his own hopeful poetics.

In the poem 'Mutra' (1952) the poet rejects a return to a static existence in favour of 'anchoring his being' (*L* 228); he defines man as 'corriendo siempre tras de sí, disparado, exhalado, sin jamás alcanzarse' (*L* 225; always running after himself, fired, exhaled, without ever reaching himself), the existentialist's thrill.

Ser (to be), then, defines man; it is that part of man that sings, that flows. This being is antithetical to ego: 'Desnudo de su nombre canta el ser' (*L* 39; Naked of its name, being sings); this being lies beyond names yet is elusively real, 'el ser sin nombre' (*L* 249; being without name); this is the 'ser total', the 'reino de pronombres enlazados' where 'yo soy tú somos nosotros' (*L* 254; total being; a kingdom of linked pronouns; I am you we are).

Analogy

Paz's poetics is grounded on the 'demon of analogy'; his syntax of metaphor, symbol and image revolves round this notion. That everything is *comparable* to everything else is in the nature of language itself; for Breton the miracle of language is summed up in the magic word *comme* (like); Mary Ann Caws calls this surrealism's theory of 'linking' and cites Eluard's 'J'établis des rapports entre...' (I establish rapports between) as the key phrase.[24]

The analogical process or the theory of correspondences can be traced back to the 'confused words' that man the poet picks up in the 'forest of symbols'; to Baudelaire, the poet digs in the 'inépuisable fonds de l'universelle analogie' (inexhaustible depths of universal analogy). We see the process at work in the very word 'forest' which forces an analogy between mind and nature, for there is no other way of talking. Analogy establishes 'the parallels between human life and natural phenomena' (Frye); consequently analogy yields the 'secret' coherence of the universe. Kathleen Raine is most clear on this tradition of 'symbolic discourse' or 'analogical thinking'; through alchemy and Swedenborg to William Blake's 'body of divine analogy'

THE NATURE MYTH 103

there runs a thread evoking 'one plane in terms of another', quite antagonistic to the 'prevailing positivism'. To Kathleen Raine (and Breton and Paz) 'matter and material object are informed from a *mental* world' (my italics). Breton himself did not use the term 'analogy' until quite late in his writing (1948), when it became his only 'intellectual pleasure', and for him the most powerful way of disturbing discursive thought and reuniting man with the cosmos. Analogy transgresses deductive laws 'pour faire appréhender à l'esprit l'interdépendance de deux objets de pensée situés sur des plans différents' (to make the spirit apprehend the interdependence of two thought objects situated on different planes). However, poetic analogy is quite empirical; it does not presuppose an 'invisible' reality. The poet is simply he who senses that 'all that is up there is like all that is down here and all that is inside is like all that is outside'. Symbolic language abolishes boundaries by its process of linking, of *ligando* (tying up); and the 'analogical approach leads to a *harmonious* vision of the world' (Cardinal and Short, my italics).[25]

For Paz the notion is equally crucial; he opposes analogy and the cyclic (myth) to causality and the linear (*Pu* 198); the former is the 'language' of nature 'interpreted' by the poet. For Paz 'la imaginación más alta es la analogía' (*C* 28; the highest imagination is analogy); the poet creates through the principle of analogy (*A* 53), and poetry expresses 'the universal analogy' (*CD* 83). The axis of his poetics is this view: 'Analogie: transparence universelle: en ceci voir cela' (*SG* 157; Analogy: universal transparence: in this see that); this is the basis of the analogical vision.

The poetic image

Analogy is the magnetic, combinatory or copulative energy of the cosmos perceived by man; the image, on a more restricted level, also 'couples' together. Paz has devoted a chapter in his *El arco y la lira* (1956) to the poetic image; but Paz's view must be apprehended through Breton's view of the image's possibilities: the spark or light given off by the image 'reveals' the hidden laws of the universe, and for Breton is a means of knowledge as well as a form of unity.[26]

For Paz, the image dominates modern poetry; it is the new 'monster' that keeps 'open' the plurality of language by fusing several layers of meaning into one. The image says 'this is that' (*A* 99), and remains concrete and immediate. The image has its most potent analogy in the lover's embrace that leads to orgasm; the lovers momentarily fuse but remain two bodies. This fusion is instantaneous, and in the image, reproduces the 'moment of awareness, the moment of perception' in all its original purity (*A* 109). The image is impervious to analysis, for it 'says' the 'unsayable' (*A* 106, 168); the image paralyses analytic thought, for the sense of an image is the experience of the image itself (*A* 110, 137, 180).

The image always creates new links between words, between words and things, between things; it reveals unexplored and unconnected aspects of the world and man. The image grants a 'sudden sense of liberation' (Ezra Pound) where *surprise* rules. Surprise is the central aesthetic prop of modernism, 'le grand ressort nouveau' (Apollinaire; the great new spring), leading to surrealism's provocative stance. Paz unconditionally seeks surprise: expressions like *imprevisto* (unexpected), *inesperado* (same), *súbito* (sudden), *repentino* (same), *de pronto* (suddenly), *insólito* (unusual) lie scattered through the poetry. For poetry awakens man to the unusual, to what lies outside his calculations: 'lo inesperado se repite y los milagros son cotidianos y están a nuestro alcance' (*L* 133; the unexpected repeats itself and the miracles are of every day and are within our reach).

Further, for Paz the image is ontological: man 'knows' himself by 'creating' the 'other' in him (language, the unexpected word); Rimbaud's desperate plea that 'life must be changed' is embodied for Paz in the transformatory action of the image. In the magic land of 'Eralabán' poetry becomes 'un insólito brotar de imágenes que cristalizan en actos' (*L* 189; an unusual budding of images that crystallise into acts); the image flows into life. In Paz's revealingly titled 'Hacia el poema' (Toward the poem), the real poem that Paz envisages (not the poem on the page) will happen when 'la imagen se hace acto' and 'la poesía entra en acción' (*L* 207; the image becomes act; poetry enters into action). There is even the possibility that the image can transcend death by intensifying temporality and fixing the *vertige* of the present moment: 'y el delirio de hacer saltar la muerte con el apenas golpe de una imagen' (*L* 218; and the delirium of making death jump with the bare knock of an image). The poetic image, then, transmutes reality and creates a *mental*, poetic reality: 'Pero también las piedras pierden pie, también las piedras son imágenes/y caen...y fluyen con el río ...' (*L* 224; But also stones loose their foothold, stones are also images that fall...and flow with the river). It is as if poetry liberates the 'stone' from its inertness and allows it to flow (to live) by restoring its symbolic or analogical resonances. The image, for Paz, is a *seed* that will change life and renew contact with the lost paradise of a natural and harmonious world: 'semilla de la imagen que crece hasta ser árbol y hace estallar el cráneo' (*L* 235; seed of the image that grows until it is a tree and makes the skull burst).

We could trace the increasing density of imagery in his poetry back to early poems like 'El desconocido' (1941; The unknown) and 'Soliloquio de medianoche' (1944) until they 'cascade' through the poetry between 1946 and 1962, paralleling his surrealist 'adventure'. He has since reduced this frequency; the long, thick and breathless lines have given way to space and white margins, but the image as ontological agency still frames the poetry; the notion of analogy still fluidly and concretely conditions the vision. The image in Paz has never been gratuitous or automatic, for though he often appeals to the ear, the meaning of words (their analogical and symbolic readings) is always active. Paz's suspicion of 'senseless music' (or automatic writing) lands him with a poetry that deals with intention. Yet he remains close to André Breton, for his aim has been to fuse thinking and feeling – that quality of 'felt thought' that Herbert Read discerned in Wordsworth. This ambition is achieved at the expense of 'ordering' his views into a system that explains itself; as Kathleen Raine writes, the meaning of images 'is their only reality'.[27]

The word, woman and poetry

In Spanish all three of these words are feminine, and Paz subtly confuses their identity; they merge as incessant analogies of each other, each always overflowing into the next. Love poetry is *also* a poem about writing a poem. But because this is poetry, the word (as in Mallarmé's joke to Degas) must be the starting point.

Paz shares the notion that the word is a Pandora's box brimming with all the potentialities of language (cf. Roland Barthes); that words have their own life, weight and value (cf. Roman Jakobson); they become independent and *live* like human beings, like women. They are fleshly, 'sensuous events'; they agglutinate, elide, collide, copulate. The poet 'yields the initiative to words' (Mallarmé); the poet does not think words, they 'think' him (Rimbaud); they take over, breathe, play, make love. All these resonances are transmitted and incorporated by Paz; this personification of the word crystallises his poetics.[28]

Let us look at this: the word is first of all a mental event: it does not designate anything in empirical reality. Consequently, it leads man to other lands, other 'truths' (*A* 190); to the 'inscape', hinting at that other, silent language of being. Poetry is the 'word' in search of the 'Word' (*CA* 7); that unsayable word which poetry points to, like a 'bridge' or an 'arrow' (*Pu* 233, *CA* 190). It is through the word that the poet seeks 'life', that state of symbolic consciousness, that 'red word of the beginning' (*S* 106).

At this level, the word replaces the lost key that has been buried since our origins; to locate this 'key' is the liberating function of poetry; to loosen the rigid associations. We could call this 'the myth of the Total Word':

> Sólo había una palabra inmensa y sin revés
> Palabra como un sol
> Un día se rompió en fragmentos diminutos
> Son las palabras del lenguaje que hablamos
> Fragmentos que nunca se unirán
> Espejos rotos donde el mundo se mira destrozado (*L* 122)

There was only one immense word without a back, word like a sun. One day it broke into diminutive fragments, fragments that will never unite. They are the words of the language we speak, broken mirrors where the world sees itself destroyed.

The clarity of these lines makes explication unnecessary: it underlines Paz's realistic *nunca*; this myth is a necessary myth.

The poet 'purifies the dialect of the tribe' by restoring life to words and insisting on a living, natural language where 'las palabras ya no son cosas y, sin cesar de ser signos, se animan, *cobran cuerpo*' (*CD* 19; words now are not things and, without ceasing to be signs, they become lively, take on a body) – here Paz's own italics stress the intent. However, this is a dynamic concept, for if the poet liberates and gives life to the word he is in turn liberated by the word: 'la palabra, al fin en libertad, muestra todas sus entrañas, todos sus sentidos y alusiones, como un fruto maduro' (*A* 22; the word, at last free, shows its core, all its senses and allusions, like a mature fruit), and, quite explicitly, 'invento la Palabra, libertad que se inventa y me inventa cada día' (*L* 10; I invent the Word, liberty that invents itself and invents me every day).

The early poem entitled 'Palabra' (Word) is almost a concordium of all the possibilities or analogies with the word as mental event: the word is a 'wound', a 'fountain', a 'mirror', a 'knife', a 'fruit', a 'flame', 'crystal light', 'salt', 'diamond', 'cloud', 'water', 'air', 'earth' – while the poet's role is to be annihilated (*L* 32;), to 'annul his self'. The real word is the unsayable one that lies beyond the poet's ego and will, yet has issued from his dark body 'riente y pura, libre' (*L* 31; laughing and pure, free). A later poem, titled 'Palabras' (words), reflects more the poet's violence and frustration with everyday 'dead' and 'used' language; 'whore' words (*L* 59) that the poet vainly tries to clean. He must turn them upside down, whip them and stuff them with sugar; only when the poet 'swallows' his own words will the sought-after word appear. In both poems, struggling with words is merely a prelude to going beyond them, *ailleurs*.

The analogy 'word–bird' points to the living, natural nature of the word in poetry. Words (and birds) fly up from horizontal temporality; the flying bird is pure song. The poem 'La rama' (The branch) illustrates this analogy; subtle clues indicate that the bird, seemingly 'real' (i.e. the word points to a real bird) is really just a *word* in a poem: this bird on a branch 'rises up' (as the word in the poem rises up from the horizontality of usual discourse) and 'disappears' into music. The real poem, like music, is invisible; the word–bird is the

> astilla
> que canta y se quema viva
> en una nota amarilla.   (*L* 48)

splinter that sings and burns itself alive in a yellow note.

The poem burns up its individual words, as fire purifies; and 'yellow' has solar connotations. Nothing is left on the branch but silence, that silence of experience that poetry articulates. Not to enrich the reading with analogy would be to read literally (the prime reading): the realists' illusion. For Paz can talk of creativity, the experience of poetry and music by talking of *birds*; it is a less explicit, more metaphorical rendering of the Romantic *topos* of the poet–lark, the poet–nightingale.

The poem 'Aparición' (Apparition) plays with the same analogy; it opens with 'vuelan aves radiantes de estas letras' (*L* 199; radiant birds fly from these letters). This word–bird is an unknown one, a 'sun' to rival the 'sun'; it amazes the poet. The bird is compared to 'light' and a 'fountain'; it sings 'blancuras atónitas de ser' (L 199; astounded whitenesses of being), then 'disappears'. This bird was 'glimpsed innocence', an apparition. The poet wonders what 'fruits' this bird feeds on; on what tree it sings 'los cantos de la altura' (*L* 199; the songs of the height); the songs are 'way above' everyday, prosaic language.

The search for the word conditions the first part of *¿Aguila o sol?* (Eagle or Sun; or Heads or Tails), aptly entitled 'Trabajos del poeta' (Works of the poet) and published in part in Breton's *Le Surréalisme, même*. This section illustrates the 'struggle' to liberate language. Inspiration arrives as an army of black insects (typed words?); they are living, hostile, aggressive, sensitive, tactile, sticky and slippery; they copulate and separate and bleed but are always full of energy. This hostile army has to be purified, the rotten elements cut away. Section VI describes the poet's *refus total*, his moral stance toward language and its decaying values. The poet despises words, steps on convention to invent a new one. He has to break with reason and with a language based on causality and analysis. He says *no* and empties himself of the *naderías* (small things) with which he is filled. He describes the result of this action: 'vaciado, lim-piado de la nada purulenta del yo, vaciado de tu imagen, ya no eres sino espera y aguardas' (*L* 151; emptied, cleaned of the purulent nothingness of the ego, emptied of your image, you are nothing but wait and you wait); he impatiently awaits the arrival of the word–bird.

But the poet's necessary critical attitude towards numbed words has not ended; the purge continues through the text; words are broken into two; they dance, scream and sing: 'En suma, en mi sótano se corta, se despedaza, se degüella, se pega, se cose y recose. Hay tantas combinaciones como gustos' (*L* 154; To sum up, in my cellar I cut, break up, throttle, stick, sew and resew. There are as many combinations as tastes). By section XI the awaited word starts appearing; the poet is thirsty to contact his being: 'Ser al fin una Palabra, un poco de aire en una boca pura, un poco de agua en unos labios ávidos' (*L* 158; To be at last a Word, a bit of air in a pure mouth, a bit of water in some avid lips). This yearned-for 'purity' announces the arrival of the poem, conveyed as a freshness, as natural: 'como abrir una puerta que da al mar...como la cascada azul... como el pájaro...y el relámpago' (*L* 158; like opening a door that gives onto the sea...like a blue cascade...like a bird... and lightning). At last he has become a bird and splits open the fruit, the wholesome, natural poem. Hence his 'scream' of pleasure (or pain), his 'surtidor de plumas de fuego' (fountain of feathers of fire) where bird, water and fire are elementally fused in an image of the intensified experience of the poem. This is the final loss of ego-consciousness and the discovery of being through a cleansed language. The poet becomes anonymous, and language–being takes over.

This personification and animation of words is constant in Paz's poetry. The poem 'Disparo' (Shot) shows that the word jumps like a horse, like a wild animal, leaving its traces every-where (*S* 21). The poet creates a series of analogies of the effect of the word on the poet:

> La oleada negra que cubre el pensamiento
> La campana furiosa que tañe en mi frente
> La campana de sangre en mi pecho
> La imagen que ríe en lo alto de la torre
> La palabra que revienta las palabras
> La imagen que incendia todos los puentes
> La desaparecida en mitad del abrazo   (*S* 21)

The black surge that covers thought, the furious bell that rings in my head, the bell of blood in my chest, the image that laughs at the top of a tower, the word that smashes words, the image that burns all the bridges, she who disappears in the middle of an embrace.

Each line is interchangeable in its rich interplay between the literal and the symbolic; from word to woman to bell to heart to music and passion and creativity. The word is the woman inside the poet who *wakes him up* to say 'remember' (*S* 22). She forces him to recall his ancestral links with the origins.

The poem 'Entrada en materia' (Entry into matter), as the title implies, deals with the poet 'descending' into matter–language to seek out his word–being. The source of poetry is sought through the real–symbolic woman's sexual organ:

> Los labios de la herida
> La boscosa hendidura de la profecía   (*S* 9)

The lips of the wound, the woody cleft of prophecy.

The poet enters 'entre tus muslos' (*S* 10; between your thighs) but is not satisfied that he has purged his 'arthritic' Spanish (*S* 12); the babel that bubbles up is not that 'original' word that he seeks; words are tauntingly both real (matter) and spiritual (mind); they have claws and fingernails but cannot be touched; they are 'reales son fantasmas son corpóreas' (real are ghosts are bodies). Only through a 'promiscuity of nouns' and names will the body and spirit – so long separated – be fused; the basic analogy for 'wholeness' is copulation; male and female (or any polarity) momentarily joined in ecstasy.

Silence, the scream and the unsayable

The poet works at the frontiers of sense. For the *symbolistes* the dream was to convert poetry into music, to release language from its duty of representing. Paz's frontiers are triple: his message lies between silence, the scream and music, for being's truth-experience is *indecible* (unsayable). Paz writes: 'entre el grito y el callar, entre el significado que es todos los significados y la ausencia de significancia, el poema se levanta' (*CA* 74; between the shout and being silent, between the meaning that is all meanings and the absence of significance, the poem rises). There are two silences; the first exists before the poem breaks it, while the second is pointed to by the 'noise' of the poem; it is the result of the poem. The first is potential writing, to be deciphered (*A* 163), a silence 'poblado de signos' (*A* 20; peopled with signs); a silence that says something, a lake full of words (*A* 147–8); this is nature's silence (*L* 40–1) and man's inner silence (*L* 109). The second silence is a 'vacío pleno' (full emptiness), for Paz claims that all words resolve themselves into the silence of plenitude (*CA* 110). This silence is poetry's utopia where the white page is a metaphor of space and being. This is why Paz calls this silence 'implicit communication' or 'latent sense' (*A* 56). The 'nothing' that it tells differentiates it from merely 'saying nothing' (*A* 56); for it is the reverse of speech (*A* 111). The poem 'Silencio' (Silence) shows how the 'music' of poetry becomes a new, mental music 'en otra música enmudece' (*L* 42); a music beyond referential language 'silencio/que dice sin decir' (*L* 251; in another music becomes silent; silence that says without saying).

For example, the body of a woman is free of writing, as clean analogically as a white page or silence. The poet penetrates this body silence through the woman's *grieta* (cleft), her *hendidura* (fissure), her 'wound', where the experiential truth is so extreme in its intensity that ordinary language is dissolved in the scream of pleasure; Paz describes this as an 'explosión no conceptual de las sílabas, goce, angustia, éxtasis, cólera, deseo. Un lenguaje más allá del lenguaje' (*CD* 85; non-conceptual explosion of syllables, joy, anguish, ecstasy, anger, desire. A language beyond language).

The 'scream' is red-hot language, the language of the senses at their limit, synonymous with the sun's 'high yellow scream' (*L* 211). The poet seeks 'tú mi Grito, surtidor de plumas de fuego' (*L* 158; you, my Scream, fountain of feathers of fire). The poem itself becomes a scream (*L* 235), and this is all that language can communicate (*S* 31); it is all that remains of Melusina's presence (*L* 249); the orgasmic *ay* of lovers (*L* 110, 202, *LE* 163); the scream that enables man to 'atravesar la muerte' (*S* 84; to cross death). This is a repetitive element in Paz: poetry is a special language 'capable of transcending the sense of this and that to say the unsayable' (*A* 105); and this ambition cuts across both his prose and poetry: 'nothing is said except the unsayable' (*S* 60). Paz's salamander is 'ungraspable', 'unsayable', the red-hot word of the origin (*S* 106).

Woman

Woman is essentially a link in the analogical chain; she cannot be uprooted from this vision. Paz asks the following question that involves the problem of isolated existence and meaning: '¿El agua es femenina o la mujer es oleaje, río nocturno...?' (*CA* 58: Is water feminine or is woman swell, nocturnal river?). The answer is, both; woman is a naturalised archetype, the central part of a sensualised nature, she partakes of all 'the natural forms', hill, tiger and sea. She is the 'presencia sensible de esa totalidad única y plural en la que se funden la historia y la naturaleza' (*C* 41; sensitive presence of that unique and plural totality in which history and nature fuse); she is the symbol of and contact with that 'lost' sacred element.

Woman, to Paz, is the only window open onto the other side of existence (*Pu* 236); and she is not only a woman, but *woman*; synonymous with mystery, heart, world and above all 'sensual apprehension of reality' (*C* 57). Woman is the embodiment of 'vital energy' and in her flow the four elements are fused; she is the feminine half of the cosmos, man's 'other' (*C* 58). But if woman is ideal, platonic idea or archetype, she must also be touched, eaten and made love to; truth is always experiential.

Woman says 'Yes' to life; she is quite literally a door onto infinity (L 137, 115). She is also the universal mother, the 'obsidian butterfly', once in contact with man when she danced until fruit and flowers and eagles budded out of her (L 193); but her magical status has been destroyed by a rotten civilisation; she is made to represent the primitive, atavistic and natural but lost relationship; she is the origin 'perverted'. This is why she is the wound through which man must penetrate to recover paradise; only she can inaugurate the 'reinado dichoso: el pacto de los gemelos enemigos' (L 195; happy kingdom: the pact of the hostile twins).

Implicit in the notion 'woman' is the analogy with the word in a poem. Paz writes *poems*; his woman is first of all a word, an idea, a memory and a symbol, not some realistic being. She is first of all the creative, fecund principle in poetry. In the poem 'Niña' (Girl) the girl of the title just has to name things and nature blossoms; and when she is silent the poet–lover is restored to his self (L 37). Consequently in Paz's universe woman can have a name, be a historical reality, a literary myth, nature, the word, the self, *anima* and so on. In 'Piedra de sol' Paz identifies with and echoes one of Breton's feminine archetypes; here she is clearly a symbol; there is no possibility of a realistic reading. Mélusine is obviously *mental*.

She appears twice in the long poem; first as part of a list, one of woman's innumerable names (L 240). The second appearance elliptically relates her role in the myth:

> Yo ví tu atroz escama,
> Melusina, brillar verdosa al alba,
> dormías enroscada entre las sábanas
> y al despertar gritaste como un pájaro
> y caíste sin fin, quebrada y blanca,
> nada quedó de ti sino tu grito   (L 244)

I saw your atrocious scales, Mélusine, shine greenish at dawn, you slept coiled in the sheets and on waking you screamed like a bird and fell endlessly, broken and white, nothing remained of you but your scream.

Paz, like Breton, reverses the Garden of Eden myth; for the

ancient goddess is destroyed by man; she becomes the 'little girl drowned a thousand years ago' (*L* 244) that poetry seeks to restore. But this Mélusine was invoked by Breton; his Nadja (in *Nadja*, 1928) compared herself to this mythic woman; in his *Arcane 17* Breton develops this association with the same visionary stance as Paz: his *cri* is Paz's *grito*, his *je vois* is Paz's *vi*. For Breton she embodies the 'lost woman' still singing in man's imagination, and if health and wholeness is the ambition she must be recovered. Breton called on Mélusine to redeem a rotten age, since she is 'la femme toute entière' (complete woman) still in contact with the elemental forces of nature. For the critic Michel Carrouges, she is the 'alliance analogique des contraires' (analogical alliance of opposites). Paz adopts a myth.[29]

At the same time, Breton was aware that individual, historical woman was oppressed and as limited by society and history as man. Breton enthusiastically took up Rimbaud's 'quand sera brisé l'infini servage de la femme' (when the infinite slavery of woman will be broken). Woman is the 'great victim' and man's monopoly of intellect and power must be ended. Woman's instinctual relation with herself and nature reveals the crucial analogue with what the poem creates out of everyday language and posits the dreamed-of poetic society.[30]

Thus woman is man's salvation from a spiritual and sensual aridity; she is the refreshing 'other' both in real life and in the poem. That is why poetry, like love, restores unity, mental–physical androgyny.

The poem and love

The poem transcends the inherent dualism and relativity of language to become 'pure' language or music, engendering a 'plurality' of meanings impossible to pin down and as fluid and open as dream-symbolism. The poem closes the abysmal gap between sign and signified where the word is the thing; it lives. Thus the poem is emblematic of paradise, an organic echo-system of analogies, a self-sufficient cosmos. The poem defies rectilinear time, for it can be read repeatedly. The poem ushers in 'absolute' or mythic time by recreating the original moment of creation and redeeming the moment. The poem is an 'electric zone', alchemically transmuting flux, embodying Breton's *alchimie mentale*. Poetry is thus knowledge, vision and reconciliation; it says the unsayable and reminds man of his true 'nature' by crystallising desire. The poem is the poet's tomb, where he loses his ego to gain his self, and where the liberated language *creates* the poet: 'Todo poema se cumple a expensas del poeta' (*L* 207; Every poem is fulfilled at the expense of the poet); or as Paz wrote years later: 'En esto que digo/Acabo' (*LE* 75; In this that I say I end).

These inevitably hazy notions underscore all Paz's writings; they are the supports of his vision. In 'Un poeta' (A poet) we see that

el saber no es distinto del soñar, el soñar del hacer. La poesía ha puesto fuego a todos los poemas. Se acabaron las palabras, se acabaron las imágenes. Abolida la distancia entre el nombre y la cosa, nombrar es crear, e imaginar, nacer.   (*L* 199)

knowing is not different from dreaming, dreaming from doing. Poetry has set fire to all poems. Words have finished, images have finished. Abolished the distance between name and thing, to name is to create and to imagine to be born.

The notion of love links all the analogies. It functions at two levels; one is thematic and descriptive, where Paz writes poems *about* love affairs, woman, desire. But love is also a structural element; Paz envisages the poem-act as analogous to the love-act. The poet makes love to words, and love is 'el diálogo corporal y espiritual entre dos seres libres' (*CA* 14; the corporeal and spiritual dialogue between two free beings). We would stress the verbal connotation of *dialogue*.

This dialogue of released desire is a natural passion (*C* 195) and a return to nature, to that 'energy' that moves the earth (*Pe* 122). In typically Bretonian terms, love is a mediation between man and nature, 'el sitio en que se cruzan el magnetismo terrestre y el del espíritu' (*CA* 58; the site in which terrestial and spiritual magnetism cross). To love in these terms is to participate, to return, to recuperate.

However, because love is such an intense passion it is condemned by all societies. For Paz all acts of what he defines as
love are immoral, scandalous (*C* 195); Paz's view of love provokes and challenges society, since it is a totally anarchic and
natural experience beyond classification, societal morality, or
common sense. But this view is 'orthodox' in that it has its own
tradition; Paz's appendix to *El laberinto de la soledad*, written in
Paris, defends the surrealist scandalous view. To defend love is
antisocial, dangerous and revolutionary (*LS* 167), and poetry
reflects this explosive love; it too bursts out in strange and pure
forms; it too breaks laws (of syntax, taste, conventions): both
love and poetry are transgressions (*LS* 164).

The axial metaphor is that of two lovers making love; Paz
declared that 'entre yo y tú la relación es la conjugación
copulativa o adversativa' (between I and you the relation is a
copulative or adversative conjugation). 'I' and 'thou' refer not
only to the lovers, but to the poet and the (female) word, the
reader and the poem. Paz adds: 'El mundo es la analogía de la
pareja primordial y sus cambios reflejan los del tú y el yo en sus
uniones y sus separaciones' (*Pu* 91; The world is the analogy of
the primordial couple and its changes reflect those of the you
and the I in their unions and separations). We return to the
source of natural energy, of copulatory rhythms.

The surrealist scandal is described by Paz in his 'Piedra de
sol'; when the poet meditates on the Spanish civil war, in
Madrid in 1937, with sirens wailing and bombs dropping, he
writes:

> los dos se desnudaron y se amaron
> por defender nuestra porción eterna,
> nuestra ración de tiempo y paraíso,
> tocar nuestra raíz y recobrarnos
> ...
> los dos se desnudaron y besaron
> porque las desnudeces enlazadas
> saltan el tiempo y son invulnerables,
> nada las toca, vuelven al principio,
> no hay tú ni yo, mañana, ayer ni nombres
> verdad de dos en sólo un cuerpo y alma   (*L* 246)

the two stripped and made love to defend our eternal portion, our

ration of time and paradise, to touch our root and recover ourselves
. . . the two stripped and kissed because nakednesses entwined leap
time and are invulnerable, nothing touches them, they return to the
beginning, there is no you nor I, tomorrow, yesterday nor names;
truth of two in only one body and soul.

The social calamity of the Spain torn by civil war can be
redeemed if man really learns to love passionately; love between man and woman recovers the 'ser total' (total being) lost
a thousand years back (*L* 246). This naked, physical act of love
breaks down the isolated ego and unites the body and the mind
separated by a life-denying Christian tradition. Paz echoes
Rimbaud's *posséder la vérité dans une âme et un corps* (to possess the
truth in one soul and body); the experience of poetry–love is
carnal–spiritual, the possession of self. In 1924 Breton wrote
that love was the perfect compensation for the miseries of the
world; in 1948 he wrote that the poetic and carnal embrace
defends the poet–lover from the same miseries. Misery is cast
aside, defused; in both Breton and Paz the word *defends* reveals
the intention.[31]

Eroticism

The woman's body transformed, internalised and symbolised
by the poet's imagination, yet still remaining a body 'out there',
tactile like a round vowel, is what Paz defines as eroticism; the
flesh made word (symbolic transformation) and the word made
flesh (the poem). Paz's eroticism is a way to the sacred; it
sanctifies the body and points towards the unnameable and
unthinkable. This is Breton's vision, according to Paz 'Breton
se propuso...consagrar al erotismo por el amor' (*CA* 62;
Breton proposed to consecrate eroticism through love); and like
a religion, eroticism reveals reality only through ecstasy (*Pu*
24). Paz shares Yves Bonnefoy's 'savoir passionnel' (passionate
knowledge), using poetry as an evident religious substitute.
Paz's eroticism is a return to nature through fusion with the
'other'; his 'videncia erótica' (erotic prophecy) turns the opaque body transparent (through imagination and desire)
revealing truth as always beyond, a *más allá/ailleurs* that is
extra-literary and experimental.[32]

The body

Only through one's body can one experience intensely, and only through the other's body can one transcend one's own. The body exists only as a relationship with another, while the ego dreams of self-sufficiency. For Paz, then, the body is truth:

El cuerpo es verdadero y la revelación que nos ofrece es inhumana, sea animal o divina: nos arranca de nosotros mismos y nos arroja a otra vida...más plena.   (CA 49)

The body is true and the revelation that it offers us is inhuman, be it animal or divine: it rips us out of ourselves and hurls us into another, more fulfilling life.

At the same time, bodies are 'jeroglíficos sensibles' (CA 49; hieroglyphics that we can feel) that the poet–lover struggles to understand. This body-language speaks a 'langage sensible' (Eluard) where the word is made real like flesh and the poet participates in the copulatory energy. Answering Breton's questionnaire on magic (1955), Paz wrote that to return to a magical view of the world would be to re-establish contact with the whole; to participate in an erotic relationship with the world (Pe 188) that Paz summarises in the fusion: 'Tocar con el pensamiento y pensar con el cuerpo' (Pe 188; To touch with thought and to think with the body); this is what Frank Kermode terms 'openly defying the intellect' and thinking 'experientially', a characteristic of twentieth-century modernism.[33]

By 1969 Paz's concern with body-thinking had solidified into a poetic where he argued that signs in a poem are 'cosas sensibles y que obran sobre los sentidos' (CD 18; sensitive things that work on the senses), endorsing what Mallarmé called écriture corporelle.The intention is clear (note the infinitive): 'hablar con el cuerpo y convertir al lenguaje en un cuerpo' (CD 18; to speak with the body and to convert language into a body). The poem transforms words from paralysis to living body. The body is what is most real (CD 23); yet because of the symbolic nature of language the body is both real and imaginary and cannot be separated either into a realistic poetics or into a 'pure' poetry: 'Todo es real...y todo es simbólico

...tocamos símbolos cuando creemos tocar cuerpos y objetos materiales' (*CD* 74; Everything is real...and everything is symbolic...we touch symbols when we believe that we are touching bodies and material objects). This leads to the basic analogy between writing experienced as a physical body (the word made flesh) and the body read like writing (for the body *speaks*); this can be rephrased as a writing throbbing with life and life read like an ecstatic poem. Paz proposes a poetics or a new passion based on the body and on eroticism, and a lived poetry where man the poet will live exuberantly in the glimpsed 'realidad magnética' (*CD* 137; magnetic reality). Paz concludes *Le Singe grammairien* by saying that the whole text was but a 'métaphore de l'étreinte des corps' (*SG* 157; metaphor of the embrace of bodies). Notice the word *étreinte*: the erotic attraction and repulsion of bodies, words and minds. This is the dream shared with Breton: 'donner corps à son rêve' (to give body to one's dream); it is a tradition, 'the rebellion of the senses', that stretches back to the Romantics, to Novalis and Rimbaud (*CD* 125).[34]

Paz's poetry inevitably traces the same steps. The body opens and reveals truth: 'el cuerpo es infinito y melodía' (*L* 35; the body is infinite and melody). The opaque, anaesthetised body is transformed through the vision into 'clarity':

> También mi cuerpo se me escapa
> Y entre las claridades se me pierde   (*L* 129)

Also my body escapes me and between the clarities it loses me.

Through the body the poet *sees*; 'el mundo ya es visible por tu cuerpo' (*L* 238; the world is now visible through your body); this is the only path: 'Voy por tu cuerpo como por el mundo' (*L* 238; I go through your body as through the world). The ancient goddess or obsidian butterfly predicts 'Allí abrirás mi cuerpo en dos, para leer las letras de tu destino' (*L* 195; There you will open my body in two, to read the letters of your destiny), for 'de mi cuerpo brotan imágenes' (*L* 194; from my body sprout images). The poet's task is defined in the poem 'Entrada en materia' as the need to 'say' what the 'sagrario del cuerpo' and the 'arca del espíritu' (*S* 13; sacred place of the body; coffer of

the spirit) 'say', in a language that is flesh and spirit, symbolic
and literal. The poem 'Lauda' expresses this fusion of body,
spirit and truth:

> Fuera de mi cuerpo
> En tu cuerpo fuera de tu cuerpo
> En otro cuerpo
> Cuerpo a cuerpo creado
> Por tu cuerpo y mi cuerpo
> Nos buscamos perdidos
> Dentro de ese cuerpo instantáneo
> Nos perdemos buscando
> Todo un Dios todo cuerpo y sentido
> Otro cuerpo perdido
> ...
> Los cuerpos abolidos en el cuerpo   (S 55–6)

Beyond my body in your body beyond your body in another body,
body to body created by your body and my body. We seek each other
lost within that instantaneous body we lose each other seeking. All
a God all body and senses, another body lost...bodies abolished in
the body.

Only through (*por*) the body can one go beyond (*fuera, perdido*).
Only the senses lead to truth, and the time of the senses is the
present instant, the 'now'; a corporeal god, the body into which
our bodies melt (i.e. re-union with nature, our nature). Liberation takes place though the body:

> El cuerpo femenino
>   Es una pausa
> Terrible
>   Proximidad inaccesible
> La demasía de la presencia
>   Fija
> Y no obstante
>   Desbordante   (LE 93)

The female body is a pause, terrible, inaccessible proximity. Excess
of presence, fixed yet overflowing.

Body excess 'speaks' the truth:

> Nuestros cuerpos se hablaron, se juntaron y se fueron.
> Nosotros nos fuimos con ellos.
>
>   (L 135)

Our bodies talked to themselves, joined and went away. We went
with them.

This is the loss of ego in the intensity of the bodies' copulation.

In *Love's Body* N. O. Brown advocates a clearly poetic solution to society's and culture's inevitable repression of desire and pleasure. Paraphrasing Blake, he writes: 'To return the word to the flesh. To make knowledge carnal again; not by deduction, but immediate by perception or sense at once; the bodily senses.' Brown calls this the recovery of bodily and unspoken meanings, for the body speaks 'silently'. This would restore a 'symbolic consciousness' deflating the common enemy 'literal mindedness'. Paz enthusiastically endorses Brown's metaphysic as 'apasionante' (*CD* 30; thrilling); Brown quotes from Paz, and bases much of his book on a close reading of Blake, Breton and Freud. Paz and Brown share the same heritage, the same tradition of 'body mysticism'. Paz ends his *Conjunciones y disyunciones* with this hope:

Tal vez la alianza de poesía y rebelión nos dará la visión...veo la posibilidad del regreso del signo *cuerpo*: la encarnación de las imágenes, el regreso de la figura humana, radiante e irradiante de símbolos.   (*CD* 142–3)

Perhaps the alliance of poetry and rebellion will give us the vision...I see the possibility of the return of the sign *body*: the embodiment of images, the return of the human figure, radiating and irradiating of symbols.

This is a poetics, in the end, of 'perhaps'. If one follows the 'perhaps' it leads to a poetics of 'embodiment', the waking-dream of a lived poetry, but always grounded in the future tense, in infinitives.[35]

Dance and music; body and spirit

Behind all the forms or analogies lies Breton's notion of magnetic energy; the body is a source of energy, as is a poem, as lovers create and squander energy. This energy is also spirit, where inner and outer, subjective and objective, body and soul (categories made nonsense by the very nature of language) are 'joined' and 'copulate'. The body becomes dance, expressing the cosmic, rhythmical energy, and poetry becomes music, the pure, non-signifying music of being.

Music's 'suggestive indefiniteness' conveys a 'spiritual' effect which transcends relative, referential, empirical language; this is a re-statement of the *symboliste* aesthetic (or dream). In this poetry, words – for brief moments – avoid contingency and 'misplaced concreteness'. Music hints, never names; it leaves spaces for the imagination, for desire. Poetry is 'toute chose non dite qui flûtise sous les vrais vers, étrangère à la parole' (Mallarmé; everything not said that flutes under real verse, foreign to the word). Music defies logic and common sense and allows the soul to sing 'naturally'; this is the mental melody of being, musical thought. Paz ends his poem 'Mediodía' (Midday) by fusing body and melody (*L* 35). This is Eluard's *pensée musicale*, a cosmic musicality, the music of analogy, of the 'universo hecho de los acordes, reuniones y separaciones, de una cosa con la otra' (universe made of chords, reunions and separations, of one thing with another). Language in a poem becomes music and dance, the 'doble mágico del cosmos' (*C* 38; the magical double of the cosmos) based on *harmony* ('acorde'). This is the original language; what is sacred in man (*C* 90).[36]

This *pensée musicale* expresses the 'soul's' rhythmic harmony:

> Canta, desde su sombra
> – y más, desde su nada – el alma.
> Desnudo de su nombre canta el ser,
> en el hechizo de existir suspenso.   (*L* 39)

The soul sings from its shade – and more, from its nothing. Naked of its name being sings, in the spell of astonished existence.

Beyond words, there is only song. From this early poem all the associations flow. This soul-song is not traditional music but a song that cannot be heard, a *music* of silence and plenitude (*L* 39). N. O. Brown states: 'The meaning is not in the words but between the words, in the silence.' Being is 'unsayable' and to name it literally would be to fix, deform and lose that fluidity that only music and dance hint at. The poem 'Silencio' conveys this:[37]

> Así como del fondo de la música
> brota una nota
> que mientras vibra crece y se adelgaza

> hasta que en otra música enmudece   (*L* 41–2)

Just as from the depths of the music there sprouts a note that while it vibrates grows and thins until it becomes silent in another music.

Man's being–truth is a natural music:

> Del silencio brota un árbol de música.
> Del árbol cuelgan todas las palabras hermosas,   (*L* 117)

From the silence sprouts a tree of music. From the tree hang all the beautiful words.

and this music takes over:

> Los dedos de la música
> La yedra de fuego de la música
> Cubre los cuerpos cubre las almas   (*L* 127)

The fingers of music, the ivy of fire of music, covers the bodies, covers the souls.

Music describes the vision that cannot be seen, that tears out eyes (*L* 117). The poem ends:

> La gran boca de la música devoró los cuerpos
> Se quemó el mundo
> ...
> Ardió su nombre y los nombres que eran su atavío
> No queda nada sino un alto sonido   (*L* 127)

The great mouth of music devoured the bodies. The world burnt... its name burned and the names that were its attire. Nothing remains but a high sound.

Music, the body's 'unheard melody', caught in the poem's liberated language, dissolves and evaporates the restricting forms, the divisions. Everything *burns* and man becomes free:

> Música despeñada
> Y ardemos y no dejamos huella   (*L* 129)

Shattered music and we burn and leave no trace.

Man finds his true self in song, in poetry. In the utopia of the poem 'Todo canta, todo da frutos, todo se dispone a ser' (*L* 203; All sings, all gives fruit, everything prepares to be). Again one must not confuse the vision with empirical reality (and inevitable failure); for being is ever elusive, always out of reach, *ailleurs*. It is all a matter of preparation, of patience and expectancy (a desperate hope?), a *disponerse*. The verb *cantar* is a constant in Paz's poetry. The long poem 'Blanco' ends on this impalpable music:

> El mundo
> > Haz de tus imágenes
> > Anegadas en la música
> > > Tu cuerpo
> > Derramado en mi cuerpo
> > > Visto
> > Desvanecido
> > Da realidad a la mirada   (*LE* 169)

The world, bundle of your images, drowned in the music. Your body spilt in my body, seen, vanished, gives reality to the glance.

The overflowing music melts the forms, the matter. Music abolishes the dichotomy inside–outside, for music is space, the silent sounds of the body, the sought-after but elusive natural language:

> Mi cuerpo oye al cuerpo de mi mujer
> (*A cable of sound*)
> Y le responde:
> > Esto se llama música   (*LE* 82)

My body hears the body of my wife, a cable of sound, and answers it: this is called music.

This silent body-language is symbolic, as Brown claims: 'It cannot be put into words because it does not consist of things.' It is music.[38]

George Steiner has traced the music–poetry analogy back to German Romanticism and Novalis' *Hymns to the Night* (much praised by the surrealists) which turn 'on a metaphor of cosmic musicality; they image the spirit of man as a lyre played upon by elemental harmonies, and seek to exalt language to that state of rhapsodic obscurity, of nocturnal dissolution from which it may naturally pass into song'. Not only does Paz title a crucial poem 'Himno entre ruinas', he calls a collection (one of his best) *Semillas para un himno*; hymn, sacred music. In all Paz's writings lies the seed sown by Novalis: and cosmic musicality, elemental harmonies, dissolution and song form a natural chain of analogies.[39]

If music is 'spirit', 'being', 'space', then dance is the body united with the spirit where dancer and dance are one. The dancer and the dance form the emblem of 'symbolic reality' (Kermode). Like music, dance is 'anti-discursive' and corresponds to the artist's effort to 'vêtir l'idée d'une forme sensible' (Mallarmé; to dress the idea in a form that can be felt). Dance and poetry are mirror-analogies:

> naces, poesía, delicia,
> y danzas, invisible, frente al hombre   (L 33)
you are born, poetry, delight, and you dance, invisible, in front of man.

The poet does not seek eternity but ecstasy:

> ¿Dura la flor? . . .
> La flor quiere bailar, sólo bailar   (L 69)
Does the flower last? . . . The flower wants to dance, only dance.

The dance is the natural rhythm, the simple life buried and lost. The ancient goddess used to dance to a standstill; then from her wound would grow leaves, flowers and fruit (L 193). Man must return to her, for she is the 'centro fijo que mueve la danza' (L 194; the fixed centre that moves the dance).[40]

Poetry–music–dance express man's inner, repressed and forgotten truth–being–desire (this clumsiness of terminology is due to the fact that we are not writing a poem). This is analogous to the energy that moves the cosmos. Once this energy is located, the usual dichotomies cease to apply and all flows: the body is liberated, energised, like the word in the poem, and this is 'carnal knowledge':

El cuerpo es surtidor de energía, una fuente de 'materia psíquica' o *mana*, sustancia que no es ni espiritual ni física...fuerza que mueve al mundo según los primitivos   (C 194)

The body is fountain of energy, a source of 'psychic matter' or *mana*, substance that is neither spiritual nor physical...force that moves the world, according to the primitives.

In 1942 Paz wrote that lovers experience 'el presentimiento de la pura energía que mueve al universo y de la inercia en que se transforma el vértigo de esa energía' (Pe 122; the presentiment of the pure energy that moves the universe and of the inertia into which the vertigo of this energy is transformed). Through his most intense body-experiences man is made aware of this energy, a sort of sap permeating the universe. This insight never deserted Paz. Poetry also canalises the 'secret force of the world' (*Pe* 126); it too is an act of love; in both poetry and love, the lover–poet touches the absolute: 'el cuerpo y el alma, en ese instante, son lo mismo y la piel es como una nueva conciencia, conciencia de lo infinito' (*Pe* 126; body and soul, in this instant, are the same, and skin is like a new consciousness, conscious of the infinite). This is another formulation of body-mysticism, like Rimbaud's possession of the body–soul as experience of truth.

Through love and poetry the poet–lover–reader re-experiences the 'original energy' (*Pe* 127), the 'vital energy' (*C* 57) that animates the universe; the red-hot word of the origin in Paz's poem 'Salamandra' is a 'grano de energía' (*S* 102; grain [seed] of energy). Language in poetry catches this *seed* of energy. It is up to the reader whether it grows or not.

Paz's new *sagesse*, his poetics, proposes a 'mental art' (*CA* 24) based on what N. O. Brown calls 'the spiritualisation of the senses, a restoration of the unsullied sense-activity of man in paradise'. Paz seeks through the body (woman, the word) an 'experiencia total, carnal y espiritual' (*CD* 65; total experience, carnal and spiritual).[41]

This desperate ambition can be compared to that of two other equally passionate and thoughtful poet–critics. Herbert Read argued for 'felt thought', where emotional intensity is embodied in a philosophical schema or system (Coleridge and surrealism?). T. S. Eliot, in his much discussed essay on the metaphysical poets, praised their 'direct sensuous apprehension of thought' where a thought becomes an experience. In this tradition we have rooted Breton and Paz together. Whatever else can be said about Paz, and for all his relative and necessary failure as a writer of individual poems, his passionate concern for poetics allows an enriching and refreshing reading. A contemporary, Yves Bonnefoy, opened one of his acute essays by identifying poetry and hope; isn't this what defines Paz's dream?[42]

Chapter 4

I The East

Dissatisfaction with one's place and time became, in the Romantics, a literary convention. Rubén Darío's vaunt is more literary than autobiographical:

mas he aquí que veréis en mis versos princesas, reyes, cosas imperiales, visiones de países lejanos o imposibles; ¡qué queréis!, yo detesto la vida y el tiempo en que me tocó nacer.

but behold you may see in my verse princesses, kings, imperial things, visions of distant or impossible countries; what do you want! I detest the life and time in which I was born.

The projection of a 'Better World over there' is a permanent Western drive, and the Cuban novelist Alejo Carpentier has fictionalised it through the alluring New World myth. It is also a quality of the imagination and desire – never satisfied, always questing and pursuing. The uprooted wanderer who seeks his true place anywhere but where he is – *fuir là-bas* – is an archetype of Romanticism, found in Baudelaire, Mallarmé, Huysmans; its echoes in Joyce are well known; and André Breton – as we have shown – placed real existence *ailleurs*, as if the dream of 'impossible places' constitutes reality.[1]

To read is to journey (there is a perennial taste for travel books and armchair travelling) but certain writers travel through words, vicariously, like Swift or Chateaubriand or Huysmans; this gives a deep-grained sense of being homeless. The difference between books 'that make you travel' (Breton) and those that genuinely recreate another reality is that between literature and anthropology. Octavio Paz is a well-travelled (read cosmopolitan) poet. His difficult relationship with the Far East must be seen in the context of this 'Western' zeal for shrinking distances in the imagination; for leaping, eyes closed, into the *exotic*.[2]

A great number of travel books are structured on a clear

'Them–Us' hinge: they serve as a cool mirror to reflect either the vices or virtues of the writer's home-land. And once this structuring is identified as a *value* conditioning the surface, the anecdotes, the descriptions – all that is seemingly exotic – these texts harden into allegories.

Here the Far East supplies blood to these anaemic dreams: romances and resonances of ancient civilisations; enigmatic cultures and a hazy luxuriousness distinguish these exotic attractions from those of the New World which are more uto-pian and Rousseauian. Henri Michaux saw through these 'effeminate and ambiguous dreams' (Huysmans), visiting both 'lost worlds'. In his account *Un Barbare en Asie* (1933) he senses his own cultural inadequacies. He is the barbarian, accepting the Chinese view of all Westerners. His acute, humorous text polarises East and West, Buddhists and Christians; he explores the divergent attitudes to sexuality, marriage, and reason; and however refreshing his inspection and meditations, the inten-tion is clear. These deeply religious Eastern cultures reject the Westerner's *despair*. Michaux remarks on this omni-presence of religion, how it permeates every act: 'Faisant l'amour avec sa femme, l'Hindou pense à Dieu dont elle est une expression et une parcelle' (Making love with his wife, the Hindu thinks of God of whom she is an expression and particle).[3]

This sense of belonging also seduced Paz. Like Michaux, Octavio Paz is a 'religious' writer, seeking through writing to recuperate a sense of vivacity and a meaning to living. Like Michaux, Paz actually went to the East.

Here Paz distinguishes himself from those seduced by a 'distant music', for instance André Breton, who disliked travel-ling so much. As early (for him) as 1924, though it is late in terms of the cults of *chinoiserie* and *japonaiserie*, Breton implores the East to solve his problems. He is aware that 'orient' is merely a symbolic and fashionable word, corresponding to 'une inquiétude de ce temps, à son plus secret espoir, à une prévision inconsciente' (an anguish of this time, to its most secret hope, to an unconscious prevision).[4]

Here 'orient' means all that is vague, exotic, or even repres-sed. Breton continues to eulogise this 'pseudo-Orient',

confirming that he lives in a 'damned civilisation'. By the time
he knew Paz Breton was more conversant with Buddhism; he
came to accept that automatic writing demands too much of its
practitioner and that it is closer to Eastern meditation, a point
that Paz also makes (who influenced whom?). He had by then
read the fashionable Suzuki; could compare Dada with Zen,
and quote Bashō (later translated by Paz). But he still insisted
on surrealism's 'sovereignty': 'mais la démarche surréaliste n'a
trouvé là qu'à s'assurer. Elle ne s'est jamais départie de son
indépendance' (but the surrealist process can but find reassur-
ance there [in the East]. It has never departed from its inde-
pendence).[5]

More specifically, through its age-old religious disciplines,
the East has attracted writers from Mallarmé and Schopen-
hauer to Emerson, Thoreau, Pound, Eliot, and the beat poets.
At this level, other, more radical, surrealists gave a different
meaning to 'orient'. This would include Artaud's rages against
putrid Western culture, against the 'contaminated' spirit; his
open letters to the Dalai Lama and the Buddhist schools
embody his violent quest for a more lived 'inner life' crushed by
European 'logic'. But though he had *read* more than Breton, his
longing for Tibet was still desperately exotic. René Daumal
actually learned Sanskrit; moved to do so as a disciple of
Gurdjieff, he evokes no vague, ambiguous orientalism. But
then, like Michaux, he was independent of Breton's magic
circle.

To move from what Paul Valéry calls his predilection for the
word 'orient' (a word that signifies, just because it is based on
books, images and hearsay, precisely because it is vague and
inaccurate, an 'orient of the mind') to what Henri Michaux and
Octavio Paz embody of the East, is to place Paz's writings in a
proper perspective. Paz lived *there*; his perceptions are coloured
by place.[6]

Octavio Paz spent seven years in the Far East. During
1952–3 he visited Japan and India, and from 1962–8 was
Mexican Ambassador to India, before resigning in protest at
the massacre of students at Tlatelolco just before the Olympic
games. His 'protest' poem, originally titled 'Limpidez', is

included in *Ladera este* (1969). Not only did Paz travel exten-
sively, in spite of the obvious linguistic and cultural barriers he
managed to penetrate the touristic 'mask' of India and incorporate some fundamental Tantric and Buddhist notions in his
own poetics. References to these years in India function on
many levels, from the anecdotal (Paz's personal impressions
and observations) to the analogical (similarities between India
and Mexico); from the satirical (on Europeans in India) to the
mythical, and from geographical local colour to metaphysical
statement. We will explore the implications of Paz's debt to
Eastern thought in his poetic 'vision'. Paz is not a Buddhist nor
a Tantrika; nor does he claim to explain what these terms mean
'objectively'. With the freedom of a poet he adapts and adopts
what suits him.

I must stress again the *heretical* nature of Paz's poetics. He
has always maintained that the poet is necessarily an outsider
to societal values. The poet is a dissident: 'La poesía moderna
se ha convertido en el alimento de los disidentes y desterrados
del mundo burgués' (*A* 40; Modern poetry has become the food
of the dissidents and exiles from the bourgeois world). This
Romantic position underpins Breton's surrealism. For example, Paz declares, silently evoking Breton: 'defender al amor ha
sido siempre una actividad antisocial y peligrosa. Y ahora
empieza a ser de verdad revolucionaria' (*LS* 167; to defend love
has always been an antisocial and dangerous activity. And now
it begins to be truly revolutionary). The 'ahora' was 1951, but
Paz's 'corazón herético' (*LE* 46; heretical heart) is that of all
poets.

Further, for Paz, the twentieth century has lost its sense of
'cohesion', its 'centre' (*A* 260). This is a 'critical epoch' that has
corroded its former unifying world 'image' without creating a
substitute. This 'espacio en blanco' (*A* 263; blank/white space)
can only be 'filled' by art. Only a 'poética' offers a solution.
This is Paz's ambitious 'mad wisdom' (*CA* 126–7), and it
assumes overt religious connotations, as Paz has recently suggested: 'The religious instinct...is congenital to mankind.'
Thus, if this new 'sacred' exists it will be discovered through
poetry (*A* 118).[7]

Because of this absence of a centre generating shared values, the poet is an exile; but the poet is not alone; Mexico itself, suffocated by alien ideologies or forms of history also lacks an authentic cultural patrimony. Mexico is 'desarraigo' (*Pu* 16; up-rooted). Paz's quest for a cultural synthesis (his cosmopolitanism) makes sense where a cultural tradition is lacking in substance.

Paz's involvement in Eastern thought flows from this cultural dilemma. In his journey from Mexico to surrealism and the East, Paz has underlined certain analogies that create a sense of unity in his preoccupations. For example, Western poetry discovered two thousand years later than Buddhism that the 'ego is an illusion' (*Pe* 172). Surrealism can be seen as an attack on the dictatorial ego through automatic writing, playing with chance and dreams, and so on. Paz lamented that Breton never turned to Buddhism as a confirmation of this central insight; and (in conversation with A. Rudolf) he has continued to stress this analogy: 'I find certain similarities with surrealism in that criticism of the world and the self which is the essence of Buddhism.' The duality of subject and object is also an illusion; Rimbaud's desire to 'possess the truth in his body and soul' (*Pe* 223) is a Buddhist constant. Paz links surrealism's automatic writing with Buddhist meditation in the demands it makes on the practitioner. Both are 'un ejercicio psíquico' (*CA* 54; a psychic exercise). The necessary detachment from the outside world, central to automatic writing, is closer to Eastern than to Western thought, even for Breton. Paz also links the collective writing of poetry, such as the *cadavre exquis*, with *renga*, the linked verse form recently used by Paz, Roubaud, Sanguineti and Tomlinson (1971), and his own paraphrase of Lautréamont's prophecy ('La poésie doit être faite par tous. Non par un' (*Poésies*, 1870; Poetry should be made by all. Not by one)) about 'creación poética colectiva' (*Pe* 156; collective poetic creation). Finally, Paz draws a parallel between Tantra's *maithuna* (ritualised copulation) and surrealism's revaluation of love between man and woman, where woman's body becomes the altar. Novalis and the surrealists' exhibition dedicated to eroticism (1959) seem related to Tantra, but, as Paz points out, the surrealists ignored the Hindu antecedent (*CD* 78).[8]

But surrealism only accidentally coincided with certain strands of Eastern thought, and then only through Paz himself. This reveals a continuity in Paz and nothing else. For Paz, the wisdom of the West is summed up in Breton's desire to fuse Marx and Rimbaud in the surrealists' programme (1935, 'Discours au Congrès des écrivains'). Could a *sanyasi* understand that? Paz asks: 'después de recobrarse de su natural estupefacción, las saludaría [las dos fórmulas] con una carcajada' (*CA* 144; after recovering from his natural stupefaction, he would greet [the two formulae] with a roar of laughter). History *cannot* be changed because it is a 'nightmare', an illusion of time; hence his (and Paz's?) derisive laughter. Here Paz diverges from orthodox surrealism.

Paz seems to have turned to Taoism and Buddhism first; but rather than trace his chronological preferences as scattered through his work, I have selected key notions that affect his poetics.

Paz values Taoism's and Buddhism's heretical position vis-à-vis the official dogmas of their day. He also emphasises Taoism's and Zen's stress on the concrete, natural man. For Paz, Chuang-tse, like a good surrealist, 'nos enseña a desconfiar de los quimeras de la razón'; for human nature is 'rebelde a todo sistema' (teaches us to mistrust the chimeras of reason . . . rebellious to all systems). Especially through its violent humour, Zen also rejects discursive thought and logic; for man is a whole, a fusion of 'la vela, el sueño y el dormir sin sueño' (*Pe* 224; sleeplessness, dream and dreamless sleep), a formula dear to surrealism. Third, it is the *experiential* bias of Eastern thought that excites Paz. Experience is the only test of truth; truths are not learned but experienced (*CA* 110). Paz yokes Zen's sudden illumination or *satori* with poetry's timeless moment as expression of that moment of revelation that defies time in the intensity of its truth. Like a surrealist, Bashō wrote his haiku not as pastimes but as 'spiritual exercises' based on 'spiritual experiences' (*Pe* 158). Zen, through this flash of awareness, reveals 'reality' (*la verdadera vida*; true life) to be beyond sequential time and death, and inside man, who 'dentro de sí lleva a la eternidad' (*Pe* 164; within carries eternity). The East proposes an inner mode; health lies not in history but inside man (*Pe* 228).[9]

This true reality, however, is always *indecible* (unsayable) except through poetry, paradox and humour. Reality cannot be named, because liberation is a critical act (Nagarjuna's negation dialectics). Buddhism identifies 'being' with *sunyata* through successive acts of negation (of self, time, language) to the joyful experience of a state beyond words (as in music) where even to translate *sunyata* as 'emptiness' is 'spiritual infidelity' (*CA* 137). Liberation is the experience of 'emptiness' as 'plenitud del vacío' (*Pe* 157; fullness of emptiness) where man is returned to that *silence* from which he (like the poem) sprang, but which is now 'charged with meaning' (*Pe* 160). This reality is a system of relationships, whether the dynamic, alternating rhythm of the *yin* and *yang* or what Paz, through Buddhism, has called a network of relationships, an impersonal reality where God is just another part of the system that is the divine system (*CA* 137). This has clear relationships with the nature of language and poetry. The only meaning lies in the relationship (reality, words); hence its illusion. Reality is unsayable, just as poetry for Paz only points towards and never names. Through these various 'religions' Paz seeks analogies with the poetic *sagesse*.

However, it is Tantra that best reflects Paz's poetics. The central act is *maithuna* (ritualised copulation). In this act, the conventional, linguistic polarities which are employed to 'understand' the world melt away, for 'reality' is one, an experiential fusion of the active–passive, male–female principles. This fusion is in terms of acts of 'real' copulation where the woman's body is an analogue of the cosmos, and sexual intercourse is a paradigm of divine ecstasy and creation. Tantra is not concerned with doctrine or philosophical novelty; it is a practice, a cult of ecstasy. As such it is violently heretical, flouting convention (like surrealism): it is a radical and heterodox shortcut to liberation. It borrows both from Hinduism and Buddhism by associating the absolute with the phenomenal in the here and now as an experience.

As Bharati says, the Tantras 'are not collections of manuals on sex' but 'doctrinal texts on spiritual emancipation'. Whether the semen is retained or not does not alter the physical-symbolic aspect of the doctrine. The target (Paz uses *blanco* (white/target) in a conventional tantric way) is always liberation, as an experience beyond the discursive processes and outside conventional learning. Tantra is anti-ascetic yet is not hedonistic. Bharati writes: 'The tantras do not teach to subdue the senses, but to increase their power and then to harness them in the service of the achievement of lasting entasy'; an aim which has Rimbaudian undertones. Rawson puts it this way: 'Instead of suppressing pleasure, vision and ecstasy, they should be cultivated and used.'[10]

Paz's earlier views on eroticism, woman and knowledge, derived largely from André Breton, find here a 'ritual' in a scandalous branch of Eastern yoga. However, actually to become a Tantrika is extremely difficult, because of Tantra's secrecy and code-language. One of the central ideas in Tantra is that of transgressing (so they eat meat, fish, smoke bhang and have sexual intercourse); but this transgression only has its real meaning in a cultural context where those customs are taboos. Paz selects what he sees fit for his poetics.

Paz refers to Tantra as early as 1954 (*Pe* 143) and 1965 (*A* 104), but it is not until *Conjunciones y disyunciones* (1969) and his 1970 preface to a Tantra show in Paris that it becomes central to his vision. He too emphasises Tantra as a total experience of body and mind (*CD* 65). For him, the ceremonial aspect, the 'sexual ritual' where bodies become symbols and symbols bodies, is axiomatic: 'tocamos símbolos cuando creemos tocar cuerpos y objetos materiales' (*CD* 74; we touch symbols when we believe that we are touching bodies and material objects). Mircea Eliade explains that it is difficult to distinguish the concrete from the symbolic in Tantra because its aim is the 'transformation de la physiologie en liturgie'. This ritual copulation leads to a reconciliation 'en la cima del acto sexual' (in the climax of the sex act) between sequential time and its negation. This is the experiential fusion of *samsara* and *nirvana*;

the perfect identity between existence and emptiness (*CD* 79). The copulatory fusion of male and female symbolically transcends all dualities, and the sex act becomes a form of meditation (*CD* 82). The resulting 'transparency' (*CD* 82) conveys the vision of the union of 'this' and 'that' as *vacuidad* (*CD* 86; emptiness). This is likened to the 'seeing-through' of conventional language and the realisation that reality is 'unique' and empty of names and value.[11]

Paz links the *mantra* – non-sensical syllables repeated during rituals (*CD* 85) – with a tradition of writers, such as Schwitters, Artaud, Michaux and Huidobro, seen as poets using invented *mantras*. This explosive language of ecstasy is the white-hot language that transcends ordinary language; it is the *grito* (scream) of Paz's long poem *Blanco* (1967). Paz touches on the metaphorical code-language used in Tantra as a language articulated on universal analogies (woman's body–reality–poem–*sunyata*) where words express the cosmos and the cosmos speaks (can be read) in the intensity of passion, the way into the signature of all things. In both Paz's view of poetry and in Tantra, erotic experience is the key (*CD* 84), for language is 'sensually' real and yet transcended (in the poem) like a woman's body in the ecstatic act of love; hence the hinge analogy: 'la escritura *vivida* como el cuerpo analógico del cuerpo físico – y el cuerpo leído como escritura' (*CD* 84; writing *lived* as the analogous body of the physical body – and the body read as writing). The poet *reads* into the world–forest, expresses the confused, sensuous network of analogies that binds man back (*religare*) into the cosmos he has separated himself from.

Paz pursued the links between Tantra and poetry in the preface to the Tantra exhibition (1970); the essential link is *meditation*. Art is seen as mental act, as a 'starting point' *towards* something beyond the artefact; art is meditation (Tantra), is a 'signo inaugural que abre un camino' (*SG* 47; inaugural sign that opens a path). Here Tantra is another expression of that ancient, hermetic tradition of 'paths' towards. The analogical similarities between the poem and the Tantric act of *maithuna* are phrased as 'body astrology', 'cosmic eroticism' and 'verbal eroticism'; elements of a magnetically unified and harmonious analogical world where meaning is only defined analogically, as an erotic relationship. Paz recreates the ancient vibrant equations where the starry sky (the living, signifying *body* of the night sky) is the semantic archetype of woman's body; where the body – zone of all sensations, feelings, thoughts – is the erotic archetype of language ; *sky* is a sign, a language, and language a body, and meaning is making love *with* these bodies (*maithuna*, the poem).

There is no explanation, only experience, for analogy defies causality; it is a 'river of metaphors' (*SG* 50), itself another analogy; river–inspiration–timeflow–tao–life; it is a word, it can correspond to the physically real and yet is *cosa mentale*.

To return to the crucial notion of art as a path, art as a spring-board, as a leap (as a window onto, in Breton's terms): Paz's ambitious poetics finds this link: 'el tantrismo evoca otra presencia que está más allá de la pintura' (tantrism evokes another presence that is beyond painting). Lurking in that proposition is Breton's often-cited *ailleurs* and his fight to free painting from representation; his scorn for 'retinal' art and realistic dross in literature; his ambition for an art based on desire and on the imagination (always beyond) as part of a greater policy to restore the open-minded magic and mystery of genuine symbolism. Paz is lucid about this property of the sign: 'El signo, cualquiera que sea, tiene la propiedad de llevarnos más allá, siempre más allá. Un perpetuo *hacia*...' (*SG* 51; The sign, whatever it may be, has the property of leading us beyond, always beyond. A perpetual *towards*...). The very notion of art dissolves, just as the body momentarily dissolves in the act of love, just as words dissolve in the experience of the poem. Art has no proper existence, it is a path, a liberty (*SG* 53).

The excitement generated by following Paz's path is evident: his faithfulness to his vision, his inner consistency, has the solidity of a religious insight; that 'religion' proposed by Breton and consolidated by Paz in ever-changing but constant frameworks.

The revelation of this symbolic fabric is the function of the poem. The poem, as energised, erotic words, describes the world as a harmonious relationship. Poetry for Paz 'is the secret religion of the modern age'. And Tantra, in Paz's reading, is another analogy for poetry, the original poetic wisdom. Paz has always sought transcendence; in 1954, writing about his generation of poets, he defines poetry as 'un ejercicio espiritual' (*Pe* 76; spiritual exercise). This is the extent of his insight and quest.

Maithuna, the copulation between Siva and Devi, repeated as a rite by the Tantrikas, is a metaphor (real and symbolic) of the uniting of opposites which reveals reality: a reality unapprehended by the intellect or its concepts. The moment of union (orgasm) is both ecstatic and empty. It is also a repetition of the first act of creation. With this in mind, we can read the poem 'Maithuna' as a preliminary to a reading of *Blanco*.

The polarities (male–female, day–night, black–white) are united through 'el acto de amor / sobre el precipicio' (*LE* 118; the act of love above the precipice) where a sense of vertigo and emptiness (the precipice) convey that ecstatic dissolution into a joyful nothingness (poetry, Tantra). Woman's reality abolishes all that is peripheral to the vision, for she is the complementary half to man's aloneness; her laughter 'soaks' the poet's forehead, his eyes, his reason (water anoints, fertilises). Experience with woman leads to vision:

> Abrir los ojos
> En tu centro   (*LE* 120)
> To open my eyes in your centre

and this vision through woman as concrete symbol of eternity obviates the need for language: 'mi lengua está/Allá' (my tongue is over there). Only paradox can convey the extreme fusion of the orgasm-vision: Paz evokes a 'burning snow'; a snow that burns woman's 'rose' (*LE* 121). Reality just *is* – 'Está' – and then is past, 'Ya', once the intense experience is over: 'El alba/Salva' (Dawn saves).

The act of love releases energy and creativity; it taps the vital source latent in poetic creation and copulation; it is *natural* energy. The surging up and out of words is analogous to that of sap rising up a stem; where the rhythm and punning creates the sense of language pulling itself out:

Y nueva nubemente sube
Savia
        (Salvia te llamo
Llama)
        El tallo
        Estalla   (*LE* 121)

And again cloudily rises the sap (sage I call you flame) the stem
bursts open [this defies translation; the close phonic affinity of the
words (Savia, Salvia; llamo, Llama; tallo, Estalla) is mimetic of a
process in which one thing passes into another].

The poem is woman's body; the poet copulates with language
(creates) as does the reader reading. Poetry is a path:
'Caminos/Hacia lo que somos' (*LE* 91; Paths towards what we
are). Poetry reveals the *ruptura* (break), the *hendidura* (cleft)
which is both sensually real (woman's *yoni* or sex) and symbolic
of the 'way through', the gate to transcendence; the white,
silent spaces between the words. In the poem 'Cuento de dos
jardines' (Tale of two gardens) Paz refers to the Mahayana
dialecticians Nagarjuna and Dharmakirti. The former's negative dialectics suggested Paz's visual pun on the negation of self,
a 'Topoema': 'Niego/Ni ego' (Negate not ego). But this time he
names them, to show how easily his woman's body allowed him
to forget them, until the act of love enabled him to refind them
through experience, not intellect:

        Olvidé a Nagarjuna y a Dharmakirti
                                        En tus pechos
        En tu grito los encontré:
                        Maithuna
                                Dos en uno,
        Uno en todo,
                        Todo en nada,
                                ¡ *Sunyata*,
        Plenitud vacía
        Vacuidad redonda como tu grupa!   (*LE* 140)

I forgot Nagarjuna and Dharmakirti in your breasts, in your scream
I found them: *maithuna*, two in one, one in all, all in nothing; *sunyata*,
empty fullness, emptiness round like your rump.

The rhythms are like a magic chant; reality is denuded of
language (the void) yet experientially as real as a woman's

haunches: hence the paradoxical language of ecstasy, 'empty fullness'.

Blanco follows the same process, but with more possible readings, as Paz suggests in his notes preceding the poem. The text is a target ('blanco') in the tantric sense, as well as the white page. It is the 'imageless' world and the void, as well as the neutralisation of all colours and the silence that follows the use of words (*A* 20); it is the absence that points to the truth (*A* 56). These are concepts derived from Mallarmé as much as from Tantra. The subtlest tantric *yantra* (a visual *mantra*) was, according to Rawson, a 'blank space'. The original edition of *Blanco* imitated a tantric scroll (according to Paz) whose unfolding would facilitate a textual 'fluidity' where the reading process would use words to go beyond words to the real meaning of the poem, which exists 'beyond' the text. Poetry aims at this 'blanco intocable' (untouchable target) while modern art in general is an attempt to find out what lies behind language. This is art's sacred function. Reading Paz through Eliade, we could say that the role of the reader is akin to that of the initiate in his penetration of the labyrinth; he is allowed various alternatives (the six readings offered by Paz); and both reader and initiate find themselves in a 'sacred space' (text) outside time. The act of reading is analogous to that of the Tantrika, granted that the target is spiritual; it is a sensual spirituality, as Paz would insist (*CD* 61).[12]

The form and typography of the poem owe much to Mallarmé but little else to Tantra, except perhaps for the fusing and separating of the left and right hand columns with the central, single lined column. This depends on how one reads the text; from left to right, cutting across the three columns, or each column at a time. The poem is a scroll that unfolds with a single central column which 'opens' and 'closes' two 'limbs' distinguished by typographical devices, such as colour and italicising. The typography is like musical notation. This spinal column might be the *kundalini* up which rises the sublimated or transformed passion until reaching the seventh *cakra* where illumination takes place. Eliade suggests that in Tantric texts the fusion and separation of the left and right columns could be the

opening of the woman's legs and the closing of them by man in
the rhythmic act of love in the tantric ritual; in Paz's text all is
analogous.[13]

Blanco is both a paradigm of the creative process and a
celebration of a ritual (the act of copulation), just as the word is
the body of the poem. André Breton's 'les mots font l'amour'
gives his definition of the poem. Thus, in accordance with
Tantra (and Breton) *Blanco* is a spiritual ladder that, through
transcending the senses, points to something that is not named,
that is 'transparent'.

As in the poem 'Maithuna', the sex act is also the poetic act.
The sperm–seed–word rises up towards the light:

> En un tallo de cobre
> Resuelto
> En un follaje de claridad   (*LE* 148)
In a stem of copper, resolved in a foliage of clarity.

But this source can only be tapped erotically when the senses
are harnessed:

> *los sentidos se abren*
> *en la noche magnética*   (*LE* 150)
the senses open in the magnetic night.

Before language can rise up (the penis, stem), the poet–initiate
has to overcome moments of 'drought'. This is inevitable, and
patience is the only answer. The poet's work at this stage is not
easy; language is an 'expiación' (expiation); language is not
innocent but contaminated with circumstance and history (*LE*
152). More than hedonism is required to achieve liberation,
and in this respect Tantra is a difficult initiatory ritual whose
process Paz has adapted to his own ends. Passion is both the
source of the initial act of love referred to and the consequent
writing of the poem.

Woman (and the water-images associated with her fertility)
is the poet's answer to sterility, complement to his isolation. By
releasing 'desire' 'en un lecho de vértigo' (in a bed of vertigo)
the poet reaches the point where he begins to *see*: 'La transparencia es todo lo que queda' (*LE* 154; Transparency is all
that remains). This is repeated at the end of the poem as the

final vision (*LE* 168). The rhythm of love-making (like the wave-periodicity) leads to the 'agua de verdad' (water of truth). The imminent arrival of the word–sperm is announced by drums (the quickening of the heart-beat); it is a 'birth', an 'ejaculation':

> Tu panza tiembla
> Tus semillas estallan
> Verdea la palabra   (*LE* 157)

Your belly trembles, your seeds burst out, the word greens.

   Woman's physical reality is also the world's. She becomes 'mujer tendida hecha a la imagen del mundo' (*LE* 159; woman stretched out in the image of the world); and the world becomes woman 'El mundo haz de tus imágenes' (*LE* 158; The world bunch/sheaf of your images), which shows the innate reversibility of analogy. This corporeal symbol (her body) is a 'knot of presences' (also a description of a poem) which is reached through the 'place of joining' (or vulva) where the male 'copulates' with the female. This act leads to the abolition of discourse (ecstasy, poetry), in a point beyond reason which is dazzling 'no pienso, veo' (I do not think, I see). So the poet's thoughts are embodied in woman, and woman is internalised in the poet as a *claridad* (clarity) annulling itself in a 'syllable' (the nonsensical language of ecstasy). The poet's mind is emptied of all but the 'spiritual' evidence, or light. The process of internalising the external, carnal woman (converting her into a syllable, mental language), of harnessing the senses for the spirit, takes place *within* the poet's eyes (*LE* 162). The body becomes symbol (during the *act* of writing the body is no longer there); this symbol is also a word and the word is a body:

> tú te repartes como el lenguaje   (*LE* 162)

you share yourself out like language

The body is the 'way' (cf. Eliade's transmutation of sexual union to liturgical song) where sexual union is 'spiritually' creative, 'fertile'. The couple copulating replicate greater cosmic unions:

> *el firmamento es macho y hembra*   (*LE* 162)

the firmament is male and female

which leads us to this crucial analogy:

> *Falo el pensar y vulva la palabra*   *(LE* 162)
> Thought a phallus, language a vulva.

Phallic thought fertilises erotic language within the poet; a sort of androgynous ghost. This act is a *natural* one: 'temblor de tierra de tu grupa' (*LE* 162; earth-quake of your hips).

Abstraction and concept become meaningful as experiences; space becomes a body, a sign, a thought (*LE* 162), and time and the world are bodies that can be touched or seen. Only through this bodily experience is the spirit born: *'pensamiento sin cuerpo el cuerpo imaginario'* (*LE* 163; thought without body, the imaginary body). This transformation from the 'real' body to the 'mental' body in the poet's mind *increases* the body's reality, leads to illumination:

> El espíritu
> Es una invención del cuerpo
> El cuerpo
> Es una invención del mundo
> El mundo
> Es una invención del espíritu   *(LE* 168)

The spirit is an invention of the body. The body is an invention of the world. The world is an invention of the spirit.

In this 'chain' of analogies spirit cannot be separated from the body but the sense can be transcended in an ecstatic union described as a 'scream': 'caer en tu grito contigo' (*LE* 163; to fall into your scream with you).

The illusory reality of the world – 'lo mirado' (the looked at) – has been transformed into reality – 'la mirada' (the look):

> La irrealidad de lo mirado
> Da realidad a la mirada   *(LE* 163)

The unreality of what is looked at gives reality to the gaze.

The illusory nature of the 'mirada' is given reality by woman's body (*LE* 169); the poem ends:

>   Tu cuerpo
> Derramado en mi cuerpo
>   Visto

Desvanecido
>Da realidad a la mirada   (*LE* 169)
Your body spilt in my body, seen, vanished, gives reality to the glance.

I have offered an 'organised' reading–the actual text is more nodal or bunched together – but the frame conditions this final liberty or plurality of readings: from passion (both sexual and poetic) to 'carnal spirituality'. Woman's bodily reality awakens dormant language, for in poetry words 'cobran cuerpo' (*CD* 19; take on a body). But once woman has been converted into a naked syllable (the flesh of language) she becomes imaginary and more real. Paz writes: 'El cuerpo es imaginario no por carecer de realidad sino por ser la realidad más real' (*CD* 23; The body is imaginary not because it lacks reality but because it is most real). Thus the poet copulates with woman through language which is woman internalised in him. Ordinary, conventional language, the 'No/Sí' of duality, has to be destroyed, just as the repetition of the *mantra* destroys the language that represents a false reality; woman is naked like a syllable because she has destroyed her conventional self through this 'sexual illumination', evoked analogically with language as

>No y Sí
Juntos
>Dos sílabas enamoradas   (*LE* 166)
No and Yes together, two syllables in love.

Here the nonsensical syllables convey the unsayable, the *blanco* of reality, in the same way as the mystic's explosive syllable of joy, *Ay*.

Paz's poem *Blanco* is not a Tantra, but it does borrow from and parallel the tantric process. Paz expands and enriches the analogies between copulation and the writing or reading of the poem; and *maithuna* becomes the common ground and prime metaphor in Paz's search for carnal spirituality.

However, though Paz adopts a tantric framework, he rejects many of the premises of Eastern thought for all his appreciation of their worth. His poem 'Mutra' was written during an early visit to India (1952). In it he contrasts the intense summer heat,

and the 'static' God-seekers of India, with his own existential
and temporal philosophy:

> no somos, no quiero ser
> Dios, no quiero ser a tientas, no quiero regresar, soy hombre
>   (L 224)
> We are not, I do not want to be God, I do not want to be in the dark,
> I do not want to return, I am a man.

The poet, severed from the mother, exiled, and in search of his
own being (desire, grounded in time), wants to experience the
temporal flow, 'rey de sí mismo, hijo de sus obras' (L 225; king
of himself, son of his works). Asked about this poem, Paz
reasserted his refusal to accept the Eastern way to the truth: 'El
encuentro de Oriente es la tentación de lo absoluto, un absoluto
que no es humano. Me resisto. No quiero ser Dios . . .' (The
meeting with the East is the temptation of the absolute, an
inhuman absolute. I resist this. I don't want to be God). This
negation of the central ascetic tradition of India finds its
justification in Paz's acceptance of tantra as heresy.[14]

There are many similar cases of 'resistance'. In 'Perpetua
encarnada' (Perpetual incarnate) Paz celebrates the 'here-
and-nowness' of the world; he is 'tied' to the world, 'in love'
with it (LE 38). He affirms that poetry is his reason for living,
since it sanctifies the word; the words that always accompany
him, his reason for being (LE 38); the poem ends in the sensual
concreteness of the poet's vision:

> Veo oigo respiro
> Pido ser obediente a este día y esta noche   (LE 39)
> I see I hear I breathe I ask to be obedient to this day and this night.

In the poem 'Vrindaban' Paz again affirms the vitality of the
senses, particularly sight: 'Yo creo/Yo veo' (LE 58; I believe, I
see). A meeting with a sadhu 'Mono de lo absoluto' (Monkey of
the absolute) crystallises the cultural distances between the
poet and India. The absolute of official religion alienates Paz:

> Desde su orilla me miraba
> Me mira
> Desde su interminable mediodía
> Yo estoy en la hora inestable   (LE 62)

From his shore he looked at me, looks at me from his interminable
midday. I am in the unstable hour.

The poet lives in time, with all its instabilities and vitalities: the
sadhu is immobile in eternity. Paz continues:

> Los absolutos las eternidades
> Y sus aledaños
>   No son mi tema
> Tengo hambre de vida y también de morir   (*LE* 62)

Absolutes, eternities, and their limits are not my theme. I am
hungry for life and also for dying.

This affirmation of 'life' as against the 'absolute' is another way
of saying that meaning for Paz lies in the act of writing itself:
'Nunca estoy solo' for 'A oscuras voy y planto signos' (*LE* 63;
I'm never alone; I go along darkly and plant signs). If creativity
is obscure, he would still rather have that than the static clarity
of the 'saint'. In the poem written around John Cage's texts,
Paz deviates from the central proposition of Mahayana Buddhism; his poem says something *slightly* different (*LE* 179). Real
knowledge is ignorance, experience:

> Recobrar la ignorancia,
>   Saber del saber.   (*LE* 81)

To recover ignorance, knowledge of knowledge.

This recalls the similar pun in 'La palabra dicha' in *Salamandra*:

> Inocencia y no ciencia:
> Para hablar aprende a callar   (*S* 32)

Innocence and not science: to talk learn to be silent.

The world of the here and now (empirical reality) contains the
absolute within it and not the other way round (as in Christian-
ity or platonism), just as silence contains language but language is not silence: *nirvana* is *samsara* but *samsara* is not *nirvana*.
Samsara equals the world of now, the chain of life and death, and
contains the 'other' but is not the 'other' unless transformed by
vision. In 'Domingo en la isla de Elefanta' (Sunday in the
island of Elephanta) *samsara* is again the starting point. Paz
demotes the divine couple Shiva and Parvati from the status of
gods to images of man's divinity (*LE* 128); for he, the poet and

his woman parallel them (Tantra) without any need for metaphysical justifications:

> Nada les pedimos, nada
> Que sea del otro mundo:
> Sólo
> La luz sobre el mar   (*LE* 129)

We ask them nothing, nothing that is from the other world: only the light on the sea.

The light, this world, the here and now, transcendence through the senses, the body: these are the elements of Paz's poetics. Only the present moment lived intensely opens 'reality': 'Je touche le présent, je plonge ma main dans le maintenant... toutes ces réalités sont un tissu de présences qui ne cache aucun secret' (*Singe* 39; I touch the present, I plunge my hand in the now...all these realities are a tissue of presences that hide no secret). No secrets, the body as evidence.

In 'Felicidad en Herat' Paz describes what he saw from the top of a mosque. His vision is not the traditional mystic's one:

> No tuve la visión sin imágenes,
> No vi girar las formas hasta desvanecerse
> En claridad inmóvil,
> El ser ya sin sustancia del sufí.
> No bebí plenitud en el vacío   (*LE* 52)

I didn't have the imageless vision, I didn't see the forms gyrate until they vanished in an immobile clarity, the already substanceless being of the sufi. I didn't drink fullness in the emptiness.

All that he saw was the blue sky, some pines and a blackbird; the world in repose, as sheer surface, as appearance; and this he calls 'happiness' and 'Perfección de lo Finito' (Perfection of the Finite). The world is a concrete, sensual surface; it is language that distorts. That is why poetry transcends its language to reveal the world as evidence, seen as naked, without words, in all its terrifying concreteness. This vision is described in 'Cerca de cabo Camorín' (Near Cape Camorin):

> Y la invisible,
> Aunque constante, pánica presencia:
> No araña o cobra, lo Innominable,
> La universal indiferencia

Donde la forma vil y la adorable
Prosperan y se anulan: vacíos hervideros   (*LE* 43)
And the invisible, although constant, panic presence: not spider nor
cobra, the Unnameable, the universal indifference where the form
vile and the form adorable prosper and annul each other: empty
bubbling springs/swarms.

This 'Unnameable' is reality when the 'forms' imported from
the binary or dual structure of language are dissolved, cancel-
led out. Reality is an empty seething. This can be called *sunyata*,
as in the poem of the same name, where reality is a presence
that consumes itself (*LE* 97). The continual use of 'sight' refers
to Paz's need or urge to redefine perception. In 'Contigo' we
have this credo:

> Soy real
> Veo mi vida y mi muerte
> El mundo es verdadero
> Veo
> Habito una transparencia   (*LE* 113)

I am real, I see my life and my death. The world is true, I see, I
inhabit a transparency.

Seeing and experiencing 'transparency' sends us back to *Blanco*
and its final intention (spiritual target/emptiness) where the
poet sees through names to the thing–reality. This is

> El uno en el otro
> Sin nombres   (*LE* 127)

One in the other without names

The poem 'Cuento de dos jardines' (Tale of two gardens) ends
with the fading-away of Paz's mental garden into 'reality':

> Se abisma
> El jardín en una identidad
> Sin nombre
> Ni sustancia.
> Los signos se borran: yo miro la claridad.   (*LE* 141)

The garden sinks into an identity without name nor substance.
The signs brushed away: I look at the clarity.

Again there is the desire to see through language; to read
between the lines, in the margins, in the white spaces; to see

clearly is to see clarity. Poetry – the criticism of language – is
Paz's way to this truth. He writes in 'Carta a León Felipe'
(Letter to León Felipe):

> El mundo se aclara
> Sólo para volverse invisible
> Aprender a ver oír decir
> > Lo instantáneo
> Es nuestro oficio
> > _¿Fijar vértigos?_   (_LE_ 90)

The world is clarified only to become invisible. To learn to see, hear,
say the instantaneous is our craft. _To fix vertigos?_

This is a 'spiritual' task demanding (as in Tantra, or the
Rimbaud of 'Alchimie du verbe') an opening of the senses
(especially vision, hearing) so that the saying can fix the instant
of revelation within the temporal flow. For Paz, the new art will
be a 'mental' or 'spiritual' art (_CA_ 24) where the reader would
participate as another creator. Paz has remained faithful to his
view of 1938 that poetry is a 'spiritual exercise'; Eastern
thought has merely provided him with another framework.

In Paz's lavish _Le Singe grammairien_ (1972) this paradoxical
view of poetry is reformulated. The poet names things in order
to dissolve their names. He discovers that the names we give
things do not stick to them. For Paz the criticism of paradise is
language (the word as the fall), and the criticism of language is
poetry. Poetry 'evaporates' words; polishes them into transparency. The world loses its differences and for an instant reality
is seen as it is. This is Paz's vision: 'si les choses sont mais n'ont
pas de nom: sur la terre il n'est aucun mesure' (_Singe_ 112; if
things are but have no names: on earth there is no measure).

In Tantra the initiate must destroy referential language in
order to experience non-duality (what lies outside language).
He enters a world of 'semantic polyvalencies' whose inexhaustible potential (poetry) shatters the normal grasp of reality
through conventions, replacing his stereotypes with, in Eliade's
words, a 'Univers à niveaux convertibles et intégrables' (Universe with convertible and integrable levels) which is poetry.
By discarding language the initiate approaches the centre by
creating a new, paradoxical language based on analogy and

metaphor. Paz's is not a poetry that *describes* a vision in the conventional Romantic sense, but one that leads the reader to that point where he is ready to experience the poem fully as a white space, a transparency where, perceptions cleansed of words, he sees reality as it is.[15]

II A reading of Octavio Paz's 'Le Singe grammairien'

Paz's *Le Singe grammairien* (1972) was published in a series which included works by René Char, Henri Michaux, Roger Caillois, Yves Bonnefoy and André Pieyre de Mandiargues (who translated Paz's only play *La hija de Rappaccini* into French) and others. This reads like a group of friends, of mutual admirers. All of them were one-time close friends of André Breton. This speaks clearly of the esteem in which Paz is held. In every volume in this enviable Skira collection, the reader's gaze is seduced by a collage of vivid images and exciting texts, impeccably printed. Paz's text is no exception.

Paz is much given to word-play. From his earliest poems, following his Mexican predecessor Xavier Villaurrutia, he has 'lapsed' or spun off into phonic variants and homologies of a given word. At times this is mere substitution – a form of sterile punning or perhaps verbal propitiation – and at others a genuine breaking-open of the word that enhances vision, as in the closing variants in the poem 'Salamandra': *Salamandra* (Salamander) to *Salamadre* (Saltmother) and *Aguamadre* (Watermother) (*S* 106). Here the metamorphic qualities of the salamander ('el dos-seres', the two-beings) are evoked in the change *mandra* to *madre* and *agua* to *sal*; a fusion of archetypal symbols.

It would not be hard to misread this title: *singe* looks like *signe* (monkey, sign). Indeed, Paz deliberately proposes this. To Julián Ríos he confided that he thought up the title in French, though the text in question is a translation from Spanish (recalling those Latin American poets like Darío, Huidobro and César Moro who wrote in French): in Spanish this pun (central to Paz's intention) would have to derive from *mono/grama* (*mono*

is Spanish for monkey) or as Ríos translates it, *simio/símil*. In
English all these puns fade away. Word-play is at the roots of
untranslatability.[16]

There is obvious irony in linking 'monkey' with 'grammar': a
variation on 'man the talking animal'. However, the reading of
the sign as 'monkey' is not based on free association. Here it is
not a matter of *aping*, or of the monkey as caricature of human
pretentiousness. There is a specialised meaning, which Paz
cites from *A Classical Dictionary of Hindu Mythology*. This monkey
is Hanuman, the flying monkey of the *Ramayana*, who is also a
grammarian. As an emblem of fertility, spontaneity and fantasy, we could add that Hanuman is a metaphor of *pensée*, the
total flow of the activities of the unconscious, without control or
regulation. Paz does not rely only on verbal signs; a colour
photo of Hanuman on the cover and another accompanying the
quotation from the dictionary dazzle the eye. It is clear that the
notion of the verbal sign points to that grander theory of
interrelated signs, of *correspondances*. Paz continually evokes this
sense of a hieroglyphic universe of thousands of differing signs,
or languages, or 'echoes' that the poet intuits or glimpses. This
text catches the interplay between eye and mind, word and
image (hence alludes to typography as aesthetics, to Mallarmé,
and Tantra) as a metaphor of this greater network.

The title of the Skira series is 'Les sentiers de la création'
(The paths of creation). Paz takes this literally and evolves a
series of analogies that govern the structure and meaning of the
text: *écrire*, *tracer* (write, trace) and *être lu*, *parcourir* (be read,
travel, in the sense that to read along a line is to take a journey).
On one level he writes about a *real* journey undertaken in India
to visit the ruins at Galta. As Paz wrote years later, the other
journey of writing brushes away the memory of the original
journey to Galta as the text spins round and round and leads
nowhere. As in *Piedra de sol*, the structure is spiral. The *only*
journey for Paz is not either the *real* one (on foot to Galta) or the
writing, but 'à la rencontre de soi-même' (to the encounter of
one's self), as it was for Breton. The quest for 'self' is always a
process; man is his own desire always projecting forward in
time.

This process (write, walk; path of life, sentence) reveals another crucial analogy (*singe*, *signe*): Hanuman in the *Ramayana* contemplates a garden as if it were a calligraphic page; a system of signs. The analogy is ancient and produces the world/book correspondence. Here the surrealists' art/life opposition takes on a more subtle tone. That is to say, life and living always interfere with the seeming purity of the text; the analogies dissolve any sense of static meaning; for the flow of the analogies is generated by temporality. André Breton's magic word *comme* (like) is at the heart of Paz's poetics: he reveals the analogies as a 'system of mirrors' (and so 'aping' reappears) whose force depends on '*passion*'. The 'étreinte des corps' (embrace of bodies), and the notion that 'words make love', *maithuna*, both underpin the erotic energy of *comme*. Paz embodies in this text the theory of correspondences ('En ceci voir cela'; In this see that) as intrinsic to the sign. All language is of its nature symbolic and free. André Breton in his *Ode à Charles Fourier* (1947) thanks Fourier for showing him that passions constitute 'un cryptogramme indivisible que l'homme est appelé à déchiffrer' (an indivisible cryptogram that man is called to decipher). This he calls a 'millenary conviction': 'all that is inside is *like* all that is outside'. This is a pseudo-hermetic cliché previously propagated by Eliphas Lévi.[17]

Paz, enamoured of intention like Breton, proposes a theory that is its own embodiment: a poem, the text in question. His poetics of temporality, of process and creativity (or 'libertad bajo palabra') is traced by the reader who also dissolves in the passion of this text, his text. A polyglottal pun suggests itself: from *singe* to *signe* to sing. The poet–reader 'sings' himself into being.

The prose poem

We now explore the conventions of readability; of the reader's expectation in terms of this text. Paz proposes a confusion of genre in his conversation with Julián Ríos. He labels this text a 'treatise' (perhaps a variation on 'manifesto') and adds:

No es un ensayo pero tampoco es una novela ni un cuento. Es un texto de cien páginas en el cual la novela se disuelve y se transforma en reflexión sobre el lenguaje; la reflexión sobre el lenguaje se transforma en experiencia erótica, y está en relato.

It is not an essay, neither is it a novel or a story. It is a text of one hundred pages in which the novel dissolves and is transformed into a reflection on language; the reflection on language is transformed into erotic experience, that is narrated.

This is not a specific generic form, but a series of transformations. The 'confusing' convention (cf. the neutral *text*) adopted by Paz echoes his intention.[18]

One way of defining the surrealists' intention is by way of defiance of normative genre; what Breton describes as 'la volonté d'affranchissement de règles caduques' (the will to set oneself free from decrepit rules). Their indifference to the aesthetics of form is the reverse of their belief in the excitement of process. Their 'passionate quest for liberty' ignores the end-result in favour of the mechanics of inspiration (whatever the method). The poetic act becomes sacred. This must be seen as part of an assault against stereotyped responses: to refresh poetry was to jolt perceptions of form, expectancies. Thus literature, the official mainstream of texts, became for Breton 'tristes chemins qui mènent à tout' (sad paths that lead to anything). We underline *chemin:* literature separated from the creative process, as pure artefact, simply bored Breton. He posited an aesthetics of 'participation in the creative act' (Balakian); quite clearly an appeal to the reader's liberty. Breton said that inspiration comes *after* writing. This reversal of expectations creates a new genre, precursor of the polyvalent *text*; that space, 'not prose, not poetry...', between the automatic text and the ordered poem.[19]

This was an act of subversion; the surrealists' 'absolute non-conformism'; their 'praise-worthy scorn' for literature generated the 'window', the 'trampoline', the 'open door' as figures for a new attitude to writing as a *means*; as a push towards that 'full' life they dreamed of.[20]

Surrealist writing must be seen in terms of Breton's stress on exploration of his *pensée* ('the real functioning of mind...') where the quest for trapping the mental flow secretes its own form. Different facets of mind might leave traces in the conventional genre; but Breton expected more, a synthesis. Most of the practitioners of *automatic writing* were clearly aware of the drawbacks; of the need to purge the texts of repetition, of awkwardnesses; even to 'arrange' it into a poem. Hence the split between poem and automatic text. I will argue that the prose poem is the best compromise between the 'formless' freedom of automatic text and the satisfying 'closedness' of the poem. This avoids Valéry's antithesis between the necessity of form and the chaos or incoherence of the 'unconscious'; for the prose poem combines the sense of limit with the exuberance of process, where *pensée* – the multilayered, intercommunicating, playful mind – flows most freely. Is not Paz in *Le Singe grammairien* close to the prose poem ('not a poem, not prose') where language and reflection on language melt erotically into a text?

Here a prose poem, a text (I almost make them synonymous) defines itself as language charged with 'mental electricity' (Breton). Was not Breton aware that there was or should have been an ideal congruence between inner and outer, source and form? Isn't the 'crystal' its emblem, as we have elsewhere observed? Breton's lyrical 'éloge du crystal' (eulogy of crystal) turns on the magical or natural and organic fusion of accident, hardness, transparency and deep aesthetic pleasure that defy categorisation and rationalisation.[21]

The prose poem has been defined as the characteristic surrealist genre; that is, as an 'undefinable genre' (Hubert) where the writing seeks a 'pure network of images'. The critic's use of 'pure' can be changed to 'direct': direct expression of *la pensée*. This is what Baudelaire envisaged in his dedication to *Le Spleen de Paris*: a dream of a

prose poétique, musicale *sans rhythme* et sans *rime*, assez *souple* et assez *heurtée* pour s'adapter aux *mouvements lyriques* de l'âme, aux *ondulations* de la rêverie, aux soubresauts de la conscience?

poetic prose, musical without rhythm or rhyme, supple and abrupt enough to adapt itself to the lyrical movements of the soul, to the undulations of the daydream, to the surprises of consciousness.

The words underlined all convey the complex free-flow of man's soul or mind. His is a subtle definition that engendered a tradition running through Rimbaud, Lautréamont, Mallarmé to Char, Michaux – and Octavio Paz. Huysmans, meditating on literature through 'Des Esseintes' in *A rebours*, selected the prose poem as his favourite form; for him it is the 'concrete sugar', the 'essential oil of art'. That the surrealists sensed this is evident in their revaluation of tradition and in their stress on being surrealists first; and only secondarily poets, painters, novelists. Anna Balakian devises a category for André Breton's prose: she calls it analogical prose. This description aptly suits Paz's multi-faceted *obra*.[22]

Octavio Paz has always sought to extend genre; his ceaseless experimentalism operates in the context of freedom, or the relief from the constriction of a historically given genre. The 'nightmare of history' fixes literature into conventions and petrifies tradition. It is not coincidental that it was the New World poets (Pound and Eliot) who revitalised the dormant English poetry of the early part of this century; for culturally the New World is more open to the relativity of history, more able to struggle out of the moulds. This cultural hypothesis can be grasped at any level. Paz's *tradición de la ruptura* (tradition of rupture) – though applicable to twentieth-century modernism – specifically relates to the Latin American's freedom from determining tradition. The tradition with which Paz, as a Mexican, identified was surrealism; surrealism as trying 'borrar las fronteras entre la vida y la poesía' (*SG* 46; to erase the frontiers between life and poetry). In his earlier *¿Aguila o sol?* (1951) – written during his 'surrealist' activities in Paris – he had embodied the surrealists' dream in a series of prose poems where *pensée* spins itself freely into its 'own' form.

Further – as witnessed in *Le Singe grammairien* – the prose poem most clearly reflects Paz's 'critical passion'; where the poet – avoiding a fixed stance deriving meaning, stable signs and their relationships from an awe of authority – sees himself instead as 'perpetual possibility'. The absence of a historically justified genre leads to the ever-present desire to abolish history (genre); hence the surrealist dream of *starting again*, and what Paz labels a 'poetics of the Now'. The choice is clear: 'submission' or 'heterodoxy' (*Pu* 219).[23]

A 'poetic of the Now' – a poetics of pleasure – is rooted in the process (which takes place *now*) of writing and reading. Breton's 'sad path' becomes in time the liberating *caminar* (to walk): a pilgrimage or quest where form has only a temporal structure given life and meaning through erotic participation. Here art – made to flow in time – parallels the act of living; there is no finality, only inexhaustible readings and exuberant *vases communicants* between life and art.

The prose poem is an activation of this liberty, for it explores signs and their vibrancies at the border of established genres. It reveals the sinuosity of the mind-flow; it is analogical prose. And because we never escape history, only *transgress* it, this becomes a voracious genre that feeds on all the others; a synthetic genre, an *obra abierta;* perhaps a utopian dream. Paz wrote in 1956 that 'el poema no es una forma literaria, sino el lugar de encuentro entre la poesía y el hombre' (*A* 14; the poem is not a literary form, but the meeting-place between poetry and man). He shares the surrealists' scorn for literary form. The throb of genuine poetry can penetrate *any form* as it pierces into and awakens man. Poems do not necessarily 'contain' poetry; poems are only good or bad *conductors* of poetry (*Pu* 102). For Paz poetry is an *energía vital* (vital energy) that always lies beyond the work, as the meaning of self is 'un más allá de sí' (a beyond itself); Breton's *ailleurs* again.

Paz also identifies a tradition of 'genuine' poets (those who 'transgressed', often writing in prose): he names Nerval, Bertrand, Baudelaire and Lautréamont as the pioneers; clearing the way for Breton, Aragon and Michaux (*A* 84). In 1966, discussing the forgotten minor Mexican 'poet' Gilberto Owen, he redefines that tradition that began with Baudelaire, wound through Rimbaud and Lautréamont, then took in Jacob, Cocteau and the surrealists. He agrees that the prose poem is hard to define; it borders on narrative, also on poetry. Then, in true surrealist tradition, he decides: 'No hay prosa' and 'todo es poesía en lenguaje' (*PEM* 16; there is no prose; everything in language is poetry). To make this quite explicit: it is not a question of prose, nor of poetry, but a question of the intensity of vision, a vital energy, an opening-out the plurality of meanings

from the deadened verbal symbols; a process that itself then
liberates the poet–reader. 'Inspiration comes *after*.' This is the
final justification for *Le Singe grammairien*. It is not a matter of
form, but typography.

In his study of Lévi-Strauss, Paz dwells on his style and
compares it with Bergson, Proust and Breton. He describes it as
a process:

el lector se enfrenta a un lenguaje que oscila continuamente entre lo
concreto y lo abstracto, la intuición directa del objeto y el análisis: un
pensamiento que ve a las ideas como formas sensibles y a las formas
como signos intelectuales.   (*CLS* 11)

the reader is confronted with a language that oscillates continually
between concrete and abstract; the direct intuition of the object and
analysis: a mind that sees ideas as sensuous forms and forms as
intellectual signs.

This quotation is crucial in its self-revelations: a style that
oscillates 'between'; a *pensée* that sees; sensuous ideas, etc. And
behind this sensuous sinuosity, there is the generating 'unity of
thought' (*CLS* 11) that informs the style. By now we can trace
Paz's 'family resemblances', for *Les Singe grammairien* embodies
this oscillation; it lies between genres, *like* a prose poem. The
new list now reads: Lévi-Strauss, Bergson, Proust, Breton and
Paz.

The text itself

For a critic to retrace the process of Paz's 'poetics of the Now'
would be to rewrite *Le Singe grammairien*. To regroup the texts
according to categories and themes would be to ignore the
crucial temporal structure. The critic is left clutching and
stressing elements wrenched from a process. Nonetheless, I
return to the primary analogies: sentence, path; reading, walking.

For Paz this is a sacred process. He embroiders the 'pilgrimage' *topos*; but the 'Holy Place' is not Galta but 'self'. But this
denies any idea of finality: man is the projection of his desire, a
perpetual possibility. There is no self, only a quest for self. So in
the writing there is no end in view. Neither writer nor reader

knows where he is going, as all futures are uncertain. This is the emotion that charges this (and all other) texts. But here Paz is being literal: 'Quête et terreur de la fin' (10; Quest and terror of the end). This journey is terrifying because it annuls the idea that the ego can create its own path. 'We' are created and given meaning by words, signs, analogies and writing. This recalls Rimbaud's awareness of the impotence of the 'Je'; not 'I think' but 'I am thought'. For Paz this is the real history of modern poetry; the liberties taken with the words 'I am'.

This lineal journey is complicated by tracing the ebb and flow of Paz's *pensée*. Paz has always sensed the pendulum-swing (call it dialectics) of his mental world. He has given it names (*soledad, comunión*), and has indicated its natural rhythm, this 'alternating current' in Mexican history (*El laberinto de la soledad*). In this text the rhythm functions as an overlapping of the original 'real' journey – transcribed as a memory – of his walk to Galta: this produces images of monkeys, ruins, stones, pariahs, an inexpressive holy man and the wretched poverty and squalor of India. Then he switches or slips into an awareness that he is *writing*, and Galta disappears; during those moments he is looking out of a window at trees, clouds, a dustbin; then another displacement, and he is watching the shadows of lovers projected onto a wall. All these levels are interrelated; they flow into each other, like a system of *vases communicants* of the whole that is 'mind'. But Paz is not giving a description of this process, but an image. A Yoga might call this 'watching your thoughts' or 'attentiveness'. As in meditation, control is relaxed, and 'chance' (the aesthetics of surprise) decides which images are to appear; just as in a reading, chance creates the interplay between text, typography, images and the reader's associative experience. A series of expressions control the spiralling rhythm of the text: light up, go out; appear, disappear; weave, unweave, etc. Thus the notion of *cheminer* is not 'straight'.

Because of this basic ebb–flow rhythm, Paz both fails and succeeds in his attempt to capture the essence of movement in the now; sometimes there are just opaque words, at others there are liberating images. Rimbaud's concept of 'fixer les vertiges' has the poet casting a spell on the perpetual motion of mind flow. The poet is always losing his thought, like Artaud; there are moments of confusion, doubt: 'ma pensée se replie' (my thought folds upon itself). Then, suddenly, in the midst of this flow, there is an eddy; Paz describes it as the centre of the *tourbillon* (whirlwind); the magic, momentarily still centre, like the eye of the cyclone. But all fixity is illusory, and the sense of stasis collapses, is swamped by the flow, and the poet–reader spins on.

Paz remains faithful to the 'timeless moment': 'La sagesse est dans l'instantanée' (15; Wisdom is in the instantaneous). This is the wisdom his poetics proposes; the sacred language of pleasure, of now, the epiphany, the vertical language that gushes up, defies gravity, like a fountain. The morality of this poetics is the patient *attente* (wait); the poem must be allowed to mature, and the poet must prepare himself and wait during futile, sterile thoughts until, behind the verbal descriptions of Galta he senses the greater whole of his psyche: 'l'ombre de nos pensées' and 'l'envers de ce que nous voyons' (22; the shadow of our thought; the reverse of what we see).

As Paz said to Julián Ríos, this text questions the nature of language; it is a reflection on language. Paz casts doubt on the conventional language–reality relationship. He realises the need to 'unwind' the verbal tissue so that reality can appear, undeformed by wordiness. All purely mental activity frustrates Paz. He quotes T. S. Eliot's 'thoughts in a dry brain' and seeks the way of breaking through the *brèche* (breach) between the lines into the white spaces. Paz adopts Breton's magazine title (*Brèche* 1961–5) because he shares the intention of breaking out of the mental prison. Here another analogy is created. The ruins of Galta are also the ruins of culture and language within the poet. The desert is mental. Like a monkey, Paz is a victim of repetitions (42).

In the hieroglyphic world of babelish tongues, the poet is forced to *decipher*, but even that – the finding or giving of meaning – is an illusion: 'l'univers est un texte dépourvu de sens' (53; the universe is a text stripped of sense). Man must find another language and this will be 'poetry', the language of bodies, of caresses, of passion. On one level words destroy reality by substituting the abstract concept for the unique thing; on another level, words recreate reality as an *image*; through this symbolic process man *invents* his reality (I have touched on this key word in Paz's poetics). This other, hidden language is discovered through the senses: 'Je peux la toucher mais je ne peux la dire' (63; I can touch it but I cannot say it). But, as in the very temporal rhythm of the text, one moment of presence (touch) is succeeded by another of absence–sterility. Time always wins. The couple making love are always moving and transforming, like words in a text. The bodies of the lovers are 'signes de la totalité qui sans relâche se divise' (signs of the totality that endlessly divides itself). The text then reaches the point of awareness where these 'bodies', so seemingly real (the conventions of realism), are also words. They are analogies of each other and exist as a dependency, as a relation. They mirror each other as well as Paz's belief in the 'universe as analogy' (87). We are back with the yeast-like word *comme*: the word that sets analogies fermenting. This freeing of words also liberates man from fixity. Because of the nature of analogy – *en ceci voir cela* – there is a desire for reconciliation with the world, with nature. Alienation, for Paz, is cultural, linguistic: 'l'abolition des différences' (the abolition of differences). If man's differences were abolished, he would be re-linked through his senses to the living cosmos as just another *signe*, just another *singe*.

This text proposes, as did *Blanco*, a dissolution of word-identity, of believing in verbal categories, values and concepts. Reality is too real; like the mental flux it is *intraduisible* (untranslatable); every detail at every moment in time would require a separate name; this monstrous proliferating science of the concrete would lead to madness (as in Borges' 'Funes el memorioso'). For writing lamely reveals resemblances and hides identity. This applies to 'things' as much as 'self'; to what is out there and what lies inside; for these very categories are conceptual, cultural.

Again the poet does not give names to things, like Adam, but dissolves names to reveal their emptiness. He sees the 'other side' of thought. He wears names out to a transparency (he crystallises words) and sees through to reality. This is poetry; it is an *intention* and is not related to form (genre) but to words: 'la critique du langage s'appelle poésie' (the critique of language is called poetry). Like Mallarmé, Paz uses words to reveal the absence of the thing named ('l'absente de toutes les roses') so that its presence (the 'rose') astonishes. To see reality as it is would be 'entrer en démesure' (to enter into excess). Paz sought that breaking of 'measure' in his 1948 poem 'El prisionero': 'desmesuras: tu medida de hombre' (*L* 109; excess: your measure of man). 'Excess' would be direct presence, astonishing and liberating. This is a variation of Rilke's quest. The world stripped of words is the world (the New World) before language categorised and evaluated; it is reality in its genesis state, the *edad de oro* (Golden Age) that Paz evoked in *Semillas para un himno* (1954) and that Breton postulated in his *Ode à Charles Fourier*. Paz has always been haunted by this paradisal vision. It was language that exiled man; language alienated and created a distance between man and nature (word and thing); but this very language can also restore the relationship as a 'bridge' back, a reconciliation.

All this is given in the literal, primal analogy: writing, tracing a path; a perpetual 'cheminement vers le sens' and 'dissipation du sens' (walking towards the sense; dissipation of the sense) as 'one' passes along the path. Thus 'poetry is empty' and there is no secret or hermetic meaning (we are always on a path, in time). He writes: 'Tout est maintenant' (140; All is now). This is the poetics of the now of pleasure, of the act of writing–reading where 'all is centre' (151). The centre is now, not at the end of the journey. Nothing happened at Galta.

The whole text has literally illustrated Mallarmé's lapidary phrase 'La destruction fut ma Béatrice' (Destruction was my Beatrice); Paz echoes both Mallarmé and Buddhism in his 'la création est destruction' (creation is destruction): to destructure man's overstructured mind. To Julián Ríos, Paz proclaimed that 'la vida es lo que cuenta' (life is what counts), but *cuenta* means both 'counts' and 'tells' ('la que...'). 'Life tells its story' is the hidden pun; a variation on 'On me pense', where the 'one' is life, time.

We have not yet mentioned one element in the text: the appearance and disappearance of *Splendeur* (Splendour). She appears in the text as a woman, a goddess of erotic love. If passion binds the world of lovers and words in poems, here this other primal analogy – woman, poem – is made explicit (97). *Splendeur* is the word *incarnate*, embodied; the woman–word that the poet can touch (caress) but not say; the reality that mocks divisive language. She is *présence*; what the poet sees after his dissolving of words. Etymologically, she shines, she is light.

Rilke, in a letter to one of his readers, defined art as the transformation of the world into *splendour*. There is an ancient ring to the rich, musical and sensuous word 'splendour'. Could Paz have read the *Zohar* or *Book of Splendour*? Its origin in thirteenth-century Spain offers a suggestive link. Perhaps there is only association in the mind of this reader, but let us explore some of the coincidences. For example, André Breton quotes from the *Zohar* in his crucial 'Signe ascendant' (1947) where he elaborates on his theory of analogy. He also quotes the pseudo-hermetic 'All that is inside is outside...' (probably derived from Eliphas Lévi as Anna Balakian has written). Further, in Breton's *Arcane 17* (1944) so central to the Paz–Breton 'conjunction', there is a defence of esoteric art because it maintains 'à l'état dynamique le système de comparaison, de champ illimité,dont dispose l'homme' (in the dynamic state the system of comparison, of limitless field, that man disposes of): or in other words, analogy, the mechanics of 'universal symbolism'. Breton links the Kabbala with Apollinaire and emphasises the relationships between esoteric arts and poetry. Later in the same text he resorts to kabbalistic method by referring to the Hebrew character פ, which means both 'tongue in the mouth' and 'word'. And in a 'kabbalistic' sense Paz's *Splendeur* condenses meanings that repeat the whole process of *Le Singe grammairien*.[24]

One of the analogies between Paz's poetics and the Kabbala is that within the profane, literal alphabet can be found a sacred text. The role of the reader–initiate (and does not Paz seek initiates?) is to strip away the appearance, the clothes. He denudes to the 'flesh'; he makes love. But this process is first of all a mental act; 'stripping' words is analogical. Is Paz also proposing a 'mental ascesis' that leads to a 'pensée pure sur le vide', as one commentator on the *Zohar* explains?[25]

In Paz as in the *Zohar* there is the same notion of 'playing' with words to get through to the 'truth'; 'start to *combine* certain letters...' is the formula that reveals 'our' language as the absence of the sacred language. But we can only *see* through to its splendour beyond language by destroying words. The metaphor is a palimpsest; that hint of another text (reality) obscured, written over. More crucially, the *Zohar* employs, like Tantra, like alchemy, like surrealism, openly erotic terms for union, out of keeping with other kabbalistic texts. Kenneth Rexroth describes the *hierosgamos* (or sacred marriage re-enacted by each couple on earth) as central to the *Zohar*: 'For the Kabbalist the ultimate sacrament is the sexual act, carefully organised and sustained as the most perfect mystical trance.' Behind the 'cloud of doctrine' or 'double talk' is a subtle 'sanctification' of the 'moment of intercourse' (Waites) in which male and female melt together and lose their differentiation: a 'supreme' moment often turned into poetry by Paz. Man alone (the poet alone, the reader alone) is incomplete: only in the 'face to face' act of love is there completion: this is a variant of the androgynous nostalgia or myth. The link between the *Zohar* and language is crucial: the male–female marriage exists on the consonantal level; between the voice and the word; the heart and the lips and so on. So Breton's 'les mots font l'amour' is kabbalistic.[26]

The *Zohar* also proposes the harmony of analogy; parts of the body correspond to parts of the universe; man's soul is a kingdom of processes that are paralleled in the 'upper world' and so on. The theory of correspondences is central to this unsystematic, openly symbolic doctrine: all is related, 'linked', as Scholem writes; there is 'no such thing as an isolated existence'. On this level the role of the reader–initiate is to decipher the symbols offered by the universe; to lift the veils of words; to *see* what cannot be described, where the vertigo of seeing finds its metaphor in the orgasm.[27]

If the Kabbala is an invitation to the ingenuity of the reader, where 'every word is capable of becoming a symbol' (Scholem), then this absence of limit on speculative subtleties clashes with the openness of the poem. The difference is crucial, for poetry is experience of the poem, irreducible to words and analysis. For poetry-reading only *borrows* from the tradition of the Kabbala; it does not pretend to 'mystical' experience, but perceives erotic experience in mystical terms.[28]

Paz parodies heterodox religious doctrines. He is a learned poet whom it is hard to gauge when literary–cultural echoes fade away. What unites Paz and Breton is a belief in a hidden universality tapped by the gnostic tradition and poetry, a 'fond commun' (Breton) or what Rexroth calls a 'fundamental identity of man's response to the great rhythms of life'. Poetry seeks to recuperate this hidden harmony, usurping the withered conventions of religion. This is what Paz *intends* through creating a poetic *sagesse*, even if this ambitious creation ends as, or is reduced to, a poem. Sufficient for us to see that the *Zohar* proposes the text as a journey of decoding where what happens at the level of language is analogous to all other levels, and *Splendeur*, the female goddess, suddenly shines through the arid text as a sensual, vivacious body.[29]

We return to seeing. Paz elevates seeing above the other senses and has included illustrations in this text that 'speak' their own language. The act of reading must also account for these, and the ways in which they contribute to the process. The over-privileging of the eye is perhaps cultural, but it is the source of the poetics in *Le Singe grammairien* and *Blanco*.

Paz once wrote: 'Vemos un poema; leemos un texto en prosa' (*Pu* 99; We see a poem; we read a text in prose). The difference is one of code: prose *seems* more natural; we forget the words while reading. In poetry, always typographical and visual, we see the words (as well as voicing the words). This (dubious) polarisation is neutralised by *Le Singe grammairien* which first of all appeals as a visual artefact. We will give two examples of this interplay between word, icon and mind.

On page 42 of *Le Singe grammairien* Paz places an ink-blot drawing by Henri Michaux, and on the facing page a battle scene from the *Ramayana*. Each image interprets the other, like

facing mirrors. In both there is a sense of frenzied activity; there
are contorted, struggling, dancing, loving and fighting bodies.
Between the pictures winds Paz's text: I excerpt 'j'habite mes
démolitions' (I inhabit my demolitions) and suddenly the pictures become *images* of the teeming, over-crowded mind-flow,
'*mes* démolitions'. This fertile, threatening inscape 'demolishes'
the security of the ego and can be seen 'frozen' in the images.
Michaux claimed that he painted to de-condition himself; to
break open the tendency to inertia and stasis. He paints to
create a sense of frenzy or movement. Like Paz, he is aware of
the sudden, sought-after 'emergencies' that irrupt through the
ego's defences. Painting and 'poem' scrape away the same
crust.[30]

On page 46 Paz places a full page picture by Victor Brauner,
faced by an ink drawing by Max Walter Svanberg. The
Brauner is entitled 'L'aube', and depicts a stylised naked
woman in an empty green room. Her face is like a cat's or an
owl's, is blue and geometric like a voodoo mask (a witch?); in
her pink fingers she holds a startled, stiff, turquoise cat. Her
nipples are bright red and her pubis is a black, inverted
pyramid. The Svanberg is an illustration from Rimbaud's *Les
Illuminations*. It resembles an Ernst collage, showing a naked
bird–lady pierced by a rhinoceros' horn, as if she is involved in
some mating rite with another bird who is pierced by a mop
with a head. This other bird is male, and is built like a stool;
solid and rigid. From him projects a dumb-bell-shaped phallus,
going between the lady's legs. They are bound together by
beads and their eyes are closed in ecstasy. The pictures 'speak'
to each other: of dawn, illumination. Somewhere in the 'dark' of
woman there is light. Paz's text embodies this dialogue by
evoking the appearance of *Splendeur* who shines, stripped of
words, in all her naked erotic mystery. Paz writes: 'tandis
qu'elle se déshabille' (while she undresses), and creates a nodal
interplay that suspends the flow of time and becomes a system
of transformations, of analogies of liberating associations.
Svanberg said that he painted 'hymns to women'; like Paz's
Splendeur. The double page comes *alive*. Breton praised the
unconscious power that Brauner's paintings unleashed in the

gazer, provoking a modification in him, 'unchaining' the imagination. Breton described Svanberg's pictorial world 'où règne le vertige' (where vertigo reigns). We come to rest on 'vertigo' again, the expression of vertiginous dissolution of forms.[31]

Paz is a passionate art critic; expressing his visual impressions in a dense, metaphorical language that borders on the prose poem, as in ¿Aguila o sol? where the description of a Tamayo painting, 'Ser natural', is a poem. In 1968 Paz returned to Tamayo and described the notion of *space* (the canvas, the white page, the mind, nature) as the common analogy in all art: 'El espacio es un campo de atracción y repulsión, un teatro en el que se enlazan y desenlazan, se oponen y abrazan las mismas fuerzas que mueven a la naturaleza' (*SG* 171; Space is a field of attraction and repulsion, a theatre in which the same forces that move nature join and separate, oppose and embrace). This space is neither inside nor outside, for it is analogical; it is the harmony of mind with nature. We should note again the flux of this theatre, where the 'embrace' (of words, bodies, stars) is the vision. In the same essay on Tamayo, Paz defines art-criticism as 'una invitación a realizar el único acto que de veras cuenta: ver' (*SG* 172; an invitation to carry out the only act that truly counts: to see). The aim is to use words to clear away deadened responses, and to see the moment in its painful, liberating uniqueness. This is the function of writing, whether the 'window' (eye) gives onto a canvas, a star, a tree, another word or a naked woman.

We may well ask 'Is all this *art?*' This perennial question hints at the powerful ways in which culture absorbs apparent exceptions. Isn't it the catch in surrealism that it became art, literature, congealed form? And isn't there an archness or an artfulness in separating *pensée* from art? And most important, isn't Paz's proposition finally *aesthetic* (rather than 'religious' or 'ontological')?

The doubts depend on each reader's faith in the original proposition 'to read is to take a journey': if the poetics is *shared* and if the reader participates as co-author, he will be sensitive to the signs – not as an ape, but as Hanuman contemplating the

hieroglyphic world. Breton's 'praiseworthy scorn' for literature
is tactical; all that really counts is whether the 'journey' is fertile
and refreshing; or whether it provokes or baffles and leads to
insight.

Octavio Paz chooses as central to Breton's poetics his praise
for Sade's comparison of Etna to a breast vomiting flames, and
his (Sade's) desire to be the volcano. For Breton this is a poetics
of 'le délire de la présence absolue...au sein de la nature
réconciliée' (the delirium of absolute presence...in the bosom
of a reconciled nature). The analogy between passion, love,
nature, man and woman, and the poem can now be hooked into
Tantra, the Kabbala and surrealism. Surrealism is truly the
'sacred' disease of the West. It is Paz who makes these secret
links, and *Le Singe grammairien* is the result. Paz, referring to
Breton's *L'Amour fou*, writes: 'Fue un "Arte de amar"...una
iniciación a algo que después la vida y el oriente me han
corroborado' (*CA* 58; It was an 'art of loving'...an invitation
into something that life and the East later corroborated). It
could not be clearer; what unites them all is the notion of
initiation into a discipline (poetry) whose ambitious claim has
little to do with 'literature'. In André Breton's words: 'la vie
humaine est à *repassionner*'.[32]

III A reading of 'Vuelta'

In 1971 Octavio Paz wrote a longish poem called 'Vuelta'
(Return). The epigraph is from Ramón López Velarde
(1888–1921), a favourite Mexican poet, on whom Paz has
written some of his most fervent criticism. López Velarde's
poem, entitled 'El retorno maléfico', written in 1921, explores
the anguish of 'homelessness' (the chaotic Mexican revolution
desolated many provincial towns). Allied to this was López
Velarde's own estrangement: his bohemian life in the capital
city, his Baudelairian satanic pose. The very fact of being a poet
separated him from his 'catholic' childhood, his 'subverted
Eden'. Within his own country there was no going 'home'; no
return. To travel is as much a mental process as a physical

movement. Paz weaves his poem around this epigraph: the quintessence of nostalgia. His own return is to his birth-place, Mixcoac, a suburb of Mexico City. The Mexican atmosphere is that of a stifling, paralysing heat:[33]

> En los buzones
> se pudren las cartas
> In the pillar boxes the letters rot.

This powerful image sparks off associations: absence of communication, the breakdown of the social structure, the pointlessness of the past. In the poem the poet walks back – in his mind – into his past; but the very notion of 'past' is illusory, a 'balcón / sobre el vacío' (balcony above emptiness). Yet the present is worse – 'me falta aire' (I lack air) – for the smog-thick air of Mexico City becomes *mental*: hospitals, asphalt, offices, paralysed architecture, cinemas, a mind–world in *decomposition*. In this perspective the past is no consolation, it is mere *bruma* (mist). Even the previous day's newspapers are more remote 'que una tablilla cuneiforme' (than a cuneiform tablet) and reveal no sense of the real past, just shredded language. The poet shifts to metaphysics:

> No hay centro
>   plaza de congregación y consagración
> No hay eje
> There is no centre, place of congregation and consecration, there is
> no axis.

This is the world as it is; de-sanctified, empty of meaning, with no umbilical cord to the centre. The visible brand of the dollar conditions all (as filthy lucre or abstract materialism).

The poet questions his status, his progress. He quotes the Chinese poet Wang-Wei (of whom more later) – his Eastern experience overbrims – and answers: 'all is won if all is lost'. Place, birth-place, is illusion: as fictive as yesterday: 'Camino hacia mí mismo' (I walk towards myself). He 'walks' into that 'innerspace': not a subverted Eden (and its nostalgic poetics) but a 'beating of time', pure temporality. Paz affirms and assumes his painful 'temporality'; for man never arrives ('Camino...') and his 'place' is the inner space of desire. He is a perpetual flow 'towards':

>   Nunca llegamos
>   Nunca estamos en donde estamos
>   No el pasado
>   El presente es intocable

We never arrive, we never are where we are. Not the past, the present is untouchable.

And even the present is fleeting ('untouchable'). Locating place as desire is the core of Paz's temporal poetics; a perception sharpened and clarified by his friction with the East. By rejecting the implications of his own name – peace, quietude, abstraction from the timeflow – Paz has created a poetics of 'passionate criticism'.

In the edition of the poem consulted here, the final 'Camino sin avanzar' – so often invoked throughout his writings – has the 'o' in bold type. Here is a clue; it is an obvious ideogram for the absent centre, the blank centre of the mandala, the mouth that speaks, the real sign behind the flowing words.

To return to the specifically literary elements in the poem there are two explicit breaches in the text; two alien voices break in typographically in brackets. The first opens onto López Velarde and the second onto the late T'ang poet Wang-Wei. Paz diverges both from the anguished nostalgia of Velarde and the sought-after tranquillity of Wang-Wei.

The conscious separation from Wang-Wei (or Paz's version of Wang-Wei), the quietist poet and Buddhist landscape painter, allows Paz to affirm:

>   Yo no quiero una ermita intelectual
>   en San Angel o en Coyoacán

I do not want an intellectual hermitage in San Angel or in Coyoacan.

The vitalism of Paz's *yo* (the pronoun is not necessary in Spanish, as person is implicit in the inflexion of the verb) gives a sense of aggressive purpose, as against the sponging away of the illusion of the ego in Buddhism. Paz, by contrast, places his ego against conventional religion; he substitutes 'exotic' Buddhism for *poetry*; action above passivity, this world against Wang-Wei's 'immobile shore' that Paz himself once yearned for. Paz rejects the fashionable refuge (San Angel, Coyoacan where Trotsky lived); for he too, like Wang-Wei, has reached his 'autumn'. For Paz there is to be no resting on his laurels as the grand poet of Mexico; he does not seek a tranquil retreat from the world in the 'Ancient Woods'. He rages for the present. And to do so is to rage for the continued enriching of experience. It is also to desire change, to be open, 'porous' to the present.

Paz has published several translations of Wang-Wei; one of his 'orientales extremos' (extreme orientals), and he admits to translating 'por pasión' (through passion). So the poem also embodies that strange dialogue with the dead (the poets) that is literature (reading). López Velarde and Wang-Wei define Paz's hunger and desires; they sharpen his poem.[34]

Wang-Wei's own poem (the one quoted by Paz) is entitled in an English version 'In answer to...'; and forms part of that Chinese 'address and answer' tradition. This bond with past poets gives the poem body, making it a complex tissue where chronology is defied and annulled by the enriching echoes. The reader adds his voice to the intimate dialogue between solitaries, out of tune with their times. Again the poem is a palimpsest, and reading is a sensitivity to these hushed and hidden voices reborn in the reader's mind.[35]

Our reading picks up another, more suppressed voice: that of the Mexican poet José Juan Tablada (1871–1945), 'este poeta que descubrió tantas cosas [que] espera ser descubierto por nosotros' (this poet who discovered so many things, who waits to be discovered by us). Paz's shrewd rereading of the Mexican tradition selects two founding fathers: López Velarde and Tablada. He admits to being 'fascinated' by Tablada's later work. Its freshness and its openness to experiment and change excite him and reinforce his hunger for the present.[36]

There are further coincidences between Paz and Tablada: Tablada introduced exquisite haiku into Spanish; he wrote ideographic and calligrammatic poems. Paz borrows and expands these 'playful', even trivial, experiments. He absorbs Tablada's message of surprise and risk, and his poetics of the image. Tablada's fertility, the many paths that he opened but did not exploit or exhaust, mirror Paz's own experimentalism. In 1945 Paz quoted Tablada – and it reads like self-quotation – in a strange identity of intent:

Todo depende del concepto que se tenga del arte; hay quien lo cree
estático y definitivo; yo lo creo en perpetuo movimiento. La obra
está en marcha hacia sí misma, como el planeta, y alrededor del sol.

(*Pe* 86)

all depends on the concept that you may have of art; some believe it
to be static and definitive; I think it is in perpetual movement. The
work is in movement towards itself, like a planet, and round the sun.

This recalls Paz's own later answer to the placid quietist
Wang-Wei.

Paz borrows techniques such as haiku, poems in counter-
point (alternating italics and lower-case), calligrammes, and
themes such as 'old mythologies' (compare Paz's *Piedra de sol*
with Tablada's 'El ídolo en el atrio'). But, in the end, what links
them specifically in Paz's 'Vuelta' is that Tablada was also a
'prodigal son' who returned home to Mexico from the East
(China and Japan). Tablada's book of poems *Li-Po y otros
poemas* (1920) links him to Paz (who also translated Li-Po);
Tablada's other book *Un día . . . poemas sintéticos* (1919) is
dedicated to Bashō (whom Paz later translated 'por pasión').
Tablada also prefaces *Li-Po* with a poem by Mallarmé, the poet
who unites in 'seed' form all Paz's later searchings:

> Imiter le Chinois au cœur limpide et fin
> De qui l'extase pure . . .
> To imitate the Chinaman with the limpid and fine heart from whom
> pure ecstasy

Here then is the absent centre, 'pure ecstasy', the structuring
voice: Tablada, China, Mallarmé, Paz, reversing chronology.
Paz rejects an attitude in Wang-Wei, but absorbs his 'limpidity'. 'Limpidity' is the title of Paz's angry renunciatory poem
over the fiasco of the Mexican Olympic games. It is a moral
quality. When Tablada returned to Mexico, in his last book *La
feria* (1928), we sense the final meaning in Paz's 'Vuelta'.
Tablada wrote:

> No tengo el delirio vano
> de querer ser universal,
> ni siquiera continental,
> me basta ser poeta mexicano.

I hold not the vain delirium of wanting to be universal, not even continental, enough to be a Mexican poet.

This move from abstract postulates and metaphysics to the 'now' of being Mexican is what Paz says but cannot write.[37]

In 1945 Paz located Tablada's poetic unity in his 'fidelity to adventure' (*Pe* 88). This attitude to art keeps a door open onto life, to *fix vertigos*. In Tablada's words:

> Arte, con tu áureo alfiler
> las mariposas del instante
> quise clavar en el papel

Art, with your golden pin the butterflies of the moment I wanted to nail to paper.[38]

To seize the instant in words: if the 'period' flavour is eliminated from these lines, Paz 'shines' through.

There is a poem by Tablada called 'El reló de sombra' (The clock of shade) in *El jarro de flores* (1922). It consists of a series of brief haiku which express the anguish and aridity of sleeplessness as 'roer el reló' (to gnaw the clock). The phrase is adapted in 'Suite del insomnio' by Xavier Villaurrutia in his book *Reflejos* (1926). He consciously invokes Tablada in his haiku 'Reloj' (Clock):

> ¿Qué corazón avaro
> cuenta el metal
> de los instantes?

What miserly heart counts the metal of the moments?

Octavio Paz changes this to a series of short, linked poems called 'Apuntes del insomnio', originally in seven sections. The opening section explicitly echoes Tablada:

> Roe el reloj
> mi corazón
> buitre no, sino ratón.   (*L* 45)

The clock gnaws my heart, not a vulture but a mouse.

Here is another version of the tradition of 'talking to the dead'. This borrowing has been pointed out by G. Ceide-Echevarría; the point is that the move from haiku through Tablada to

Villaurrutia and Paz is one from a tradition of natural harmony
(the Japanese haiku) to that of Paz's anguished, arid temporality in the 1940s. After his 'Eastern' experience, Paz returned to
Mexico with a *poetics* of temporality, his earlier anguish transformed into a visionary poetics.[39]

Postscript

It is tempting to try to keep up with Paz's writings and revisions, but the temporal nature of his questing poetics makes it impossible.

It is ironic that since I wrote the last section on what was then called the symbolic poem 'Vuelta', Paz has published a collection entitled *Vuelta* (Barcelona: Seix Barral, 1976), as well as transforming the abandoned *Plural* into a magazine called *Vuelta* (no. 1, December 1976). We have not amended our text for it would have no end; there is an inbuilt 'obsolescence' at the heart of all criticism on a still active writer.

Paz does not respect his own texts; he is constantly revising, correcting, shortening and excising. This is his right (and we recall W. H. Auden's deletions) but it does also suggest an impermanence at the roots of his texts. Is this related to changes of fashion? Or to a maturing poetic consciousness, to a sharper sense of craft? Or is it the poet guiding time's natural elimination of waste and froth? We will explore some of these suggestions.

The original version of 'Vuelta' (1971) had 140 'lines' (including spatialised words). The 1976 version printed in *Vuelta* has 168. And here we enter the slippery ground of the morality of the definitive text (so acute in studies of César Vallejo, for example). Some of Paz's additions to the 1971 version are mere tidying up, others obey rhythm, others are visual and some are harder to evaluate. We will compare some sections:

1971	1976
Me falta aire	Me falta aire
me falta cuerpo	me falta cuerpo
Mediodía	me faltan
puño de luz	la piedra que es almohada y losa

que golpea y golpea   la yerba que es nube y agua
    Caer en una oficina   Se apaga el ánima
o sobre el asfalto   Mediodía
                                 puño de luz que golpea y golpea
                                 Caer en una oficina
                                     o sobre el asfalto

I lack air, I lack body. Mid-   I lack air, I lack body, I lack
day, fist of light, that beats   the stone that is pillow and
and beats to fall into an office tombstone, the herb that is
or onto asphalt.   cloud and water the soul put
                                 out. Midday, fist of light, that
                                 beats and beats to fall into an
                                 office or onto asphalt.

Apart from the typographical re-organisation (which prompts the question why a poem is so spatialised, what necessity determines the order; is it visual, to do with breath, a musical score for voice?), we have to ask which version is best. Paz has heightened the notion of what is *lacking*, reinforcing the appeal to sound and the play on the absent archetypes. The later version is more explicit and elaborate in a rhetorical and literary way with a typical Pazian (by now I can use this adjective) surge of word sound: the p's, b's, and g's give a consonantal enriching of texture, like a litany. The earlier version seems cryptic (but better?).[1]

A few lines later we find this contrast between two lines and five lines, where Paz has clotted the lines, creating a more urgent sense of nightmare:

1971   1976
  Germinación de pesadillas   Germinación de pesadillas
en el vientre de los cines   infestación de imágenes leprosas
                                 en el vientre los sesos los pulmones
                                 en el sexo del templo y del colegio
                                 en los cines

Germination of nightmare in   Germination of nightmare,
the belly of cinemas.   infestation of leprous images
                                 in the belly, brains, lungs, in
                                 the sex of the temple and the
                                 college, in the cinemas.

Paz's disgust or despair evidently required a greater clarity: the group cinema–belly (linking social escapism and digestion) is expanded to become body, church and school; since it is the whole society that Paz curses, this explicitness is necessary.[2]

A new section that attacks the political set-up in Mexico in terms of rigid, Aztec-like statues (suggesting false gods) is magnificent in its consonantal thickness (it uses Aztec words) and gains by being read aloud. But it does not modify our original reading of the poem. Paz seems more aware of the poem's importance and makes his moral stance more explicit. It is as if he is sensitive to greater public responsibility. Is this the emergence of a more political poet?

This revisionist attitude is not new; it is present like a flaw in his very texts; this much has been hinted in this book. Judith Goetzinger and E. R. Monegal have studied aspects of this.[3]

I end by returning to the original affinity between André Breton and Octavio Paz, and stress three crucial affinities:
(1) Poetry as self-defence; poetry as the perfect 'compensation' for endured miseries. Breton asserted this in 1924 and always held it.[4]
(2) Poetry as a 'sacred fever'; both poets share a 'religious' intention.[5]
(3) Poetry as a *moral* activity, a stance based on Breton's daunting intransigence about principles; what Ferdinand Alquié called the primacy of the moral point of view, an 'exigence éthique' (ethical exigency). We quote Paz:

...Las imperfecciones de algunas obras...provienen casi siempre, más que de ausencia de talento, de una *falta* espiritual del poeta. La moral, en el sentido profundo de la palabra, interviene más de lo que se piensa en la creación artística. He escrito *moral*. Quizá debería haber dicho: amor, entrega a la obra, arrojo, integridad espiritual.

(Pu 135)

the imperfections of some works...come nearly always, not from absence of talent, [but] a spiritual fault in the poet. Morality, in the deep sense of the word, intervenes more than one thinks in artistic creation. I wrote moral. Perhaps I should have said: love, surrender to the work, daring, spiritual integrity.

I could compare Paz's description of this new morality with what Boris Pasternak said about good and bad poetry: 'and I became convinced once again that, generally speaking, verses, good and bad, do not exist, but there are only good and bad poets, that is, whole systems of thought which are either productive or which spin in the void'.[6]

It is on this interpretation that my study of Paz stands or falls, on Paz's 'whole system of thought'. Here, at this serious level, Paz has fulfilled Breton's wish: 'ma plus grande ambition serait d'en laisser le sens théorique indéfiniment transmissible après moi' (my greatest ambition would be to leave the theoretic sense indefinitely transmissible after me).[7]

Notes

Introduction

1. H. Bloom, *The Anxiety of Influence: A Theory of Poetry* (New York: O.U.P., 1973), 13, 29, 35. H. Gersham, 'On Malcolm de Chazal', *Symposium*, XXIV, 4 (Winter 1970), 316.
2. J. Guillén, 'La stimulation surréaliste', *La Nouvelle Revue Française*, 172 (April 1967), 896.

Chapter 1

1. André Breton, *Entretiens* (Paris: Gallimard, 1952), 285; André Breton, 'Editorial', *Le Surréalisme, même*, 3 (Autumn 1957), 2; André Breton, *Perspective cavalière* (Paris: Gallimard, 1970), 239; Guillén, 'La stimulation surréaliste', 896.
2. J. L. Bédouin, *La Poésie surréaliste* (Paris: Seghers, 1964).
3. J. T. Bodet, *Tiempo de arena* (Mexico: F.C.E., 1961), 343; J. T. Bodet, 'Nadja', *Contemporáneos*, II, 5 (October 1928), 194–9.
4. Paz, 'Cultura de la muerte', *Letras de México*, I, 33 (November 1938), 5; 'El teatro de X. Villaurrutia', *Sur*, 105 (July 1943), 96–8.
5. Paz, *Poesía en movimiento, México 1915–1966* (Mexico: Siglo XXI, 1966), 16; X. Villaurrutia, *Obras* (Mexico: F.C.E., 1966), 772; J. Ríos, *Solo a dos voces*, (Barcelona: Lumen, 1973), n.p.n.
6. Ortiz de Montellano in E. J. Mullen (ed.), *Contemporáneos: Revista mexicana de cultura* (Salamanca: Anaya, 1972), 70–2.
7. Jorge Cuesta, *Poemas y ensayos* (Mexico: U.N.A.M., 1964), 65, 222, 224, 222, 369.
8. The surrealist map in P. Waldberg, *Surrealism* (London: Thames & Hudson, 1965), 24.
9. Antonin Artaud, *México* (Mexico: U.N.A.M. 1962), 69, 82; Antonin Artaud, *Les Tarahumaras* (Décines, Isère: Barbezat, 1963), 152, 196.
10. I. R. Prampolini, *El surrealismo y el arte fantástico de México* (Mexico: U.N.A.M., 1969), 53.
11. André Breton, *Le Surréalisme et la peinture* (Paris: Gallimard, 1965), 233–4; Rafael Valle, 'Diálogo con Breton', *Universidad de México*, 29 (June 1938), 6; Roger Caillois, 'André Breton: divergencias y convergencias', *Espejo*, 2 (1967), 126.
12. Prampolini, *El surrealismo y el arte fantástico*, 66.

13. André Breton, *La Clé des champs* (Paris: Pauvert, 1967), 42–9, 62.
14. Agustín Lazo, 'Reseña sobre las actividades sobrerealistas', *Cuadernos de arte*, 3 in *Universidad de México* (March 1938), n.p.n.; Adolfo Samara, 'El surrealismo, igual a cero', *Letras de México*, 28 (June 1938), 4; Arqueles Vela, 'André Breton, globe-trotter aux pas perdus', *Ruta*, 1 (June 1938), 47, 48.
15. Rafael Solana in *Las revistas literarias de México* (Mexico: I.N.B.A., 1963), 98; Paz, *Poesía en movimiento*, 20.
16. Cardoza y Aragón, 'Demagogos de la poesía', *Taller*, 8–9 (January–February 1940), 48, 50; Ramón Gaya, 'Divagaciones en torno al surrealismo', *Romance*, 1, 2 (15 February 1940), 7; Anon., 'Nota', *Romance*, 1, 2 (15 February 1940), 7; Prampolini, *El surrealismo y el arte fantástico*, 44.
17. Benjamin Péret, 'Los mitos', *El hijo pródigo*, IV, 14 (15 May 1944), 113, 118, 114.
18. Larrea, collected in *Del surrealismo a Machupicchu* (Mexico: Mortiz, 1967).
19. Carlos Monsiváis, 'Octavio Paz en diálogo', *Revista de la universidad de México*, XXII, 3 (November 1967), 8.
20. Elías Nandino, 'Después del surrealismo... ¿Qué?', *Estaciones*, 4, 3 (Autumn 1956), 406.
21. Salvador Echevarría, 'Derroteros de la poesía contemporánea', *Estaciones*, 1, 1 (Spring 1956), 23, 24; Salvador Reyes Nevares, 'Notas sobre el surrealismo', *Estaciones*, 1, 3 (Autumn 1956), 329, 330.
22. Margarita Michelena, *Notas en torno a la poesía mexicana contemporánea* (Mexico: Asoc. Mex. por la libertad de la cultura, 1956), 33; Raúl Leiva, 'Piedra de sol', *México en la cultura*, 449 (27 October 1957), 2; Silva Villalobos in *Metáfora*, 2 (May–June 1955), 37.
23. J. E. Pacheco in *Narradores ante el público* (Mexico: I.N.B.A., 1966), 33; in *Estaciones*, 7 (Autumn 1957), 360; 'Un momento estelar de la poesía mexicana', *México en le cultura*, 624 (26 November 1961), 3; 'Descripción de *Piedra de sol*', *Revista iberoamericana*, 74 (January–February 1971), 144.
24. Claude Couffon, *Hispanoamérica en su nueva literatura* (Santander: Publicaciones de la isla de los Ratones, 1962), 80; Roberto Vernegro, 'Una entrevista con Octavio Paz', *Sur*, 227 (March–April 1954), 61.
25. Vernegro, 'Una entrevista' 64; Paz, 'Carta a F. Gamboa', *Plural*, 17 (February 1973), 36; Anna Balakian, *André Breton: Magus of Surrealism* (N.Y.: O.U.P., 1971), 212.
26. René Daumal, *L'Evidence absurde* (Paris: Gallimard, 1972), 155.
27. *Almanach surréaliste du demi-siècle* spec. no. of *Nef*, 63–4 (March–April 1950), 29–31; J. L. Bédouin includes 'Haute fréquence' in *Vingt ans de surréalisme, 1939–1959* (Paris: Denoel, 1961), 311–13; *Lexique succinct de l'érotisme* (Paris: Losfeld, 1970); André Breton, *Perspective cavalière* (Paris: Gallimard, 1970), 238–42.

28. See G. Brotherston, *Latin American Poetry: Origins and Presence* (Cambridge: C.U.P., 1975), 138–9.

29. Couffon, *Hispanoamérica*, 79; Paz, 'Benjamin Péret', *Les Lettres Nouvelles*, VII, 24 (October 1959), 26; María Embeita, 'Octavio Paz: poesía y metafísica', *Insula*, 260–1 (July-August 1968), 14.

30. Paz, 'Constante amigo', *Taller*, 4 (July 1939), 53.

31. Vernegro, 'Una entrevista' 63; Breton, *Entretiens*, 282; P. Audoin, *Breton* (Paris: Gallimard, 1970), 115–16; S. Alexandrian, *André Breton par lui-même* (Paris: Seuil, 1971), 54; Monsiváis, 'Octavio Paz en diálogo', 8.

32. J. P. Sartre, *Situations II: Qu'est-ce que la littérature* (Paris: Gallimard, 1948), 222; André Breton, *Arcane 17* (Paris: Pauvert, 1947), 174; J. H. Matthews, *Surrealist Poetry in France* (Syracuse: Syracuse Univ. Press 1969), 6.

33. Luis Suarez, 'Octavio Paz habla desde París', *México en la cultura*, 560 (6 December 1959), 2; Benjamin Péret in J. L. Bédouin, *Benjamin Péret* (Paris: Seghers, 1961), 106, 107; André Breton, *Clair de terre* (Paris: Gallimard, 1966), 157; André Breton, *Manifestes du surréalisme* (Paris: Pauvert, 1962), 63; Breton, *Arcane 17*, 83.

34. Breton, *Entretiens*, 278.

35. Augusto Lunel in *México en la cultura*, 311 (6 March 1957), 2; Paz in *Plural*, 17 (February 1973), 36–7; Paz, 'Sobre el surrealismo hispanoamericano: el fin de las habladurías', *Plural*, 35 (August 1974), 75.

36. Paz on Sade in 'Corriente alterna', *Universidad de México*, xv, 6 (February 1961), 15–20.

37. Raúl Leiva in *Revista de Guatemala*, 2 (July–September 1951), 167; *Selected Poems of Octavio Paz*, trans. Muriel Rukeyser (Bloomington: Indiana Univ. Press, 1963); Paz, *La centena (Poemas 1935–1968)* (Barcelona: Barral, 1969).

38. Maurice Nadeau, *Histoire du surréalisme* (Paris: Seuil, 1945), 33.

39. Geoffrey Gorer, *The Life and Ideas of the Marquis de Sade* (London: Panther, 1964), 81.

40. Maurice Blanchot, *Lautréamont et Sade* (Paris: Editions de Minuit, 1964), 24, 25, 73.

41. Breton, *Entretiens*, 141.

42. Breton, *Clair de terre*, 165.

43. J. H. Matthews, 'The Right Person for Surrealism', *Yale French Studies*, 35 (December 1965), 95; Paul Eluard, *Donner à voir* (Paris: Gallimard, 1939), 82.

44. Paz, 'Corriente alterna', 15, 16, 15.

45. André Breton, *Anthologie de l'humour noir* (Paris: Pauvert, 1966), 55; Paz, 'Corriente alterna', 20.

46. André Breton, *L'Amour fou* (Paris: Gallimard), 14; J. E. Cirlot, *A Dictionary of Symbols* (London: Routledge & Kegan Paul, 1962), 71.

Chapter 2

1. Breton, *Manifestes*, 40, 32.
2. Breton, *Manifestes*, 154; Breton, *Le Surréalisme et la peinture*, 46.
3. Paz, *Claude Lévi-Strauss o el nuevo festín de Esopo* (Mexico: Mortiz, 1967), 24.
4. Paz, 'Vigilias: fragmentos del diario de un soñador', *Taller*, 7 (December 1939), 13.
5. Paz, *Marcel Duchamp* (Mexico: Era, 1968), 28, 59–60.
6. André Breton, *Point du jour* (Paris: Gallimard, 1970), 7.
7. Breton, *Entretiens*, 213.
8. Breton, *Entretiens*, 78, 135.
9. See J. Bernard, 'Myth and Structure in Octavio Paz's "Piedra de sol" ', *Symposium*, XXI, 1 (Spring 1967), 5–13; J. E. Pacheco, 'Descripción de "Piedra de sol" ', *Revista iberoamericana*, 74 (January–March 1971), 135–46; R. Nugent, 'Structure and Meaning in Octavio Paz's *Piedra de sol*', *Kentucky Foreign Language Quarterly*, 3 (1966), 138–46.
10. J. H. Matthews in *Comparative Literature Studies*, I, 2 (1965), 100.
11. Rimbaud cited by Y. Bonnefoy, *Rimbaud par lui-même* (Paris: Seuil, 1970), 131; Rubén Darío, *Cantos de vida y esperanza* (Madrid: Anaya, 1964), 71; Breton cited by M. A. Caws, *The Poetry of Dada and Surrealism* (New Jersey: Princeton Univ. Press, 1970), 88.
12. Paz, 'Eroticism and Gastrosophy', *Daedalus*, CI, 4 (Fall 1972), 81.
13. N. O. Brown, *Love's Body* (N.Y.; Random House, 1966), 255.
14. Elena Poniatowska, 'Octavio Paz; roca solar de la poesía', *México en la cultura*, 450 (3 November 1957), 3.
15. Paz, 'Pablo Neruda en el corazón', *Ruta* (4 September 1938), 25–33; Paz, 'Respuesta a un cónsul', *Letras de México*, 90 (15 August 1943), 5.
16. Breton, *L'Amour fou*, 61; Paz, 'Benjamin Péret', 27.
17. Roland Barthes, *Writing Degree Zero* (London: Cape, 1967), 94; Northrop Frye, *Fables of Identity* (N.Y. Harcourt, Brace & World, 1963), 18.
18. Paz, *Claude Lévi-Strauss*, 95; Breton *Clair de terre*, 69; André Breton, *Signe ascendant* (Paris: Gallimard, 1968), 118; Breton, *Clair de terre*, 179.
19. Paz, 'Vigilias', Eluard, *Donner à voir*, 80.
20. Eluard, *Donner à voir*, 81.
21. Breton, *Manifestes*, 167–8; Eluard, *Donner à voir*, 80; see E. J. Wilson, '*Abrir/cerrar los ojos*: a Recurrent Theme in the Poetry of Octavio Paz', *Bulletin of Hispanic Studies*, XLVIII, 1 (January 1971), 44–56.
22. Eluard cited by L. Perche, *Paul Eluard* (Paris: Ed. Universitaires, 1964), 42–3.
23. Alexandrian, *André Breton par lui-même*, 55; P. Jaccottet, *L'Entretien des muses* (Paris: Gallimard, 1968), 79; Paz, *Poesía en movimiento*, 11.

24. Paz, 'Diario de un soñador: vigilias', *El hijo pródigo*, VII, 24 (15 March 1945), 147.

25. Guillermo Sucre, 'La fijeza y el vértigo', *Revista iberoamericana*, 74 (January–March 1971), 47–72.

26. Breton, *Arcane 17*, 206.

27. Breton, *Signe ascendant*, 66, 32.

28. Rachel Phillips, *The Poetic Modes of Octavio Paz* (Oxford: O.U.P., 1972), 109; Cirlot, *A Dictionary of Symbols*, 71; Breton, *Point du jour*, 99; Breton, *L'Amour fou*, 49, 14; Alexandrian, *André Breton par lui-même* 46; Audoin, *Breton*, 57; Matthews, *Surrealist Poetry in France*, 113.

29. Paz, *Poesía en movimiento*, 4; Audoin, *Breton*, 112.

30. David Gallagher, *Modern Latin American Literature* (Oxford: O.U.P., 1973), 74.

31. Gaston Bachelard, *La Psychanalyse du feu* (Paris: Gallimard, 1968), 174.

32. Ramón Xirau in *Universidad de México*, 5–6 (January–February 1955), 28.

Chapter 3

1. Paz, 'Vigilias', *Tierra nueva*, II, 7–8 (January–April 1941), 38; Breton, *Signe ascendant*, 99; Paz, 'Vigilias', 38.

2. Breton, *L'Amour fou*, 85, 107–8.

3. Paz, *Claude Lévi-Strauss*, 119–20.

4. A. Rimbaud, *Oeuvres complètes* (Paris: Gallimard, 1972), 251, 106, 252, 117.

5. Paz, 'El mar (Elegía y esperanza)', *Taller*, 3 (May 1939), 41–4.

6. Perche, *Eluard*, 60.

7. Eluard, *Donner à voir*, 146, 157; Balakian, *André Breton*, 39.

8. Bachelard cited in J. Chevalier (ed.), *Dictionnaire des symboles* (Paris: Laffont, 1969), 67.

9. Breton, *Clair de terre*, 95, 113, 164.

10. C. G. Jung, *Memories, Dreams, Reflections* (London: Collins, 1971), 68; Breton, *Clair de terre*, 69.

11. C. G. Jung, *Psychological Reflections* (London: Routledge & Kegan Paul, 1971), 51.

12. E. Carballo, 'Octavio Paz: su poesía convierte en poetas a sus lectores', *México en la cultura*, 495 (25 August 1958), 3.

13. Breton, *Clair de terre*, 111, 112, 113.

14. M. L. Mendoza, 'Algunas preguntas a Octavio Paz', *El gallo ilustrado* (5 August 1962), 1; Y. Bonnefoy, *Du mouvement et de l'immobilité de Douve* (Paris: Gallimard, 1970), 121.

15. Bonnefoy, *Du mouvement de Douve*, 208.

16. Breton, *Manifestes*, 359–60.

17. Breton, *Signe ascendant*, 8, 99, 102, 109, 112, 113; C. Browder. *André Breton: Arbiter of Surrealism* (Geneva: Dras, 1967). 130.

18. Guillermo Sucre, 'Poesía crítica: lenguaje y silencio', *Revista iberoamericana*, 76–7 (July-December 1971), 577.

19. Breton, *Signe ascendant*, 122, 124.

20. André Breton, *Les Pas perdus* (Paris: Gallimard, 1949), 171, 167, 168, 169.

21. Breton, *Clair de terre*, 175; R. Jean, *Paul Eluard par lui-même* (Paris: Seuil, 1968), 41–2.

22. Saúl Yurkievich, *Fundadores de la nueva poesía latinoamericana* (Barcelona: Barral, 1971), 259.

23. Julio Cortázar, 'Comme étoile de mer', *Le monde* (15 January 1971), 17.

24. Breton, *Signe ascendant*, 16; André Breton, *Les Vases communicants* (Paris: Gallimard, 1967), 133; Caws, *The Poetry of Dada*, 30.

25. J. Pierre, *Le Surréalisme* (Lausanne: Edition Rencontre, 1967), 18; Frye, *Fables*, 32; Kathleen Raine, *Defending Ancient Springs* (Oxford: O.U.P., 1967), 108–12; Breton, *Signe ascendant*, 7, 8, 9; R. Cardinal & R. S. Short, *Surrealism* (London: Studio Vista, 1970), 34.

26. Breton, *Manifestes*, 361; Breton, *Les Vases communicants*, 134.

27. Herbert Read, *Wordsworth* (London: Faber, 1954), 119; Raine, *Defending Ancient Springs*, 108.

28. Barthes, *Writing Degree Zero*, 54; R. Jakobson, 'Qu'est-ce que la poésie?', *Poétique*, 7 (1971), 308; Mallarmé and Rimbaud in R. Gibson, *Modern French Poets on Poetry* (Cambridge: C.U.P., 1961), 157, 158.

29. André Breton, *Nadja* (Paris: Gallimard, 1964), 147; Breton, *Arcane 17*, 83, 84, 91, 92, 105; Michel Carrouges, *André Breton et les données fondamentales du surréalisme* (Paris: Gallimard, 1950), 285–6.

30. Rimbaud, *Oeuvres*, 252; Breton, *Arcane 17*, 85.

31. Rimbaud, *Oeuvres*, 117; Breton, *Manifestes*, 31; Breton, *Signe ascendant*, 124.

32. Bonnefoy, *Du mouvement de Douve*, 206; Paz, 'El más allá erótico' in C. Fuentes (ed.), *Los signos en rotación y otros ensayos* (Madrid: Alianza, 1971), 181.

33. Frank Kermode, *Continuities* (London: Routledge & Kegan Paul, 1971), 2–22.

34. Breton, *Arcane 17*, 67.

35. Brown, *Love's Body*, 124, 265.

36. Mallarmé in Gibson, *Modern French Poets*, 182; Eluard in Jean, *Paul Eluard*, 129.

37. Brown, *Love's Body*, 259.

38. Brown, *Love's Body*, 265.

39. George Steiner, *Language and Silence* (Harmondsworth: Penguin, 1969), 65.

40. Frank Kermode, *Romantic Image* (London: Collins, 1971), 79–81.

41. Brown, *Love's Body*, 247.

42. Read, *Wordsworth*, 119; T. S. Eliot, *Selected Prose* (Harmondsworth: Penguin, 1965), 109; Bonnefoy, *Du Mouvement de Douve* 185.

Chapter 4

1. Rubén Darío, *Prosas profanas* (Madrid: Espasa-Calpe, 1964) 10–11.
2. Breton, *Les Pas perdus*, 98.
3. J.-K. Huysmans, *A rebours* (Paris: Union Générale d'Editions, 1975), 284. Henri Michaux, *Un Barbare en Asie* (Paris: Gallimard, 1967), 49.
4. Breton, *Point du jour*, 47.
5. Breton, *Entretiens*, 283.
6. Paul Valéry, 'Orientem versus', *Verve*, 3 (October–December 1938), 13.
7. Paz, 'Eroticism and Gastrosophy', 81.
8. A. Rudolf, 'Octavio Paz: an Interview', *Modern Poetry in Translation*, 11 (Autumn 1971), 20; Paz (with J. Roubaud, E. Sanguineti and C. Tomlinson), *Renga* (Paris: Gallimard, 1971).
9. Paz 'Chuang-tse, un contraveno', *México en la cultura*, 430 (16 June 1957), 1.
10. A. Bharati, *The Tantric Tradition* (London: Rider, 1965), 173–4, 290; P. Rawson, *Tantra* (London: Arts Council of Great Britain, 1971), 5.
11. M. Eliade, *Le Yoga: immortalité et liberté* (Paris: Payot, 1954), 252.
12. Rawson, *Tantra*, 88; Eliade, *Le Yoga*, 227.
13. Eliade, *Le Yoga*, 253.
14. Carballo, 'Octavio Paz', 3.
15. Eliade, *Le Yoga*, 250.
16. Ríos, *Solo a dos voces*, n.p.n.
17. Breton, *Signe ascendant*, 113, 8.
18. Ríos, *Solo a dos voces*, n.p.n.
19. André Breton, *La Clé des champs* (Paris: Pauvert, 1967), 81; Breton, *Manifestes*, 44; A. Balakian, *Surrealism: the Road to the Absolute* (N.Y.: Noonday Press, 1959), 115; Breton, *Point du jour*, 186.
20. Breton, *Manifestes*, 63, 37.
21. Breton, *L'Amour fou*, 14.
22. R. Hubert, 'Characteristics of an Undefinable Genre: the Surrealist Prose Poem', *Symposium*, 22 (Spring 1968), 27; Charles Baudelaire, *Petits poèmes en prose* (Paris: Gallimard, 1973), 22; J. K. Huysmans, *A rebours* (Paris: Union Générale d'Editions, 1975), 304–5; Balakian, *André Breton*.
23. Paz, *Children of the Mire: Modern Poetry from Romanticism to the Avant-Garde* (Cambridge, Mass.: Harvard University Press, 1974), 5, 157.

24. Rilke cited by P. Jaccottet, *Rilke par lui-même* (Paris: Seuil, 1976), 65; Breton, *Signe ascendant*, 7; Breton, *Arcane 17*, 150, 171.

25. R. Weil, 'Le Zohar' in *Encyclopédie des mystiques* (Paris: Laffont, 1972), 107.

26. K. Rexroth, 'Introduction' in A. E. Waites, *The Holy Kabbalah* (Secaucus, New Jersey: University Books, 1960), xi; Waites, *The Holy Kabbalah*, 361, 381; Breton, *Les Pas perdus*, 171.

27. G. Scholem, *Major Trends in Jewish Mysticism* (London: Thames & Hudson, 1955), 223.

28. Scholem, *Major Trends*, 210.

29. Breton, *La Clé des champs*, 201; Rexroth in Waites, *The Holy Kabbalah*, xii.

30. H. Michaux, *Emergences-Résurgences* (Geneva: Skira, 1972), 9, 43, 65.

31. Svanberg cited by S. Alexandrian, *Surrealist Art* (London: Thames & Hudson, 1970), 222; Breton, *Le Surréalisme et la peinture*, 121, 241.

32. Breton, *L'Amour fou*, 85; Breton, *Arcane 17*, 197.

33. 'Vuelta' in Ríos, *Solo a dos voces*, n.p.n.

34. Paz, *Versiones y diversiones* (Mexico: Mortiz, 1974), 189, 7.

35. *Poems of Wang Wei*, trans. with an introduction by G. W. Robinson (Harmondsworth: Penguin, 1973).

36. Paz, *Poesía en movimiento*, 444.

37. J. J. Tablada, *Obras I* (Mexico: U.N.A.M. 1971), 477.

38. Tablada, *Obras*, 365.

39. Tablada, *Obras*, 44; Villaurrutia, *Obras*, 43; G. Ceide-Echevarría, *El haikai en la lírica mexicana* (Mexico: Col. Studium, 1967), 98–9.

Postscript

1. Paz, 'Vuelta' in Ríos, *Solo a dos voces*, n.p.n.; 'Vuelta' in *Vuelta*, 21.

2. Ríos, *Solo a dos voces*; Paz, *Vuelta*, 22.

3. J. Geotzinger, 'Evolución de un poema: tres versiones de "Bajo tu clara sombra"', *Revista iberoamericana*, 74 (January–March 1971), 203–32; E. R. Monegal, 'Relectura de *El arco y la lira*', *Revista iberoamericana*, 74 (January–March 1971), 34–46.

4. Breton, *Manifestes*, 31.

5. Breton, *Les Pas perdus*, 15.

6. F. Alquié, *Philosophie du surréalisme* (Paris: Flammarion, 1955), 47.

7. Breton, *Manifestes*, 346.

Bibliography

Since there are fairly reliable and readily available bibliographies for specialists, I concentrate on Octavio Paz's main books, on those translated into English and on those critical studies that I have found rewarding and which are not cited in the footnotes.

Bibliographies

Bernard, J. 'Bibliography' in 'Mexico as Theme, Image, and Contribution to Myth in the Poetry of Octavio Paz'. Unpublished Ph.D., University of Wisconsin, 1964
Flores, A. 'Bibliografía' in A. Flores (ed.), *Aproximaciones a Octavio Paz*. Mexico: Mortiz, 1974
Roggiano, A. 'Bibliography by and on Octavio Paz' in I. Ivask (ed.), *The Perpetual Present: The Poetry and Prose of Octavio Paz*. Norman: University of Oklahoma Press, 1973; orig. in *Revista iberoamericana*, XXXVII, 74 (1971), 269–97

Works by Octavio Paz

A la orilla del mundo y Primer día, Bajo tu clara sombra, Raíz del hombre, Noche de resurrecciones. Mexico: Compañía Editora y Librería Ars, 1942
Libertad bajo palabra. Mexico: F.C.E., 1949
El laberinto de la soledad. Mexico: Cuadernos americanos, 1950; 2nd edn revised F.C.E., 1959, 3rd edn. 1964
¿Aguila o sol? Mexico: F.C.E., 1951
Semillas para un himno. Mexico: F.C.E., 1954
El arco y la lira. Mexico: F.C.E., 1956; 2nd edn revised 1967, with 'Los signos en rotación' orig. publ. Buenos Aires: Sur, 1965
Piedra de sol. Mexico: F.C.E., 1957
Las peras del olmo. Mexico: U.N.A.M., 1957
La estación violenta. Mexico: F.C.E., 1958
Libertad bajo palabra. Obra poética, 1935– 1958. Mexico: F.C.E., 1960; 2nd edn revised 1968
Salamandra (1958–1961). Mexico: Mortiz, 1962
Cuadrivio. Mexico: Mortiz, 1965
Puertas al campo. Mexico: U.N.A.M., 1966

Poesía en movimiento. México 1915–1966 (with A. Chumacero, J. E. Pacheco, H. Aridjis). Mexico: Siglo XXI, 1966
Blanco. Mexico: Mortiz, 1967
Claude Lévi-Strauss o el nuevo festín de Esopo. Mexico: Mortiz, 1967
Corriente alterna. Mexico: Siglo XXI, 1967
Marcel Duchamp o el castillo de la pureza. Mexico: Era, 1968
Ladera este (1962–1968). Mexico: Mortiz, 1969
La centena (Poemas 1935–1968). Barcelona: Barral, 1969
Conjunciones y disyunciones. Mexico: Mortiz, 1969
Posdata. Mexico: Siglo XXI, 1970
Topoemas. Mexico: Era, 1971
Renga (with C. Tomlinson, J. Roubaud, E. Sanguineti). Paris: Gallimard, 1971
Los signos en rotación y otras ensayos (ed. Carlos Fuentes). Madrid: Alianza, 1971
Traducción: literatura y literalidad. Barcelona: Tusquets, 1971
Le Singe grammairien. Geneva: Skira, 1972
El signo y el garabato. Mexico: Mortiz, 1973
Versiones y diversiones. Mexico: Mortiz, 1974
Los hijos del limo. Barcelona: Barral, 1974
Teatro de signos/transparencias (selected and mounted by J. Ríos). Madrid: Fundamentos, 1974
Pasado en claro. Mexico: F.C.E., 1975
Vuelta. Barcelona: Barral, 1976

Octavio Paz in English

The Labyrinth of Solitude (trans. L. Kemp). N.Y., Grove, 1961
Selected Poems (trans. M. Rukeyser). Bloomington: Indiana University Press, 1963; 2nd edn *Early Poems*. N.Y.: New Directions, 1973
Sunstone (Piedra de sol) (trans. M. Rukeyser) in *Configurations* (trans. P. Blackburn, D. Levertov, C. Tomlinson etc.). London: Cape, 1971. Also trans. P. Miller, Toronto: Contact Press, 1963; trans. D. Gardener, York: Cosmos Press, 1969; trans. S. Berg in *Triquarterly*, 13/14, fall/winter 1968–9
Marcel Duchamp or the Castle of Purity (trans. D. Gardener). London: Cape Goliard, 1970
New Poetry of Mexico (ed. M. Strand with W. S. Merwin, D. Justice etc.). N.Y.: Dutton, 1970
Configurations (trans. P. Blackburn, D. Levertov, C. Tomlinson etc.). London: Cape, 1971
Eagle or Sun? (trans. E. Weinberger). N.Y.: 1971
Claude Lévi-Strauss. An Introduction (trans. J. S. & M. Bernstein). London: Cape, 1972
The Other Mexico (trans. L. Kemp). N.Y.: Grove, 1972

Renga (trans. C. Tomlinson). N.Y.: Brazilier, 1972

The Bow and the Lyre (trans. R. Simms). Austin: University of Texas Press, 1973

Alternating Current (trans. H. Lane). N.Y.: Viking, 1973

Conjunctions and Disjunctions (trans. H. Lane). N.Y.: Viking, 1973

Children of the Mire. Modern Poetry from Romanticism to the Avant-Garde (trans. R. Phillips). Cambridge, Mass.: Harvard University Press, 1974

Works on Octavio Paz

Baciu, S. *Antología de la poesía surrealista latinoamericana*. Mexico: Mortiz, 1974

Bernard, J. Ph.D. thesis (*see* Bibliographies)
'Myth and Structure in Octavio Paz's "Piedra de sol"', *Symposium*, XXI, 1 (Spring 1967), 5–13

Brotherston, G. *Latin American Poetry. Origins & Presence*. Cambridge: C.U.P., 1975

Céa, C. *Octavio Paz*. Paris: Seghers, 1965

Cohen, J. M. *Poetry of this Age 1908–1965*. London: Hutchinson, 1966

Flores, A. *Aproximaciones a Octavio Paz* (with essays by J. G. Ponce, R. Xirau, C. Fuentes, J. Franco, J. Ortega, E. Pezzoni etc.). Mexico: Mortiz, 1974

Franco, J. *An Introduction to Spanish American Literature*. Cambridge: C.U.P., 1969

Gallagher, D. *Modern Latin American Literature*. Oxford: O.U.P., 1973

Ivask, I. (ed.). *The Perpetual Present. The Poetry and Prose of Octavio Paz*. Norman: University of Oklahoma Press, 1973 (with essays by G. Sucre, M. Durán, T. Segovia, E. R. Monegal etc.)

Monegal, E. R. 'Octavio Paz: crítica y poesía', *Mundo nuevo*, 21 (March 1968), 55–62

Nugent, R. 'Structure and meaning in Octavio Paz's *Piedra de sol*', *Kentucky Foreign Language Quarterly*, XIII, 3 (1966), 138–46

Phillips, R. *The Poetic Modes of Octavio Paz*. Oxford: O.U.P., 1972

Revista Iberoamericana (special number on Paz), XXXVII, 74 (January–March 1971) (with essays by G. Sucre, E. R. Monegal, J. Franco, J. E. Pacheco etc.)

Sucre, G. *La máscara, la transparencia*. Caracas: Monte Avila, 1975

Xirau, R. *Tres poetas de la soledad*. Mexico: Antigua Librería Robredo, 1955

Octavio Paz: el sentido de la palabra. Mexico: Mortiz, 1970

Yurkievich, S. *Fundadores de la nueva poesía latinoamericana*. Barcelona: Barral, 1971

Interviews with Octavio Paz

Carballo, E. 'Octavio Paz: su poesía convierte en poetas a sus lectores', *México en la cultura* 495 (25 August 1958), 3

Couffon, C. *Hispanoamérica en su nueva literatura*. Santander: Publicaciones de la isla de Ratones, 1962

Couturier, M. In *La Quinzaine littéraire*, (1–15 March 1971), 14–15

Embeita, M. in *Insula*, 260–1 (July-August 1968), 12–14

Fell, C. in *Plural*, 50 (November 1975), 7–16

Guibert, Rita in *Seven Voices*. N.Y.: Knopf, 1973

Monegal, E. R. in J. Ortega (ed.), *Convergencias/divergencias*. Barcelona: Tusquets, 1973

Monsiváis, C. in *Revista de la universidad de México*, XXII, 3 (November 1967). 1–8.

Ríos, J. *Solo a dos voces*. Barcelona: Lumen, 1973

Rudolf, A. in *Modern Poetry in Translation*, 11 (Autumn 1971), 19–21

Vernegro, R. in *Sur*, 227 (March–April 1954), 61–4

There is a record of Octavio Paz reading his own poems: *Octavio Paz. Voz viva de Mexico*. Mexico: U.N.A.M., 1961

Index